Contents

Wing Commander Frank Arthur Brock RN OBE.

The authors dedicate this book with thanks to Francie without whom it would not have been written

Introduction

Like many young boys in those post-World War II days, my brothers and I grew up with a large dressing-up box generously supplied, mainly with toy armaments but in our case these also included a British Army tank telescopic gun-sight, some real helmets and some of the half firework-shell cases, similar to those described in the book. My favourite toy was a submachine gun. Bright red plastic and clockwork powered, it discharged in less than a minute and with pleasing reliability, 100 shot rolls of the green paper-backed Brock's caps – technically, 'amorces' or toy percussion caps.

We and our friends played British vs Germans or Cowboys vs Indians. Virtually all boys in the country carried at least one real knife in their pockets, often two – pen knives and sheath knives. The idea of stabbing anyone in those days would never have entered our heads but my father, who only a few years earlier had been trained as a commando, taught me by the age of six the rudiments of disarming any ne'er-do-well of similar size approaching me with a knife – something, mercifully, I have never had to put to the test.

Despite subsequently having spent a lifetime of peace and tranquillity, taking on the role of a warrior at an early age led my thoughts, not infrequently in those days, onto the battlefield although on rainy days, if I was lucky, my mother Anne would supervise me looking into her ancient oak chests filled with papers, medals, newspapers, books, photographs, an Intelligence-issue knuckleduster and pieces of Zeppelin and Zeppelin bomb shrapnel, where I began to learn about her father – Frank Brock – and his family.

When I entered adulthood there would have been several people alive who knew him, had even fought with him, yet I failed to take the opportunity to find, meet or talk to any of them. By the time my interest had matured and sharpened to a point where I knew what questions to ask, it was of course, too late. A failure that became increasingly frustrating as the realisation of the extent of his role in World War I became apparent: a British officer who significantly hindered our enemy's aims and, in the process, gave the Allies two of the best feel-good moments of that terrible conflict.

I spent a fascinating few years working at Brock's Fireworks in the 1980s and inevitably my interest in Frank, his achievements and those of his forebears, grew stronger. This book has been in gestation for decades. Throughout, there was a growing conviction, that Frank's life story deserved to be told but to explain such a man, the book needed to set his life in context, within the family from which he emerged, centuries of the Brock firework enterprise.

A century and a half ago and for many decades, the name of Brock was one of the best-known 'brands' around the globe. With their new artforms the Brocks, 'artists in fire', entertained tens of millions – the highest rulers and potentates to the lowliest of their subjects - and pioneered new military, naval and industrial pyrotechics. The family business played a part in bolstering governments and monarchs. It helped British diplomacy and played a role for a time at the heart of the British imperial project. It even lent its name as part of a metaphor, enriching spoken and written English, where it was used on a daily basis for decades.

It seemed to me that this tale had the potential to be of interest, not least to Frank's descendants and to his wider family. Above all it was a hidden part of British and even world history. It was worth preserving and I feared that unless I tried to do so, it was in danger of being lost forever.

I would like to start by thanking my friend and collaborator Henry Macrory, with whom I visited Zeebrugge and without whose skill, hard work and growing respect for Frank's memory, it would probably not have happened. In researching Frank's life for several decades, I have received generous help from many around the world. In listing them here I hope that none have been missed but if so, I apologise in advance.

***

I would like to thank Lord Ashcroft for his generous foreword. He is the proud owner and curator of the largest collection of VC medals ever gathered. If the centuries of Brock family history set Frank's emergence and extraordinary natural skills as a pyrotechnist in context, then this foreword does the same for the inspiring courage that he demonstrated on St. George's Day 1918 in a battle that was described by Churchill as 'the finest feat of arms' and was said at the time by an admiral to have saved the Royal Navy's honour.

The Flemish military historian Johan Ryheul, who lives near Zeebrugge, has spent decades studying the minutiae of the hour-long Raid. This was not an easy exercise given the intensity of the fighting and the myriad of confusing and contradictory accounts that followed its aftermath. His fluency in both English and German has allowed him to study the reports of both nations and I am very grateful to him for sharing his conclusions.

In recent years, staying with my generous sister-in law - the widow of my late brother Philip, another of Frank's grandchildren - I was able easily to visit the nearby National Archives which I mined for many weeks but eventually had to leave despite believing there were probably several more nuggets left for others to find. I also spent days visiting the Churchill Archives in Cambridge and have made several visits to see Alan Wakefield and his team at the Imperial War Museum in London where, in all institutions, I have been helped greatly by their patient and professional staff.

I would like to thank them and in a similar vein, the following establishments and individuals who encouraged and helped by patiently answering my questions spread over many years: the historians Deborah Lake, Ian Gardiner, Paul Kendal, Ernest Coleman, Christopher Sandford, Ian Castle, John Glanfield and Guy Warner. The composer Matthew Beatie and the archives of the Royal School of Music; the National Museum of the Royal Navy; the Archive Department and Research Centre of the Fleet Air Arm; the Museum of London; the National Army Museum; the RAF Museum; the British Library; Jürgen Bleibler of the Zeppelin Museum, Friedrichshafen; Dr. Arnulf Scriba of the Deutsches Historisches Museum; Dr. Thomas Menzel of the German Military Archives in Freiburg and also the German Federal Archive Military Museum in Berlin; the Federal Library of Berlin; the Library of Philadelphia; the National Museum of Scotland; the Canadian Aviation & Space Museum; the Museum of Croydon; Croydon College; the Metropolitan Police; the University of Cambridge Department of Chemistry Library; Erin O'Neill of the BBC Archives; the Department of History, Melbourne University; Keele University; the Centre for the History of Medicine, Mayo Clinic; the Archives of the University of Minnesota Libraries; the Rugby Football Museum; Richmond Rugby Football Club; the British Amateur Boxing Association; Devonshire Park, Eastbourne; the Eastbourne Herald; the Ordnance Survey; Kate Pool of the Society of Authors; the Crystal Palace Foundation.

I have also been encouraged by help from the following, whom I would like to acknowledge and thank: my sister and brother, two of Frank Brock's grandchildren, Celia Burgess and Lt. Col.(rtd.) Mark Shelford; Sue Joslin and lots of my Brock cousins on both sides of the Atlantic; Soroya Cerio and Catista Lucy of Dulwich College; Professor McKitterick of Cambridge University; Sarah Mahaffy; Peter Buckman; Kate McLennan; Barry Sturman;

Jeremy Jameson, Jason Billing, Sir Reginald Tyrwhitt and Lord Fisher of Kilverstone, the descendants of, respectively, Rear Admiral Murray Sueter, Noel Pemberton-Billing and Admirals of the Fleet Sir Reginald Tyrwhitt and Lord 'Jacky' Fisher; Eugene Leouzon; Drs. Saad Abdalla and Jiri Pavlu; Colin Mackenzie; Clare Litt; John Bennett and the late Jack Drewes; Cheryl Foulsham and her team at the Oxford Duplication Centre who worked devotedly to enhance the ancient images; the Oxfordshire County Council Libraries.

The Times of Philadelphia reported in July 1876 on the Philadelphia Exposition's recently fired Brock's display. The article appeared under the headline Gunpowder & Glory. This is the inspiration for the book's title and it is appropriate that the publisher should be the Philadelphia based Casemate, the British arm of which is established in my local city of Oxford, where the editors Ruth Sheppard and Isobel Fulton have used their extraordinary powers of endurance, professionalism and good humour to guide the book into print, for which I give unreserved thanks.

Finally, I would like to thank my wife Xianfu without whose superhuman patience, kindness and encouragement in the face of endless delays and setbacks, together with information technology skills of the first water, none of this would have been possible.

Foreword

All my life I have had a passion for bravery. As a boy I listened wide-eyed to my father as he told me of his exploits on D-Day, when he and his comrades ran into anti-tank, mortar, machine-gun and rifle fire on Sword Beach. By the time I reached my teens, my fascination for gallantry had become addictive. From war comics I graduated to war films and then to books on military history. Shortly after my fortieth birthday, by which time I had been fortunate enough to make some money as an entrepreneur, I bought a Victoria Cross at auction. From that modest start I built up the largest collection of Victoria Crosses and George Crosses in the world. These are now on display at the Imperial War Museum in London. I have also written five books on bravery, and have lectured on gallantry up and down the country. My simple aim is to highlight great acts of courage and to ensure that the brave men who carried them out are not forgotten.

I am therefore delighted to have been invited to write the foreword to this first-ever biography of Frank Brock. As well as being an outstandingly courageous man, he was one of the most significant figures of World War I. As a member of the famous Brock's fireworks clan, he was a pyrotechnical genius. When Zeppelins began bombing Britain in 1915, the Germans hoped to bring the country to its knees. They reckoned without the likes of 'Fireworks' Brock. He used his skills to develop an incendiary bullet capable of destroying the previously invincible airships. Soon afterwards, using Brock bullets, William Leefe Robinson became the first pilot to shoot down a Zeppelin over Britain. The VC he won in the process is now part of my collection, providing me with a tangible link to the remarkable Commander Brock.

During the course of the war, Brock's fertile mind spawned numerous other military innovations. In particular, his giant 'Dover Flares' played a crucial role in combatting the U-boat menace in the English Channel. But he was far more than a back-room 'boffin'. He was also a man of action – a superb shot, an intrepid pilot and an expert in unarmed combat. Early in the war he slipped into Germany on an intelligence-gathering mission, knowing he would be shot as a spy if caught. His courage on that occasion was a foretaste of the incredible bravery he displayed during the Royal Navy's raid on Zeebrugge in April 1918. The aim of that St George's Day operation was to render the port of Bruges in German-occupied Belgium inoperable as a U-boat base. Brock not only invented an impenetrable smoke screen which was key to the mission's success. He also insisted on going ashore with the raiding parties where, like my father on Sword Beach more than a quarter of a century later, he ran headlong into a hail of enemy shells and bullets. 'My dear Brock, of imperishable memory and Victoria Cross bravery,' was how the former First Sea Lord, Jacky Fisher, described him after the raid.

Frank Brock was my kind of hero, and it is high time that his extraordinary story was told. With the 100th anniversary of the Great War, this is an appropriate time to tell it. Prepare to be inspired.

Michael Ashcroft

Prologue

Come on, You Boys

Beneath a night sky that was too bright for anyone's liking, the ageing warship sped across the Channel at the head of a ragtag armada of destroyers, launches, old submarines and Mersey ferry-boats. The men on board knew that their chances of making it home again were not high. By common consent, their mission was one of the most audacious and suicidal ever undertaken by the Royal Navy.

For all the tension, one man on board showed little outward sign of concern. As HMS *Vindictive* steamed towards the Belgian coast on the evening of 22 April 1918, Commander Frank Brock remained his usual unflappable self. He was by nature a supreme optimist. No one was more confident than he of returning home safely.

Frank Arthur Brock was already a legend among the men on the ship. Had Ian Fleming conjured up James Bond 35 years before he did, he might have used him as the template for 007. At 33 years old, he was a large, powerful, broad-shouldered man of dark good looks. He could fly an aeroplane and was a superb all-round sportsman, excelling at football, rugby, golf, swimming and boxing. On top of this he was a first-class shot, as proficient with a revolver as with a rifle or a shotgun. During a remarkable career he had helped catch terrorists in India and risked his life on an intelligence-gathering mission behind enemy lines. The word 'derring-do' summed up his raw courage and his love of adventure. His initials – FAB – seemed entirely appropriate.

But this daring young naval officer could have been more than the basis of 007. He might equally well have been the model for Q, the Secret Service quartermaster who supplied Bond's gadgets. For on top of his other attributes, Frank was an inventor of outstanding talent. One of his ideas played a crucial role in protecting the nation from Zeppelins, the giant German airships which Kaiser Bill had hoped would bring Britain to its knees. Another was used with devastating effect to counter the threat from U-boats. His most recent brainchild, deemed essential to the success of the raid in which he was about to take part, was an artificial fog or smoke screen, vastly more efficient than any that had come before, which would cover the approach of the British flotilla as it neared the enemy-occupied Belgian coast.

That he had such a creative mind was not surprising. Invention, innovation and a flair for the theatrical ran in his blood, for he had been born into Britain's most famous fireworks family. The Brock clan had practised the art of pyrotechnical wizardry for eight generations. More than two centuries earlier Frank's five times great-grandfather, John Brock, a self-proclaimed 'artist in fireworks', had painted London's night skies with his dazzling displays of sky rockets, spinners, serpents, vertical wheels and firecrackers. By the time of Frank's birth, Brock's was the most successful maker of fireworks in Britain, enthralling hundreds of thousands of people a year with their world-famous exhibitions at London's Crystal Palace.

Frank himself had joined the company as soon as he left school, immersing himself in the science of fireworks and the art of showmanship. For 13 years he travelled the world putting on elaborate shows in front of vast crowds. One of his specialities was staging pyrotechnical depictions of great naval battles such as the battle of Trafalgar and the destruction of the Spanish Armada. As he busied himself in the darkness on the deck of *Vindictive*, it may have occurred to him that that night's raid would make an excellent subject for a Crystal Palace spectacular.

But in the meantime, there was the rather more pressing matter of winning the war against Germany. After nearly four years the conflict remained as fierce and as costly in lives as ever. This was not the war as portrayed in the adventure stories Frank had read as a boy; this was carnage on an industrial scale, falling like a scythe on his generation. Tonight's top secret 'stunt' was the most dangerous mission he had undertaken and was born out of desperation and necessity. It was nothing less than an attempt to keep Britain in the war.

German submarines remained a severe threat to British shipping and were based in large numbers at Bruges. This ancient Belgian port, eight miles inland from the North Sea, was an invaluable outpost for the Germans, being some three hundred miles closer to Dover than their naval ports in the Heligoland Bight. By making use of it, the German Navy was able to threaten Britain's Atlantic sea traffic and her lines of communication with the continent to deadly effect. By one estimate, Bruges-based submarines were responsible for the destruction of more than 2,500 Allied vessels during the war, amounting to some 4,400,000 tons. Unless Bruges could be neutralised, warned the First Sea Lord, John Jellicoe, Britain would be forced into submission.

Then, as now, Bruges was connected to the sea by canals leading to the coastal towns of Zeebrugge and Ostend, and these were the key to the operation. The plan was to scuttle blockships in the harbours of both towns, so sealing the canals and rendering Bruges inoperative as a naval base. If successful, the raid would box in numerous German torpedo boats and destroyers as well as up to 30 submarines.

But could it be done? Sailing into an enemy-occupied port would be difficult enough under any circumstances, even under the cover of Frank Brock's smoke, but the problem was made infinitely more difficult at Zeebrugge because the harbour there was screened by a vast sea wall known as 'The Mole'. Around one and a half miles long, it was the longest such structure in the world and bristled with batteries of German guns. The essence of the British plan was for storming parties from *Vindictive* to attack the Mole at midnight, knock out the German guns and create a noisy diversion. Amid the chaos, the blockships, laden with concrete, would be sailed into the canal entrance and scuttled. With their job done, the survivors – and it was not anticipated that there would be many – would make a dash for home, again using Frank's artificial fog for cover.

Described by one who knew him as 'a powerfully built, dashing and resourceful man with big-hearted enthusiasm which carried everyone with him' and in another friend's diary as 'courteous, with very good manners – a salty tongue in private – and the most pleasant public personality, a "true English gentleman" who acted at all times with the utmost decorum and restraint until the moment came to blow someone or something up', Frank should not have been part of the mission at all. His superiors thought him too valuable to the war effort to risk his life at Zeebrugge, and pleaded with him to stay away. But he was adamant he was going to play his part. He had heard about a system of metal tubes mounted on the Mole which he believed to be the latest in enemy sound-ranging equipment used for locating hostile artillery. If circumstances permitted, he would snaffle some of the equipment and bring it back to Dover, using it to create an improved British version. To achieve this, he argued, successfully, that he would have to join a storming party on the Mole, regardless of the danger.

At 10.30 on the night of the raid, as hot soup was ladled out to the men aboard *Vindictive,* the flotilla split into two, with the Ostend force peeling off and heading for its separate destination. Zeebrugge was now just 15 miles away.

In 90 minutes it would be St George's Day, and Frank had every intention of doing justice to St George's memory.

At 20 minutes to midnight, motor launches ahead of the flotilla started deploying Frank's artificial fog. The German gunners on the Mole were confused. They could hear but not see the approaching armada. Frank's invention was working a treat. Three hundred yards out from the Mole, *Vindictive's* telegraphs call for full speed ahead and she emerged from the smoke screen. The German gunners were briefly stunned into disbelief. Then they opened fire with every weapon at their disposal.

At one minute past midnight – just 60 seconds behind schedule – *Vindictive* pushed up against the Mole. Projectiles of every kind ripped into her steelwork. Men fell wounded and dying in terrifying numbers. The survivors clambered on to the Mole and advanced under continuous shell and small-arms fire towards the German guns.

Even now Frank was under no obligation to go with them. At the very least he had the option of holding back until it was relatively safe to go ashore. But he was a man in a hurry and a man without fear. Armed with two pistols and a cutlass, he jumped down onto the Mole. Turning to the men behind him he shouted 'Come on, you boys' and charged into the smoke and bullets like the intrepid rugby forward he was.

CHAPTER I

A Whiff of Black Powder

The process that would one day lead to the creation of Brock's Fireworks, and start Frank Brock on his extraordinary career, probably began between two and three thousand years ago over a campfire in China. Saltpetre, found there in large quantities, was used from ancient times as both a medicine and a food preservative. Some early cook, combining it by chance with two other common kitchen ingredients, sulphur and charcoal, would have been fascinated by the way the mixture glowed and sparkled in the fire.

So it was that gunpowder, as we call it today, joined that impressive list of early Chinese inventions, which also included paper, printing, the compass, the crossbow and, some would argue, the parachute. (Legend has it that in around 2200 BC Emperor Shun used conical hats to break his fall when jumping from the roof of a blazing barn.)

The Chinese named this intriguing black powder *huo yao*, meaning 'fire chemical' or 'fire drug', and used it initially in their search for the secrets of eternal life. As early as AD 142, an alchemist named Wei Boyang wrote of experiments with a mixture of three powders – he did not name them but they were almost certainly the ingredients of gunpowder – that would 'fly and dance' violently when heated. Although the powder failed to unlock the secret of immortality, it was apparently useful for treating skin diseases and as a fumigant to kill insects.

Back at the campfires, the early cooks had long been troubled by semi-human monsters called *shanxiao*. These naked creatures lived in the mountainous regions of western China. They spied on travellers through the foliage and crept out when they were not looking in order to steal salt, which they sprinkled on the crabs and frogs they roasted for sustenance. If confronted, they hit back by afflicting the camp dwellers with fever. The best way to send these ogres packing was to throw a piece of bamboo into the fire. The heat burst the bamboo, and the resulting crack caused them to scurry off into the undergrowth. For centuries the *pao chuk* ('exploding bamboo') was an essential aid to trouble-free travel.

In due course some enterprising individual (supposedly a Chinese monk named Li Tian) worked out that a far louder and more satisfying bang could be achieved by stuffing pieces of bamboo with 'fire chemical'. The gases produced by the burning powder caused a build-up of pressure which blasted the bamboo apart so fiercely that no lurking *shanxiao* in his right mind would set foot near a campfire again. So was born the firecracker or *pao chang*. Legend has it that Li Tian used his invention to eradicate the floods and droughts which afflicted the east of the Hunan Province, setting off fireworks to disperse the evil spirits that caused them, and enabling a grateful populace to live and work in peace and prosperity.

By the time of the Song Dynasty (960–1279) it was possible to buy fireworks from street traders to set off at home. Li Tian's success in Hunan Province was striking proof that the bang (*bian pao*) they made was enough to scare away the most persistent of ghosts. This made them popular at weddings, birth celebrations, funerals, festivals to mark the lunar new year and celebrations of military victories. They were often made out of red paper, since evil spirits were supposed to be frightened of the colour red. The redder the paper and the louder the bang, the more the cowed demons retreated into the shadows.

The art and science of firework-making rapidly developed into a profession. Before long, someone figured out how to make a fuse (*yin hsien*) by twisting a piece of paper sprinkled with gunpowder into a long string. Someone else discovered that if one end of the tube was closed up, the firecracker would shoot off in all directions, spouting flames and sparks. These primitive rockets were known as ground rats (*ti lao shu).*

The work of these so-called firework masters was not all plain sailing. Singed beards were the least of their worries as they experimented with different mixtures. A contemporary chronicler noted in *Classified Essentials of the Mysterious Tao of the True Origin of Things*:

> Some have heated together sulphur, realgar and saltpetre with honey; smoke and flames result, so that their hands and faces have been burnt, and even the whole house where they were working burned down.

Their doggedness eventually paid off, and the firework masters became highly regarded for their ability to mount dazzling displays of light and sound. Early in the 12th century the Chinese army mounted a pyrotechnical display for the emperor which opened with 'a noise like thunder'. Fireworks played against the indigo sky, while dancers in exotic costumes pirouetted through the coloured smoke. The display went down well with the emperor, but success was not guaranteed. A record from 1264 states that a ground rat frightened the Empress Dowager Gong Sheng when it disappeared under her throne during a feast held in her honour by her son, Emperor Lizong of Song. The festivities ended abruptly and the fireworks masters responsible were jailed.

It did not require a great leap of the imagination to realise that gunpowder could also be used in warfare. A reference to a crude Chinese gunpowder catapult dates back to 1046, and in the decades that followed Chinese soldiers regularly fired ground rats at their enemies, confusing advancing infantrymen and terrifying horses. By 1083 'flying fire lances' or *fei-ho* were being produced in their thousands. Gunpowder was wrapped in paper 'in a lump like a pomegranate', sealed with pine resin and attached to the shaft of an arrow. The archer lit a fuse projecting from the lump and launched the arrow at the enemy. These explosive arrows were reportedly used successfully against the Mongol invaders in the 13th century.

There may even have been attempts at manned flight. According to Chinese legend, an official named Wan-Hu assembled a rocket-propelled chair with which to launch himself into the sky. He attached 47 rockets and two large kites to the chair, and at the given moment 47 assistants lit the fuses before beating a hasty retreat. There was a tremendous explosion, and when the smoke cleared Wan-Hu and his chair were nowhere to be seen. They had presumably been blown to bits, but in acknowledgement of the lingering belief that Wan-Hu launched himself into space, the Soviets named a crater on the far side of the moon after him in 1966.

There inevitably came a time when the knowledge of fireworks spread to the west. Marco Polo is sometimes credited with their arrival in Europe during the 13th century, but the appearance of gunpowder in England and elsewhere almost certainly pre-dates his travels. It has been suggested that Crusaders and Knights Templar returned from their journeys abroad with the secret of a monstrous new weapon that could breathe fire, but it is equally possible that Europeans discovered gunpowder independently. One way or another, an English scholar named Roger Bacon knew of gunpowder (or blackpowder as he called it) by the 1260s. He wrote in his *Opus Majus* of:

> … a child's toy of sound and fire which is made in various parts of the world with powder of saltpetre, sulphur and charcoal of hazel-wood. This powder is enclosed in an instrument of parchment the size of a finger, and since this can make such a noise that it seriously distresses the ears of men, especially if one is taken unawares, and the terrible flash is also very alarming.

In Europe as a whole, Italy led the way in pyrotechnics, as it did in so many other artistic endeavours of the time. Fireworks are recorded as having accompanied a religious mystery play in Vicenza as early as 1377. In his book *Pyrotechnic*, published in 1540, Vanuzzio Biringuccio, an Italian engineer, described how in former times it was the practice in his native Siena to put on shows using figures of wood and plaster that emitted fire from their mouths and eyes. He wrote that the festivities included *girandoles*, or whirling decorated wheels packed with fireworks which were suspended from a rope hung across a street or square. He added that from these 'forceful and horrible materials bringing harm and terror to men, a happy and pleasing effect is also produced and, instead of fleeing from it, the people willingly go to see it.'

A significant Italian contribution to pyrotechnics was the development of explosive-filled canisters, or shells, which were fired into the air and detonated at maximum height. This innovation laid the foundations of modern aerial displays. Italian fire masters also experimented with a slower-burning explosive mixture that produced showers of radiant sparks when lit. They used the new compound to create the forerunners of many modern fireworks, including fountains, spinners, cones, wheels, Roman candles and sparklers. In 1379, an Italian named Muratori used the word *rochetta* when he described the fire arrows propelled by gunpowder in medieval times. This is believed to be the first use of the word which later became 'rocket' in English.

In England, the first recorded use of primitive fireworks was at the coronation of Henry VII's bride, Elizabeth of York, in 1487. The barge at the head of the Lord Mayor's procession which met her on the river 'carried a dragon spouting flames of fire into the Thames.' A similar pyrotechnic effect was deployed nearly half a century later when Anne Boleyn was conveyed by water from Greenwich to London prior to her coronation in 1533. One of the galleys escorting her carried 'a great, red dragon, constantly moving and casting forth wild fire, and round about the said galley stood terrible, monstrous and wide men, casting of fire and making a hideous noise.'

By the late 16th century, fireworks had grown in sophistication and were becoming an established part of England's cultural life. Their rising popularity was fuelled by Elizabeth I, who was so enamoured of them that she appointed an official 'Fire Master of England'. The first recorded full-scale display in Britain was held in her honour at Warwick in 1572 in the form of a mock battle. The event, organised by the Earl of Warwick, did not go entirely to plan when rockets over-shot a timber and canvas fort built especially for the occasion and landed on the roof of a cottage in the town. The blaze rapidly spread to adjoining houses, injuring one Henry Cooper and his wife. Despite this unexpected diversion, Elizabeth was thrilled by the show and in generous mood she sent for the couple the next day and gave them £25 to pay for their repairs.

Things went more smoothly three years later when Robert Dudley entertained her with a firework extravaganza at Kenilworth Castle. A contemporary account by Robert Laneham told of 'a blaze of burning darts flying to and fro; beams of stars coruscant; streams and hail of fire sparks; lightnings of wild-fire on the water and on the land; flight and shooting of thunderbolts, all with such continuance, terror, and vehemence, the heavens thundered, the waters surged and the earth shook.' It was said that people could hear the display 20 miles away. Among them, quite possibly, was 11-year-old William Shakespeare, who lived close by with his parents and siblings in Stratford-upon-Avon.

Shakespeare made several references in his plays to fireworks, as when Don Amado declared in *Love's Labour's Lost*: 'The King would have me present the Princess with some delightful entertainment, or show, or pageant, or antic, or firework.' In a remarkable flight of fancy, a 19th-century historian, W Grist, suggested that Sir Toby Belch's line to Malvolio in *Twelfth Night*, 'Marry, hang thee, Brock,' was inspired by a meeting between the bard and a member of the Brock firework family. Since the Brocks' recorded association with fireworks did not begin until nearly a century after *Twelfth Night* was written, we can safely conclude that Shakespeare's sole intended meaning was 'Go hang yourself, you stinking badger'.

Theatres during the playwright's time were often equipped with both fireworks and thunder-sheets to produce dramatic stage effects. In his tragi-comedy *The right, excellent and famous Historye of Promos and Cassandra*, printed in 1578, the dramatist George Whetstone included stage directions which called for the entrance of 'two men apparelled like greene men at the mayor's feast, with clubs of fireworks'.

The 'Green Men' he referred to played an important part in English firework custom. Their role was to walk at the head of processions 'strewing fire from large clubs' and scattering 'fireworks' (in this case probably meaning sparks) to clear the way. As at Anne Boleyn's wedding, they were generally dressed from head to toe in green ivy and other foliage to protect themselves from flying sparks. These early fire-workers liked to salute each other with the words 'Stay green!' and may have been the inspiration for many of Britain's 'Green Man' pubs. An account of a pageant in Chester on St George's Day, 1610, described two such fireworkers:

> There appeared two men in green ivy, set with work upon their other habit, with black hair and black beards, very ugly to behold, and garlands upon their heads, with great clubs in their hands, with fireworks to scatter abroad to maintain the way for the rest of the show.

The popularity of fireworks grew rapidly during the 17th century and it was not uncommon for £1,000 or more (around £200,000 in today's money) to be lavished on state-run displays. According to *A History of Colleges in and around London*, published in 1611, there were living in the city many 'men very skillful in the art of pyrotechny and fireworks'.

Pyrotechnical literature was also much in demand. In 1635 the English mathematician and gunner John Babington published one of the first descriptions in English of recreational fireworks. His book, *Pyrotechnia, or a Discourse of Artificiall Fireworks*, was essentially a do-it-yourself manual, and was probably responsible for innumerable lost eyes and fingers. It contained guidance on how to make and fire rockets and how to stage a duel between St George and a fire-breathing dragon. Babington also set down the first written instructions for making a Jack-in-the-Box, which included filling a box with 'fisgigs or serpents'. Having lit the fuse, 'after a pretty distance of time you shall heare a sudden noyse and see all those fisgigs flying some one way, some another. This toy has given great content to the spectators.'

Guy Fawkes provided another fillip to the burgeoning firework industry. Within a few decades of his attempt to blow up the Palace of Westminster in 1605, Gunpowder Treason Day, as it was at first known, had become the chief English state commemoration. (The gunpowder used in the plot, incidentally, was bought from one John Pain, whose business may have grown, centuries later, into Pains Fireworks, one of the Brock family's chief competitors.) A display in 1647 at Lincoln's Inn Fields in London commemorated 'God's great mercy in delivering this kingdom from the hellish plots of papists.' Effigies of Fawkes and the Pope were burned and rockets were fired to symbolise 'popish spirits coming from below' to enact plots against the king.

Anti-Catholic fervour was again fuelled by the Great Fire of 1666, which was widely regarded as a papist plot to destroy London with pyrotechnics. Fireworks allegedly belonging to Catholics were put on show in the capital's coffee houses as evidence of plots to create further conflagrations.

The arrival in England of a Swedish artillery officer, Major Martin Beckman, gave fireworks another boost. A highly skilled pyrotechnist, his specialities included building papier-maché obelisks, pillars, pyramids, the figures of men, or whatever other object might suit the occasion, and filling them with fireworks to create dazzling effects. He also appreciated the value of water in enhancing the spectacle of fireworks, an idea first tested on the Thames in 1613 to celebrate the marriage of King James I's daughter, Elizabeth, to Frederick V, Count Palatine of the Rhine. One observer was so impressed by this display that he was moved to write that 'Arte hath exceeded Nature.' Another commentator, John Chamberlain, was not so sure:

> The fireworks were reasonably well performed, all save the last castle of fire, which bred most expectation and had most devices, but when it came to execution had worst success.

As the 'King's Ingenier' (the title 'engineer' was applied to firework masters and makers of 'engines of war' for centuries before it gained its present meaning), Beckman masterminded Charles II's coronation fireworks in 1661. In the process he nearly killed himself, being 'severely injured by an accident at an explosion in the preparation of fireworks to be shown on the water in the king's honour.' Of the display itself there is sadly no record. Samuel Pepys, who might have been expected to provide a full account, was suffering from a hangover and only heard the fireworks in the distance, although he wrote that on the night of the coronation a 'fire-brand' was thrown into a carriage 'by which a woman was blinded.' The show was presumably a success because Beckman went on to oversee James II's coronation fireworks in 1685. Staged on the Thames, these were an unqualified triumph, 'a Wonder-full and Stupendious drama', in the words of one observer, at which rockets soared and exploded around 42ft-high pyramids and an artificial sun.

In 1688 Beckman supervised a display to celebrate the queen's delivery of a son. He subsequently organised several other displays, including one in St James's Park to mark the return of William III to London in 1695. Over the course of a long career he raised the standard of public displays to a new level of professionalism and was the first Fire Master of England to be knighted.

Unfortunately the more informal and less dignified celebrations held on Gunpowder Treason Days were rapidly becoming an excuse for rowdy behaviour and drunken brawls. Apprentice boys took to demanding money from coach passengers for alcohol and bonfires, and effigies of the pope were burned with increasing fervour. A grim touch was added in London in 1677 when the belly of the pope's effigy was filled with live cats 'who squalled most hideously as soon as they felt the fire.' Another account from that period spoke of 'the numerous platoons and volleys of squibs discharged' amid shouts that 'might have been a cure for deafness itself.' Much damage was done as builders of bonfires went to any lengths, legal or otherwise, to gather firewood. One observer noted:

Ill is sure to betide the owner of an ill-secured fence; stakes are extracted from hedges, and branches torn from trees; crack, crack, goes loose paling; deserted buildings yield up their floorings; unbolted flip-flapping doors are released from their hinges as supernumeraries; and more burnables are deemed lawful prize than the law allows.

In 1682, London militiamen had to break up violent confrontations on Firework Night, and several proclamations banning bonfires and fireworks were issued in the following years, 'much mischief having been caused by squibs.' An Act of Parliament in 1697 enforced earlier bans on the throwing of squibs, crackers and rockets, and imposed fines of up to £5 and even hard labour in a house of correction for infringements.

No large-scale displays were held to mark the coronations of Queen Anne, George I and George II, although a spectacular show was held on the Thames off Whitehall in 1713 to celebrate the end of the War of the Spanish Succession. Set on a raft of barges 400 feet in length, its features included 'large and small Bees swarms, half of which were set with lights to swim on the water.'

The tailing-off of elaborate, state-organised displays at around this time coincided with the growth in popularity of public parks and pleasure gardens in and around the big cities. At weekends, families flocked in their thousands to these open spaces in search of entertainment. The diversions on offer ranged from the sedate (manicured walks, classical concerts, displays of horsemanship, exhibitions of paintings and tea-drinking to the accompaniment of French horns) to the salacious (bare-knuckle bouts, cock-fighting, bear-baiting and prostitution). In the more genteel gardens, the ladies were 'fragrant with powder,' gentlemen were requested 'not to smoak' and the entrance of servants in livery was prohibited. At the less reputable venues, patrons risked losing their belongings to pickpockets, footpads and 'light-fingered knaves,' and, as a shocked correspondent informed the *St James's Chronicle*, unaccompanied men were liable to be approached by women asking: 'Pray, Sir, will you treat me with a dish of tea?'

Vauxhall Gardens in London was a typical magnet for the crowds. In 1665 Pepys went there on 'the hottest day that ever I felt in my life … pleasantly walking, and spending but sixpence, till nine at night.' Within a few decades tightrope walkers, concerts, taverns, and pavilions with brightly-painted supper boxes ensured that most visitors to the Vauxhall Gardens spent a good deal more than sixpence.

The Marylebone Gardens, with their gravelled walks and neat hedges, were another popular destination. The ubiquitous Pepys went there too, writing in May 1668 that 'we abroad to Marrowbone, and there walked in the garden, the first time I ever was there, and a pretty place it is'. Visitors were charged sixpence to enter the eight-acre site and had to pay a further fee if they wished to use the oval bowling green at the centre of the gardens.

Showmen were constantly on the look-out for new ways of parting the crowds from their money at these and other pleasure gardens (one impresario enthralled visitors to Marylebone Gardens with a masquerade which featured 'an ape of the largest kind, which was offensively dexterous') and in due course several canny entrepreneurs saw the advantage of adding firework displays to the existing commercialized entertainment.

Among them was a young man named John Brock, who had been born in around 1677 in London's Clerkenwell. He was reputedly an eccentric individual who wore a cloak and wide-brimmed hat in the manner of Guy Fawkes. Quick to recognise a money-making opportunity, and with an indubitable flair for pyrotechnics, he set up a fireworks business towards the end of the 17th century in the north London suburb of Islington, and used his expertise to entertain visitors to Marylebone Gardens.

He could not have foreseen that his business would continue to provide a handsome living for his descendants nearly three centuries later, or that the knowledge accrued by his firm would one day play an important part in defeating a determined enemy in the most terrible war the world had known.

John Brock, drawn by the artist John Hassall (1868–1948).

CHAPTER 2

Fireworks in Their Blood

Firework shows in John Brock's day were frequently an unsavoury business. It was an age in which bull-baiting, bear-baiting, dog-fighting and cock-fighting were hugely popular forms of entertainment, and if the odd human participant came a cropper too, as when Christopher Preston, the proprietor of the notorious Bear Garden at Hockley-in-the-Hole in Clerkenwell, London, was attacked and half-devoured by one of his own bears in 1709, so much the better. 'Scratch John Bull and you find the ancient Briton who revels in blood,' remarked *The Pall Mall Gazette*.

Fireworks in themselves, though electrifying to 18th-century spectators, did not satisfy the bloodlust prevalent in many sections of society, but if combined with the barbarous mistreatment of helpless animals they were sure-fire crowd-pleasers. A flyer advertising entertainment at Hockley-in-the-Hole in the early 1700s gave a taste of the grisly delights on offer:

> A Mad Bull dressed up with fireworks is to be turned loose; likewise a dog dressed up with fireworks; also a bear to be turned loose. N.B. a cat to be tied to the bull's tale.

In or about 1712 the then proprietor of Hockley-in-the-Hole began putting on attractions in Marylebone Gardens, close to John Brock's business premises. He imported to Marylebone many of his less edifying specialities, including cock-fighting, bull-baiting, gambling and boxing matches between female contestants. With fireworks readily available just up the road to spice things up, it was easy money. As John's descendant, Alan Brock, wrote nearly two and a half centuries later:

> It is a matter rather of interest than of pride that I refer to the probability that an ancestor of mine was responsible for the fireworks employed in these repulsive exhibitions, from his place of business in the neighbouring Islington Road. One is glad to remember that there were other, and more reputable, outlets for the family's pyrotechnical activities close at hand in the pleasure gardens that had sprung up in the neighbourhood.

There is a German saying that once a man has smelt black powder he will be unable to stay away from it for the rest of his life, and no doubt this was true of John Brock. Exactly when he set up business in Islington as an 'artist in fireworks' is lost to time, but according to some accounts he did so in 1698 when he was twenty-one years old. It is more than likely that as boy he would have witnessed and have been inspired by the displays staged on the Thames by that great Fire Master, Martin Beckman, and it is possible that he supplied some of the fireworks that thrilled the crowds celebrating the end of the War of the Spanish Succession in 1713. Certainly he would have wanted to involve himself where possible in more wholesome attractions than those inspired by the owner of Hockley-in-the-Hole, and he may well have had a hand in the illuminations and fireworks in Marylebone Gardens held to celebrate King George I's birthday in May 1718.

The gunpowder he used was supplied by the Chilworth Gunpowder Mills near Guildford in Surrey, a business established by the East India Company in 1626 on the banks of the Tilling Bourne, and it was Chilworth gunpowder that did for him. Some kind of disaster befell him on the significant day of 5 November 1720 – according to one account it happened while he was checking a mine which had not gone off – and what remained of him was buried in the family plot at St James's Church, Clerkenwell. His wife Eleanor survived him by several years, but his daughter Mary followed him into the London clay three weeks later. The particulars of her death are not known but she was perhaps a victim of the same explosion.

Not that there was anything out of the ordinary about firework fatalities in those reckless times, and it was by no means the last catastrophe to strike the Brock family. No regulations existed to control the making, storage or distribution of fireworks, and accidents to both workers and the public were frequent. Several people often worked together in the same room of a crowded building, typically in a heavily populated area. Gunpowder was kept in open containers, and finished or partly-finished fireworks were left to dry by a fire in an open grate.

One reason for this cavalier approach was that under statutes enacted in the seventeenth century in the wake of all that rowdy behaviour, and still in force until 1860, the whole industry was technically illegal. Indeed, every time the state laid on an exhibition, it was in the odd position of employing people to break the law. Although the rules relating to fireworks were seldom enforced, a consequence of the industry being outside the law was that no regulations were drawn up to control it. A year and a half after John Brock's death, another firework manufacturer, Mr Goodship, was killed when his premises off London's Chancery Lane exploded in a noisy constellation of shells and mines, like demons unleashed from Martin Beckman's tomb. According to a newspaper report:

> As he was making some fireworks, the Gunpowder took fire and blew him up, by which means the house was fired, and that adjoining somewhat damaged. More Mischief had been done, but that there was timely help. The Man is so hurt that his life is despaired of.

That was the end of the road for Goodship's Fireworks and they were never heard of again. Brock's Fireworks, by contrast, went from strength to strength. Though only nineteen years old, John Brock's son, also named John, took over the Islington premises after his father's death, and kept a firm grip on the firework market in North London. No doubt his products continued to be used at some of the more unsavoury places of entertainment, but he preferred to concentrate his skills on developing spectacular shows in London's pleasure gardens. With their wide open spaces, these made ideal venues for the erection of tall frames on which to effect increasingly magnificent and artistic displays.

While no precise record exists of the company's activities prior to 1750, typical set-piece displays by London fireworkers of the time included 'Jupiter discharging lightning and thunder,' 'Two gladiators combating with fire and sword,' and 'Neptune finely carv'd, seated in his chair, drawn by two sea horses on fire-wheels, spearing a dolphin.'

The earliest written records of the Brock family's involvement with fireworks, other than those associated with the Chilworth Gunpowder Mills, date to the 1750s when they were responsible for elaborate shows held at the Marylebone Gardens, using architectural scenery and musical accompaniment to enhance pyrotechnical set-pieces which featured cascades and showers of fire.

For many people, fireworks were still a rather intimidating novelty. One display, which followed a masquerade in Marylebone Gardens in September 1751, was introduced with a semi-apology: 'The playing of the fireworks will not incommode the ladies.' Nor did they meet with everyone's approval. In a denunciation of fireworks in *The Gentleman's Magazine* in 1749, Dr Johnson wrote:

> The first reflection that naturally arises is upon the inequality of the effect to the cause. Here are vast sums expended, many hands, and some heads employed, from day to day, and from month to month…and in what is all this to end? In a building that is to attract the admiration of ages? In a bridge, which may facilitate the commerce of future generations? In a work of any kind which may stand as the model of beauty, or the pattern of virtue? But nothing of this kind is designed; nothing more is projected than a crowd, a shout, and a blaze; the mighty work of artifice and contrivance is to be set on fire for no other purpose that I can see, than to show how idle pyrotechnical virtuosos have been busy…how many

lasting advantages might be purchased, how many acres might be drained, how many ways repaired, how many debtors might be released, how many widows and orphans, whom the war has ruined, might be relieved, by the expense which is about to evaporate in smoke, and to be scattered in rockets?

Several years later Johnson became incensed when some promised fireworks in Marylebone Gardens – probably one of John Brock's enterprises – were cancelled because of rain. Convinced it was a 'mere excuse to save their crackers for a more profitable company,' he persuaded some young hotheads to smash the lamps around the orchestra and to try to ignite the fireworks themselves. Their efforts failed, and for once the truculent Johnson was thwarted.

A more appreciative visitor to Marylebone was George Frideric Handel. He was one of many leading musicians whose works were performed in the gardens at around this time. It is not unreasonable to assume that he attended a Brock's display at least once, and that such a visit might have provided inspiration for his famed 'Music for the Royal Fireworks'.

As the century wore on, the younger John Brock, and later his son James, began providing firework entertainment at the prestigious Vauxhall Gardens, whose elegance and comparatively safe environment kick-started the civilization of Georgian London. They also put on shows at the Ranelagh Gardens in Chelsea, at the less select but no less popular Spa Gardens in Bermondsey, and at the Mulberry Garden in Clerkenwell. Fierce competition

'A View of the Canal, Chinese Building, Rotundo in Ranelagh Gardens with the Masquerade', 1759.

meant that such displays were nearly always lavish, so much so that they were occasionally deemed a nuisance by those who lived nearby. During the 1770s, Marylebone residents tried to stop the fireworks, and an outraged lady named Mrs Fountayne (perhaps a disciple of Samuel Johnson) produced a rocket-case found in her garden as evidence of the disruption. The local magistrate, John Fielding, dismissed the protests and the displays continued.

The Brock family were by now pre-eminent among British fireworkers. They worked closely for a time with the renowned Italian pyrotechnist Giovanni Battista Torre (known as 'Fireworks Macaroni') who staged spectacular displays at Marylebone in which actors and dancers mimed scenes from classical myths against a background of sparkling special effects. In her novel *Evelina*, published in 1778, Fanny Burney described being frightened by one such display, masterminded by Torre, and probably assisted by the Brocks:

> The firework was really beautiful, and told, with wonderful ingenuity, the story of Orpheus and Eurydice: but, at the moment of the fatal look, which separated them for ever, there was such an explosion of fire, and so horrible a noise, that we all, as of one accord, jumped hastily from the form, and ran away some paces, fearing that we were in danger of mischief, from the innumerable sparks of fire which glittered in the air.

A generation later, Thomas Brock the elder – great-grandson of the firm's founder – moved his business to the east of London in 1782. He also worked

'A View of the Grand South Walk in Vaux Hall Gardens with the Triumphal Arches, Mr Handel's Statue', 1753.

with Torre and helped with two of his signature pieces, 'Mount Etna' and 'Forge of Vulcan', which featured erupting volcanoes with streams of lava pouring down their sides. In his journal of reminiscences, *A Book for a Rainy Day*, the antiquarian John Smith recalled being taken to see the fireworks in Marylebone Gardens in the 1780s and 'thinking them prodigiously grand.' The Brock family may also have assisted with some of Torre's displays at Versailles, in particular the extravaganza which celebrated the marriage of the Dauphin to Marie Antoinette in 1770.

During this period Torre established numerous pleasure gardens in France, including Torre's Vauxhall near the Porte Saint-Martin in Paris. As a result 'vauxhall' became a generic in the French language for 'pleasure garden'. Curiously, the word also embedded itself in the Russian language. The destination of the first Russian railway was a pleasure park known as 'Vauxhall Gardens' at Pavlovsk, south of St Petersburg. Passengers took to referring to this station as 'vokzal', and in due course all new stations were called 'vokzals', as they are to this day.

The first time fireworks were let off across Britain to celebrate a national event was the Golden Jubilee of King George III on 25 October 1809. Some 34 towns and cities, including Manchester, Hull, Edinburgh and Dublin held displays, and many used fireworks supplied by Brock's. (The authorities in Warwick, possibly mindful of the mishap witnessed by Elizabeth I more than two centuries earlier, expressly forbade them.) At Woolwich a salute of 50 guns was followed 'by the discharge of an immense number of very fine rockets set up into the air by fifties.' The king and queen spent the evening at Frogmore where they hosted a fete to which 'every family in Windsor' as well as 'one hundred of the young gentlemen of Eton College' were invited. A local newspaper reported:

> A more striking spectacle was never witnessed than that presented by the fireworks which, reflected in the lake in a thousand directions, heightened inconceivably the splendour of the scene.

The 19th century proved even more successful for Brock's Fireworks than the 18th, although it was not without its setbacks. In advertising his displays, the fifth generational William Brock – who operated from Whitechapel in what was later to become the 'east end' of London – revelled in the wildly extravagant language much favoured in Georgian times to boost his reputation. In June 1812, in announcing a display at the Mermaid Gardens, Hackney, he boasted in the *Morning Chronicle* that 'the greatest feast for the eye ever exhibited is a superb firework by that unparalleled artist, Mr Brock, Engineer.'

An advertisement for a display at Ipswich in 1818, which, incidentally, was one of the first to use the term 'Roman Candle', lauded the said Mr Brock 'whose indefatigable study and attention of his profession, enables him to produce devices hitherto unknown to the Art, and with a richness and brilliancy surpassing all precedent.' The bill described Brock's as 'an old-established firm of ripe experience'.

William's flier for a show at Highbury House, Islington, on 8 September 1823 – in which he described himself as 'Engineer to Vauxhall' – was in similar vein:

> Mr Brock begs to return his grateful acknowledgements to the Nobility and Gentry of Highbury, Islington and its Vicinity, and the Public in general, for the distinguished approbation his Fire Works was honoured with last time; and anxious to continue the pre-eminence which a thorough knowledge of his profession has given to his Exhibitions, will, in the present, produce such variety of New Devices and Fires as cannot fail of giving universal satisfaction, and evince to a discerning Public his superiority in the Art.

Ever inventive, William also helped to develop the Christmas cracker by coating a minute particle of chemical on a cardboard strip to produce a snap. These made their first appearance at around the time of the battle of Waterloo and were originally known as Waterloo Crackers. But his work was not all plain sailing, and disaster struck on 3 September 1825 when his Whitechapel factory was destroyed by an explosion. More than a century after his great-great-grandfather had blown himself up on Guy Fawkes Day, firework safety regulations remained as lax as ever. It is telling that not only was the factory located in a heavily populated residential area, but that William himself lived within a few yards of the factory with his wife Mary and their four sons and four daughters. On top of that, the explosion was caused by two boys in his employ who had very little experience of gunpowder and who had been left alone in the factory while the rest of the workforce went off for breakfast. *Bell's Weekly Messenger* provided a graphic account of what happened:

> Yesterday morning, about half-past eight o'clock, Whitechapel Road, and the numerous streets that abound there, were thrown into the greatest state of agitation, by the inhabitants experiencing a most tremendous shock, as if caused by a volcano or an earthquake. The houses for a considerable distance were deserted by their inhabitants, and men, women, and children were seen running about in all directions, under the impression that the world was at an end. It was soon ascertained that their alarm was produced by the explosion of the factory of Mr Brock, the artist in fireworks at No 11, Baker's Row, Whitechapel Road, nearly opposite the London Hospital.
>
> The following particulars relative to this direful disaster have reached us: Mr Brock has resided for the last five years in Baker's Row, and at the back of his dwelling-house is his repository for fireworks, where they are manufactured. This building is about 50 feet by

20 feet, and contains three magazines, which are lined with lead, and would be perfectly secure from fire, should it occur, on any of the adjoining premises. In these receptacles were deposited all the powder, composition, and, in fact, all the combustible matter, and Mr B. was remarkable for the method he had taken to prevent any accident occurring on his premises. A few weeks since he had taken two boys out of the poor-house to instruct in the art of firework making, and he kept them chiefly employed in filling and ramming the cases of the sky-rockets, serpents, squibs, etc.

Yesterday morning, at the time above stated, Mr Brock and his men left the factory to go to breakfast, leaving the two boys engaged at the work-board, ramming the sky-rockets. They had scarcely sat down to their meal when they, as well as the inhabitants around them for some distance, heard a sort of rumbling noise as if of some distant thunder, and the next moment a tremendous and deafening explosion followed, and the air was illumined with lights of various descriptions, and accompanied by continued reports. The concussion thus occasioned was so great that the inmates in the different houses were shaken from their seats, many of whom were sitting at their breakfast, and the tables and tea-things were upset and broken to pieces. The window frames were all forced out, and the brickbats and materials were flying about in every direction. The roofs of Mr Brock's manufactory, and the factory of Mr M'Devitt adjoining, were blown to a considerable height, and the falling materials did considerable mischief.

After the agitation was somewhat subsided, an inquiry into the cause of the accident took place, when it appeared from the statement of the two boys (who were blown a considerable height and were much injured) that they were at work ramming the rockets, when the ramrod struck against the funnel, and the friction caused a spark, which flew into the bowl of gunpowder that stood near them; this soon exploded, and ran like a train to all the other fireworks in the factory, and at length communicated to the magazines, which caused the disaster. Mr Brock, however, declares that it could not have arisen in that way, as the nipple of the funnel was copper, therefore a friction would not cause a spark. One poor woman, sister to the beadle, who lives next door to Mr Brock, was so dreadfully injured by the broken glass that she lies in the London Hospital, without hopes of recovery. Ten houses were seriously damaged, and over sixty had their windows broken from top to bottom.

In the words of William himself, the accident 'nearly annihilated his prospects of providing for a numerous family,' but somehow he managed to pick up the pieces (literally) and rebuild his business. One of those who helped him back on his feet was Tom 'Bravo' Rouse, the larger-than-life 'mine host' of the Eagle Tavern in City Road. The Eagle, immortalised in the nursery rhyme 'Pop goes the Weasel', had extensive grounds which were used for concerts, balloon ascents, optical shows known as cosmoramas and, somewhat surprisingly, annual contests between wrestlers from Devon and Cornwall. In the wake of the explosion, Rouse offered to hold a benefit night for William, allowing him free use of his grounds to stage a firework display.

William Brock Snr., 1779–1849. Described in his literature as 'Engineer to Vauxhall, the original Ranelagh and Spa Gardens, Bermondsey'.

William was overjoyed. Praising Rouse for the 'sympathy that characterises the man and does honour to the heart', he announced an exhibition 'comprising a series of New and Elegant Devices, which from a long life of practice and chymical knowledge of his profession, cannot fail of giving the satisfaction always attendant on his efforts.' The evening was evidently a success, for Rouse continued to host 'Brock's Benefits' for William, and later his younger brother, Thomas, for years to come. A cynic might suggest that other factors, such as the bar receipts or side-show takings, lay behind Rouse's generosity, but in any event he acquired a taste for 'benefits'. In ensuing years he held one for the 'blind Hebrew brethren in the East', another for 'The Laudable Pension Society of Bethnal Green', and a third for 'Decayed Druids and their wives and orphans'.

Helped by the likes of Rouse, William saved the family business and continued his experiments with renewed vigour. Two years after the explosion he announced that he had achieved a breakthrough in firework colouring. Prior to the 19th century, the only colours that could be produced by fireworks were orange from black powder, and white from metal powders. Various tricks were tried to suggest colour, such as placing coloured-glass screens in front of the fireworks, but none was satisfactory. In the early 1800s French pyrotechnists experimented with metallic salts to manipulate colour (strontium for red, barium for green, copper for blue, sodium for yellow).

William kept abreast of their advances and may even have been ahead of his French counterparts. By the mid-1820s, continuing to diversify his business, he had developed a brisk trade in the sale of coloured fires to the theatres – his 'red fire' sold at £1 and 4 shillings a pound, equivalent to about £250 per kilo in today's money. One way or another he was able to declare in 1827 that he had invented devices 'superbly adorned with a variety of colours, the result

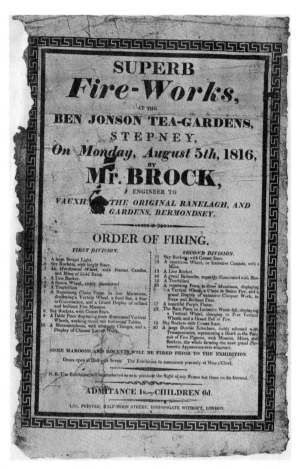

Poster or 'bill' advertising a Brock's display in 1816. Ben Jonson's fame was being used to promote this pleasure garden. Living at the same time as Shakespeare and regarded as one of the finest writers of his era, Jonson is buried in Westminster Abbey.

of chymical research, amongst which will be produced (a recent discovery of Mr Brock's) an Emerald Green Flame.'

In due course, in the now time-honoured family tradition, he passed on his accumulated knowledge of fireworks to his eldest son, another William, who, like the five generations of pyrotechnical Brocks before him, styled himself in the firm's literature as 'an artist in fireworks'. The younger William took charge of the firm in the 1840s, and ran it with the same enthusiasm as his father. In an advertisement for his annual firework gala in 1858 at the New Globe Tavern and Pleasure Grounds in Mile End Road, he boasted that the display 'for correctness, execution and brilliancy will not be surpassed by the production of any Public Garden in the Metropolis.' Brock's were

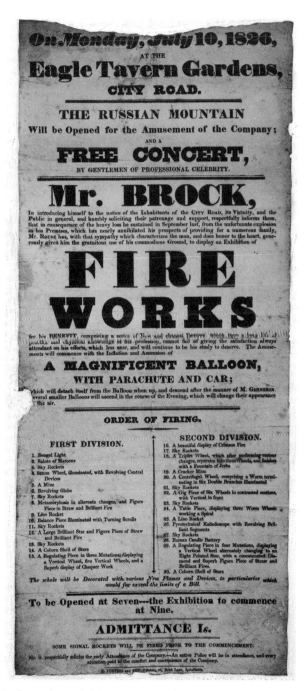

Bill advertising display in the Eagle Tavern, City Road in 1826. This is the tavern associated with the popular song 'Pop Goes the Weasel' – 'Up and down the City Road, in and out of the Eagle'.

William Brock Jnr., 1813–1869.

by now so renowned that nobody, except perhaps a handful of rival fireworkers, would have thought to dispute this claim.

But times were changing. By the middle of the 19th century, most of the pleasure gardens which once hosted firework displays had disappeared beneath the tide of bricks and mortar of the ever-growing cities and towns. The most ambitious pyrotechnical efforts, in the limited space available, were dwarfed by comparison with the great national displays staged in the London parks for the Jubilee of George III and the Coronation of Queen Victoria. In addition, state-sponsored displays held to mark the end of the Crimean War in 1856 were widely criticised for being over-lavish with public money. A new direction was needed, and the Brock's were more than up to the challenge.

CHAPTER 3

Taking the Palace by Storm

During the 1860s, William's third son, the seventh generational Charles Thomas Brock, became the new driving force behind the business. A tall, imposing young man with a full black beard, he had all the skills, vision and entrepreneurial spirit of his forebears. From an early age it was his ambition to raise the art of fireworks 'to a level never before dreamed of, even in the palmiest days of the eighteenth century'. His nephew Alan would write of him:

> Possessed of a curiously impulsive temperament, fruitful of ideas, he planned on an heroic scale. Everything he undertook must be not only the best, but the biggest – or at least bigger than had been achieved before.

Charles's greatest achievement was to usher in an extraordinarily lucrative era of pyrotechny at the Crystal Palace. The gigantic prefabricated building of iron and glass had originally been erected in London's Hyde Park to house the Great Exhibition of 1851, but had since been transported and rebuilt in the south London suburb of Sydenham. With its 293,655 panes of glass, its glittering indoor fountain and its ten double staircases leading to an array of upper galleries, it ranked not only as the most grandiose show-place in England, but also as one of the marvels of the age, perfectly conveying the magnitude and assurance of the Victorian era. 'The sight of the Crystal Palace was incredibly gorgeous, really like fairyland,' wrote Queen Victoria in her diary when she made her first visit there. (The queen, concerned by the hundreds of sparrows nesting in the glass roof and leaving messy deposits on the exhibits, sought the advice of the Duke of Wellington, who famously replied: 'Try sparrow-hawks, ma'am.')

Charles was quick to see the potential of the Crystal Palace in its new suburban location. To use his own words, its 'terraces, fountains and foliage offered unrivalled advantages for the display of grand effects.' His proposal in

Charles Thomas Brock, 1843–1881.

1865 to hold regular displays there did not at first find favour with the mutton-chopped mercantilists on the Crystal Palace board. One reason for this was that the old London pleasure gardens, and by association fireworks, had become linked in the public mind with prostitution. Conservative to a man, the Palace directors thought fireworks were not quite 'proper' and would lower the tone of what Thackeray had called 'that blazing arch of lucid glass'. Such was their distaste for pyrotechnics that they had banned firework makers from a trade exhibition at the Palace in 1862. They had taken a similarly dim view of a suggestion to hire the world-famous French tightrope walker, Blondin. 'Suppose he was to fall?' one of the directors had asked fearfully, anticipating the bad publicity that an accident might provoke. To which Blondin's manager, Harry Colcord, replied: 'Blondin, fall from a rope! He can't!'

The Palace's designer, Sir Joseph Paxton, was even more of a fuddy-duddy than the directors. He was not only opposed to fireworks but to music as well. 'Music!' he retorted, when told that people would tire of the Palace without amusements. 'Have we not Mr Schallehn's band in the Music Court?' and complained that the Palace would become a bear garden if any other musicians were permitted to play there.

Like Blondin, who in time became one of the Palace's most popular attractions, (appearing there against a background of fireworks) Charles refused to take 'no' for an answer. He told the directors he was confident there would be 'a large attendance of the better classes' at his displays and assured them that fireworks were 'really not of an immoral tendency'. He also pointed out that no further events need take place if the first one was a failure. He perhaps used his masonic connections (he belonged to Temple Lodge 101) to pile on the pressure, and after months of procrastination the directors finally capitulated. In consequence, Brock's held their first Crystal Palace display – a 'Grand Competition of Pyrotechnists' organised by Charles's father, William – on 12 July 1865.

Charles wrote afterwards that the event 'far exceeded my most sanguine expectations.' Twenty-seven thousand people attended the show, spurring the delighted Crystal Palace directors to give the go-ahead for five more displays that season, swelling the total to 202,949. Contracts for future exhibitions, with Brock's as 'sole pyrotechnists', were drawn up. It was a watershed year for the firm, and from then on the Crystal Palace displays became the acknowledged standard of perfection for firework-makers across the globe. Single-handedly Charles changed the public perception of fireworks and made them respectable again.

Even now, he could not have foreseen that the Crystal Palace fireworks would become the cultural phenomenon that they did. On the back of the Crystal Palace breakthrough, he opened a new factory in a seven-acre field at Nunhead, in what is now south London, and began making fireworks on a previously undreamt of scale in the trade – 'the vast expanse of the locale of my displays necessitating extraordinary expenditure of material.' The firm's profits soared and Nunhead, which was conveniently just five miles from the Crystal Palace, was dubbed 'the headquarters of pyrotechny' by the press. (Journalists noted gleefully that by a macabre coincidence a sign proclaiming 'This way to the cemetery' stood close to the factory gates.) Local historian William Harnett Blanch enthused:

> Many are aware of the vast improvements that have been made in the quality and effectiveness of Mr. Brock's displays, of the marvellous delicacy, variety, and brilliancy of his coloured lights, the heights to which they are propelled, and the great distances they are made to float in the upper air.

With each season the Crystal Palace shows grew more elaborate as Charles developed the tricks of the trade he had learned from his father into what was virtually a new art form. On Sydenham Hill the startling scream of the 'whistling rocket' was heard for the first time. Silver fire-wheels up to thirty feet in diameter made their debut in front of astonished spectators. So did the final 'Good Night' in letters of dripping fire. Displays often took 70 men up to three days to prepare on site, and acquired a new brilliance thanks to the introduction of metal powders and chlorates into the pyrotechnical mixes. On a typical evening a team of up to 200 Brock's operators fired 2,000 rockets, 120 shells, 600 Roman candles and 400 coloured lights.

The highlights of the shows were another of Charles's specialities. These were the great set-pieces or 'fire pictures', usually depicting famous victories or battle scenes such as the siege of Gibraltar or the battle of Chesapeake Bay. Over the years these pictorial extravaganzas expanded from 20 feet to 600 feet in width, leaving the crowds open-mouthed in wonder and never disappointed. They were vast enterprises, involving an army of artists, pyrotechnists, carpenters, and display operatives. The huge quantities of material needed ranged from the frames used to construct the sets to the two-pointed nails used to hold the lances. For the larger displays, more than five tons of material were consumed at a cost of around £10 a minute for a half-hour show. This included up to 14 miles of quick-match (cotton soaked in a gunpowder solution to prime fireworks). As the firm liked to point out, this was enough to stretch from the Crystal Palace to Charing Cross and back.

Seats on the terrace, facing a vast sweep of Kent and Surrey countryside fading into the evening shadows, cost just sixpence. The first indication that a display was imminent came at dusk when the warning boom of a maroon was sounded to clear the grounds behind the main set-piece. The show began a quarter of an hour later, usually with a flight of hundreds of rockets. As one visitor, Frederick Willis, observed in his memoir, *A Book of London Yesterdays*:

> What fireworks they were! Brock's let themselves go at the Crystal Palace. The audience never applauded in the usual way. All they could do was to emit a long-drawn 'Oooooo' of admiration. This chorus was as gratifying as any ordinary applause. 'Ooooo!' – and then, aside, 'Isn't it beauuuutiful?'

Sydenham Hill being one of London's highest points, the blue, red and gold of the rockets could be seen for miles around, as could the golden candles of fire spilling gracefully and dripping to earth. On still nights the rumble of exploding gunpowder could be heard in central London. 'No pen can adequately describe the wondrous magnificence of it all,' ran the Brock's literature in an echo of the purple prose William Brock had deployed so effectively half a century earlier. 'No artist could do justice to its dazzling brilliance. There is one way only: to witness it yourself.'

Within three years the Crystal Palace firework displays had become the biggest attraction in Britain. As one newspaper proclaimed: 'There is no form of entertainment which pleases so many persons far and near at so small a cost as Fireworks.' The number of events rose to 18 a year, always held on Thursday evenings or on Bank Holidays, and usually accompanied by music from the Crystal Palace Band. In those pre-cinema, pre-television days, nothing could match these shows for sheer excitement and spectacle. For hundreds of thousands of people they became a brief, glorious escape from the realities of industrial England. 'Parents bring your children! Children bring your parents!' ran the Brock's advertisements.

A correspondent for *Punch* magazine wrote:

I rapturously applauded the Maroons and Balloons, the *Saucisons* and Asteroids, and Magnesium lights (which Mrs Malaprop, near whom I had the honour of sitting, would call Sausages and Asterisks and Magnesia), the Cascades and Fountains, the Comets and Rockets, the Batteries and Salvoes, the Temples and the Palm Trees, and all the rest of the successful splendours achieved by Mr Brock, who seems fired by a noble sky aspiring ambition constantly to surpass himself.

The Racing Times published the overheard comments of a husband and wife who were watching one of the Thursday night displays:

Woman: 'Oh, John, isn't it lovely?'
Man: 'Why, yes, it's pretty good.'
Woman: 'Good! But it's lovely, lovely, lovely! I've never seen anything like it before.'
Man: 'Perhaps not, but you'll get used to it by and by. It's as good as this every night in Heaven.'

The one downside to the extraordinary success of the Crystal Palace venture was that it sparked an irreversible rift between Charles and his father, William. The latter apparently disapproved when Charles entered into a contract with a Parisian company to hold shows at the Palace, and resisted all attempts to placate him. When he died in 1869 he had reportedly not spoken to his son for three years. Charles regretted the estrangement for the rest of his life.

Despite this domestic upset, Charles remained single-minded in his efforts to ensure that the Sydenham Hill exhibitions remained the most popular and most talked about form of entertainment in the country. He trademarked the name 'Crystal Palace Fireworks', and garnered publicity by evolving a formula of concerts and fireworks for special occasions and distinguished visitors. It was not long before he began attracting royalty to the VIP stand at the Crystal Palace. In July 1867 the Sultan of Turkey, on his first visit to England, went there with the Prince of Wales to see a Brock's display arranged in his honour. According to *The Times*, it was 'probably the grandest display of fireworks ever witnessed in Europe.'

The Sultan was so impressed that there and then he appointed Charles pyrotechnist to the Ottoman Court and asked him to establish a fireworks factory outside Constantinople. Unable to find the time to go to Turkey himself, Charles sent a man named Bell to train local men in the art of pyrotechnics. Things did not go to plan. As Bell's steamer set sail for England at the end of his visit, his students attempted to honour his departure by staging a firework display on rafts on the River Bosphorus. Unfortunately they managed to set fire to a raft. Everything – rafts and fireworks alike – went up in one massive explosion. No more was heard about a factory in Turkey.

The following year the Prince of Wales again attended a Crystal Palace display, this time with his brother, Alfred, Duke of Edinburgh. Charles had by now become adept at thinking up random reasons for royal fireworks festivities, and the show celebrated the latter's return from a voyage round the world in HMS *Galatea*. It included a full-size representation of the vessel in full sail, illuminated in fireworks. The prince enjoyed himself so much at these shows that he took on the unofficial role of VIP tour guide to the Crystal Palace fireworks. Reinforcing the royal seal of approval, he returned in 1869 to watch a display in honour of the visit of the Viceroy of Egypt, and again in 1871 to celebrate the visit of Grand Duke Vladimir of Russia.

In December of that year the prince fell seriously ill with typhoid fever and for several days his life hung in the balance. As he lay delirious in his bed at Sandringham, the future Poet Laureate, Alfred Austin, chose to publish some verse intended to capture the severity of the situation. The lines were considered to be above his average.

> Across the wires the electric message came,
> He is no better, he is much the same.

After numerous crises, the prince made a full recovery, and prayers were offered up in thanks throughout the land. It was an indication of the esteem in which he held the Brock's shows that the following summer he and several other members of the royal family attended a firework display at the Crystal Palace to celebrate his return to health. It was the firm's most ambitious production yet, and a record crowd of 60,000 came to the event. There was no keeping the prince away. An even more elaborate display, the Czar's Fete, was held two years later to honour the visit to England of Czar Alexander II of Russia and the Czarina. The prince was again in attendance, this time in the company of the Princess of Wales.

Another appreciative guest was the Shah of Persia, Nasr-el-Din. He was so impressed by the fireworks during a visit in June 1873 that he postponed his departure from London so that he could see another display.

He arrived on the second occasion on an ordinary 'shilling day', paying his money at the turnstile like everyone else so that he could mix with the crowds. He confided to the manager, when the latter caught up with him, that he had not spent a happier evening in all of Europe. When he was recognised, the Crystal Palace band struck up a popular tune and the palace crowd sang along lustily:

> Have you seen the Shah?
> Smoking his cigar?
> Twenty wives and two black eyes
> Have you seen the Shah?

This enthusiastic rendition is said to have started the patriotic singing that took place at the Crystal Palace over many years.

The Shah of Persia with the Prince and Princess of Wales witnessing Brock's grand firework display at the Crystal Palace, July 1889. 'Well did Messrs. Brock merit the Prince's eulogiums'. (*Penny Illustrated Paper*, 13 July 1889). 'At the close of the fireworks the Prince of Wales sent for Mr. Brock, warmly congratulated him on a "glorious display" and presented him to the Shah, who shook him by the hand and expressed his delight with what he had seen.' (*The Pictorial News*, July 1889)

Never one to rest on his pyrotechnic laurels, Charles kept dreaming up new ideas to draw in the crowds. One effect, introduced in 1870, was that of two comets travelling down a wire from the top of one of the Crystal Palace towers to the terrace below. Later the comets were replaced by a dragon, then by Mother Goose, and in 1872 by a 'Fiery Bicycle'. In 1875 Charles suggested 'The Descent of Jove the Thunderer'. This, he decreed, would be enacted by a living man sliding down the wire, clad in a skin-tight suit made of reflecting metal mirrors and illuminated by a frame of fireworks. He tested the idea himself, apparently successfully, but things did not go as planned on the actual night. The name of the performer hired to carry out the feat was given in the programme as Signor Gregorini, although in reality he was an actor called Bill Gregory. Having begun his descent from the northern tower,

'Signor Gregorini' became stuck half-way down and had to remain there for the remainder of the display. His Anglo-Saxon comments as squibs and crackers exploded all around him were overheard by some of the spectators and reportedly left no doubt as to his real country of origin. In the interests of safety, this particular act was abandoned, but not before the story of 'Signor Gregorini's' mishap had gone round the world. The *Mount Ida Chronicle* of New Zealand commented:

> No fatal accident occurred, but it is hoped that before Jove the Thunderer again assumes the position of a flying angel some steps will be taken to prevent the possibility of his becoming one of these aerial beings permanently.

A more successful innovation was the reproduction in fireworks of famous buildings. These included the Crystal Palace itself, as well as the Arc de Triomphe, the Mosque at Delhi and the cathedrals at Worcester, Salisbury and Strasbourg. Natural catastrophes were also staged, such as avalanches, tempests and the volcanic eruption that destroyed Pompeii.

So successful were the displays that in 1869 the Crystal Palace directors agreed that Charles Brock should receive all gate receipts for one night a year 'as a mark of their appreciation of his unfailing efforts and outstanding achievements in the field of pyrotechny during the past five seasons'. These annual displays became known as 'Brock's Benefits', and were a convenient way of using up the substantial number of fireworks that had failed the firm's quality control tests during the year. They were added in, so guaranteeing a huge show.

The term 'Brock's Benefit' quickly became a metaphor for any loud, smokey or dramatic incident. If someone had the misfortune to be struck on the head or in the eye in late Victorian England, they were as likely as not to declare: 'Lumme! It was like Brock's Benefit!' The same went for everything from a thunderstorm to the clatter of falling pans in a kitchen. According to one newspaper, a man in a train was heard remonstrating with a pipe-smoking passenger: 'Look 'ere mate, this isn't Brock's Benefit.' The term was even used to describe rowdy parliamentary debates, as when the *Daily Herald* described a Commons speech on Irish Home Rule by Sir Edward Carson as 'like a Brock's Benefit at the Crystal Palace'. Ditto a particularly robust Budget in 1909. In due course it would become an everyday phrase in the mud of Flanders and the Somme, earning itself a place in both the *Oxford Dictionary of Phrase and Fable*, and *Brewer's Dictionary of London Phrase and Fable*. Later still, it became part of the Royal Air Force's official vocabulary, being used to describe any intense display of flares, searchlights and anti-aircraft fire. As *The Sportsman*

'The Destruction of Pompeii', July 1886. See Appendix II for a description of this piece. (*The Graphic*, July 1886)

observed in 1892: 'Brock's Benefit is almost as familiar among Englishmen, and quite as well known among Londoners, as Bank Holiday.'

By the 1870s the Brock name was so ingrained in Britain's cultural iconography that it began making its way into contemporary literature. In 1876 *All the Year Round*, a periodical founded and owned by Charles Dickens, a story was published called 'Blind Guy Fawkes', which included a vivid description of a fireworks party:

> We are in a great square on a November night, dim walls enclosing it. Rockets are shooting far into the wintry sky, Roman candles are jetting out stars of many-coloured flame. Catherine-wheels whizz round on tree trunks; squibs are spurting out their short but sparkling life; crackers banging and barking on the ground, noisy, demonstrative, and soon extinct, like fussy politicians; and, besides all these, there is plenty of high pyrotechnic art from Mr Brock's famous laboratory – set-pieces, Chinese trees, fiery fountains and the like. Plenty of noise, plenty of fire, and plenty of light.

Later in the decade Oscar Wilde wrote a short story, 'The Remarkable Rocket', partly inspired by a Brock's display he had attended, while Edith Nesbit, author of *The Railway Children*, often referred in her stories to the Crystal Palace fireworks. She wrote in *The Book of Dragons:*

> George and Jane had sixpence each, and they spent the whole amount on a golden rain, which would not light for ever so long, and when it did light went out almost at once, so they had to look at the fireworks in the gardens next door, and at the ones at the Crystal Palace, which were very glorious indeed.

It was the same with plays and shows. When Toole's Theatre near London's Charing Cross staged a burlesque version of Goethe's *Faust*, the Brocken Mountain became a 'Brock'un' pyrotechnic display, although on the first night, as one theatre critic noted drily, 'the fireworks declined to go off, and the burlesque ended with a fizzle.'

In 1870 Charles, who had added military pyrotechnics to the firm's activities, won a lucrative contract to supply the armies of Napoleon III with two million cartridges and fuses for the Franco-Prussian War. He built three large sheds at Nunhead for the assignment, expanded his workforce and completed the order with impressive speed, the staged contract being administered on behalf of the French government by the ancient clothiers, grain merchants and industrial conglomerate S.W. Silver & Co. This profitable deal put the firm on such a secure financial footing that by the middle of the decade he felt confident enough to declare in advertisements: 'Displays undertaken in any part of the world.'

Some of the foreign displays Charles masterminded were even grander than those at the Crystal Palace, particularly a series of spectacular shows he laid on for the Prince of Wales's 17-week tour of India between November 1875 and January 1876. Charles himself could not find the time to travel to India in person, but instead he sent his younger brother, Arthur, to run the operation with a team of eight other Brock's specialists. They took with them fireworks to the value of £35,000 (around £3.5 million in today's money).

Though only 17, Arthur did not let the side down. The prince – by now a seasoned Brock's aficionado – was greeted by dazzling displays at every major venue, including Bombay, Madura, Colombo, Madras, and Jaipur. The illuminations of the Taj Mahal and of the 300-foot-high Rock of Trichinopoly in southern India were two of the outstanding events of the visit. *The Graphic* reported:

> All the principal points of the Rock were lighted up with lines of light, while the summit was ablaze with magnesium and coloured fire. The summit heaved forth rockets like a volcano, Niagaras of fire burst over the various terraces, while in the tank below the rock were innumerable water fireworks, the lake being alive with fire devices of every hue.

As soon as the Indian tour was over, Charles signed a contract for four displays in Philadelphia's Fairmount Park to celebrate the 100th anniversary of America's independence. On this occasion he chose to go himself, accompanied by both Arthur and another brother, 21-year-old William. For three young men with plenty of time on their hands, it was an exhilarating and eye-opening experience. The park's centennial exhibition showcased all the latest New World innovations, and among items unveiled for the first time were Heinz tomato ketchup, a Pullman Palace car and a Remington typewriter. When shown Alexander Graham Bell's new telephone, Dom Pedro II of Brazil is said to have exclaimed: 'My God, it talks,' and was equally astounded when it 'spoke' to him a minute or two later in Portuguese.

But of all the attractions at Fairmount Park, Brock's Fireworks created the biggest stir. The displays were on a scale not previously attempted in the western hemisphere and, as one American newspaper put it, set a standard that 'far surpassed anything of the kind seen in this country.' Tragedy struck during the first show when a Brock's operator named Taylor was killed by the premature detonation of a twelve-inch shell. His leg was blown off above the knee, and although all three brothers offered themselves up for the then almost untried operation of direct blood transfusion, he could not be saved.

The rest of the visit was a triumph. On 4 July alone, some 250,000 people paid half a dollar each to walk through the turnstiles, and of these the vast majority came primarily for the pyrotechnics. The display set the bar for future Independence Day celebrations. It was unintentionally made all the more spectacular when the threat of rain led to some of the set-pieces, which included temples, portraits of George Washington, mounds, volcanoes, stars, patriotic mottoes, pyramids, and other structures, being discharged almost simultaneously.

Despite its rushed nature, the show was rapturously received. 'Gunpowder and Glory' was how *The Times* of Philadelphia headlined it the next morning. *Frank Leslie's Illustrated Newspaper* said of the final show:

> The magnificent, and in this country, unparalleled display, ended with a simultaneous *girandole* of two thousand large rockets, which, bursting in mid-air, poured an aerial bouquet of peerless grandeur. The pieces exceeded in extent, diversity, and magnificence anything ever attempted in that line on this side of the Atlantic.

It was perhaps ironic that displays held in celebration of America's independence from the British Empire had been devised and executed by three Englishmen, but no one seemed to notice or to care. The president of the exhibition, Joseph Hawley, wrote to Charles: 'The displays were highly creditable to you for the skill and ingenuity of their preparation and the novelty and beauty of the devices.'

Charles himself was delighted by the Philadelphia success, and saw America as a land of opportunity. He wrote to his mother:

> Our displays surprised and astonished [the Americans] and well they might. I think when we first came over we had some fear of bowie knives and pocket revolvers [but they] seem to me to have that in them that would make them a fine industrious people … they are sober, hard-working and intelligent men … they don't know everything, far from it, and many a great fortune could be made here. Capital and original brains is wanted, the brains most especially.

Fireworks, of course, were nothing new to the Americans. They had been around from the time of the earliest settlers (in 1608 Captain John Smith 'fired a few rockets' to impress the natives during the difficult first days of the Jamestown colony) but the four Brock's Fireworks' spectaculars in Philadelphia in 1876 are often credited with having done more than anything else to start the taste for big displays on the American continent.

Later the same year Charles, William and Arthur went to India to supervise displays in Calcutta, Delhi and other cities to mark the proclamation of Queen Victoria as Empress of India. The Prince of Wales was again present at the celebrations, and once more Brock's fireworks were an integral part of the pomp and ceremony. Some £4,000 went up in smoke at each event.

The Delhi celebrations were attended by the greatest ever gathering of Indian rulers and princes. They were enlivened by a stampede of 182 government elephants, which trampled several people and created an unplanned for cloud of dust. Charles always regarded it as fortunate that the stampede was sparked by the firing of the imperial 101-gun salute, and not by the fireworks, as would undoubtedly have been the case had the pyrotechnics preceded the salute. The Brocks' party later travelled north, and the display they put on in Rajputana so impressed the Maharaja of Jaipur that he despatched a contingent of state elephants to bring Charles, William and Arthur to his camp so that he could present them with pearl, emerald and gold pendants. Arthur later recalled that on one of his visits, the Maharaja had been 'so pleased with his work that he pressed him to remain as his guest in the palace, with a guard of honour, saddle horses and a hunting elephant at his disposal. After a stay of six weeks, upon taking his leave, a magnificent collar of pearls with a diamond pendant was fastened round his neck, whilst two of his lucky subordinates received similar though smaller presents.'

Brock's Fireworks were by now an integral part of the imperial establishment, and occasions such as those at Delhi and Calcutta emphasised their increasingly significant role in enhancing the thrill of empire and in showing off British ingenuity and creativity to people in far-flung corners of the world.

The Maharaja of Jaipur – the Brocks' client and host. (Wikimedia Commons)

A well-organised pyrotechnic show was an opportunity to represent the Raj as bringing order, discipline and pomp to the empire's most populous and valuable colony. What better way to enthral, impress and command respect from the empire's subjects than to stage brilliant, multi-coloured displays, imported from London, often featuring, among other things, a sparkling likeness of the great Queen Victoria herself, 60 feet high, and gazing down in a regal blaze of splendour while a military band played the national anthem.

The same went for Australia. Brock's established itself there in the 1880s and always strived to enhance reverence for the mother country. Its Australian displays frequently ended with firework depictions of the crown, the Prince of Wales's feathers and the motto 'God Save the Queen'.

The firm stirred patriotic hearts at home as well as abroad, and was held up by many as one of the bastions of British greatness. The *Daily Graphic* noted: 'One thing we do manage in England better than anywhere else is our fireworks. Brock is almost a pillar of our constitution … the fireworks at Crystal Palace in general and Brock's Benefit in particular are national institutions, and Englishmen are justly proud of them.' The paper added that the Londoner who had not at one time or another said to himself that he must go to the Crystal Palace to see the fireworks was 'almost as rare as the man who was not moved by the sight of his native land.'

Pyrotechnical likenesses of Queen Victoria and of other eminent people – 'firework portraiture' as it was known – were introduced by Charles in 1879. The effects were astonishingly accurate. Among those whose images were reproduced in fire before the Crystal Palace crowds were Cetewayo, King of the Zulus, and Tāwhiao, the Maori king. Both visited Sydenham and were astounded to see themselves depicted in this way. (The Maori King was also amazed by the size of the assembled crowd, and told Charles he had not realised there were so many people in the world.) Some of the pyrotechnic portraits were ignited electrically from the royal box by the originals, often after they had enjoyed a sumptuous dinner with the seemingly ever-present Prince of Wales. Sadly Queen Victoria herself was not there when a Brock portrait of her failed to fire properly and winked suggestively at the crowd. One hopes that she would have been amused.

Thanks largely to the royal patronage of the Crystal Palace displays, fireworks become a universally acceptable form of entertainment from the 1870s onwards, to be enjoyed at every level of society. For the wealthy, it became increasingly fashionable to hold displays at private gatherings. In 1872 alone, Brock's organised events on the estates of a dozen or more members of the aristocracy, including the Duke of Bedford and Lord Dartmouth. No request was turned down. In 1874 Charles travelled to Moscow to help with the celebrations of the Duke of Edinburgh's marriage to the Grand Duchess Maria Alexandrovna of Russia, although the planned firework display was eventually cancelled because of the unstable political situation.

Charles Brock's other great achievement was to help frame the Explosives Act of 1875, which was to have a profound influence on the working conditions of people employed in the UK fireworks industry. In conjunction with Sir Vivian Majendie, the Chief Inspector of Explosives, he produced a 3,000-word report which contained numerous recommendations for improving safety, including a proposed ban on the employment of young boys and girls in the industry. He also invited members of a Royal Commission to visit his Nunhead factory, where he showed them a number of pyrotechnic experiments aimed at making firework production and transport safer.

So lax were the existing regulations that in 1874 a team of Brock's employees had been allowed to demonstrate the art of making fireworks in front of packed crowds in the central transept of the Crystal Palace. Surrounded by boxes of gunpowder, they had shown forty separate operations, from the rolling of small paper cases to the filling of large shells and rockets. As Charles's nephew, Alan, wrote some 70 years later:

> The idea of doing such work before a crowd of sightseers, all bent on a close-up view, would be today a pyrotechnist's nightmare, but, of course, in those days no gentleman – or lady – smoked in public.

As if to emphasise the need for legislation, a barge carrying three barrels of benzoline and five tons of gunpowder blew up in the Regent's Canal, close to London Zoo, early one October morning in 1874. All three men on board were killed, and scores of houses were badly damaged. According to one report, the explosion could be heard 25 miles away, and 'dead fish rained from the sky in the West End.' It was probably the greatest explosion in London up to that point and was a timely incitement to action.

Soon afterwards almost every suggestion in Charles's report was embodied in the Explosives Act, 1875. From then on, fireworks could only be made with a licence, and strict limits were imposed on the amount of explosive material and the number of workers in each building. Factory huts were required to have a door at each end, and there had to be a minimum distance between buildings. In addition, measures were introduced to reduce the risk of accidental sparks, including the provision of linoleum floors, and of non-inflammable outer garments for workforces.

Charles was all too conscious of the accidents which had befallen some of his ancestors and many of their rivals when he pressed for the changes. By the end of the 1870s, thanks in no small part to his diligence and determination, things had come a long way since his four-times great-grandfather had blown himself up in Islington. In due course the measures he advocated spread across the world, although it took more than a century for them to reach China, the birthplace of fireworks, where their introduction in the late 20th century belatedly reduced the number of deaths from accidents.

By 1880 his health was failing but he appeared to rally, at one point holding a great supper for the employees in the rolling shed that had been built at Nunhead for the Franco-Prussian War work. On another day in late July he took a lease on a small property known as the *Rookery* in Merstham, driving over to the factory each day in a pony phaeton; thinking, no doubt, that the country air and daily drive would benefit his health.

Like many Brock men before him, Charles did not live to a great age. Beset with business worries in his latter years, including a failed attempt to set up a fireworks factory in the United States near Coney Island, and a protracted legal struggle relating to the licence for a new factory in South Norwood, he died in 1881 aged 37, leaving a widow but no children. He had changed the way that fireworks were made, transported and displayed but his greatest legacy was to have established such high standards in the industry that for decades afterwards British pyrotechnists were far ahead of their competitors in other countries.

On his death, his brother Arthur, aged just 23, but already a veteran of numerous successful displays in India, Philadelphia and at the Crystal Palace, took over the business. Like Charles, he had energy, enthusiasm and entrepreneurial talent. His earliest memory was of watching his father at work in the laboratory concocting new colours for fireworks, and at school he had made fireworks for his friends, using a coffee-mill to mix the ingredients, on one occasion losing half his eyebrows in the process. He was, to use his own words, 'the concentrated essence of seven generations of firework manufacturers' and he was determined that Brock's Fireworks would prosper as never before under his leadership.

He was also keen to start a family. At around the time he took over the firm he met and fell in love with Annie Dewdney from Ugborough in Devon. Riding to hounds whenever she was able, Anne reputedly had 'a fine seat', 'the best legs in Devonshire' and was described by friends as a 'perfect Devon girl' with her English rose colouring. They married in 1883 and a year later, on 29 June 1884 – Arthur's 26th birthday – the first of the couple's nine children was born: Frank Arthur Brock, the future hero of Zeebrugge.

CHAPTER 4

The Shakespeare of Pyrotechnics

The world into which Frank Brock was born was an exciting place. In the year of his birth, long-distance telephone calls were made possible for the first time using submarine cables – the first building blocks for today's world wide web – pioneered by S. W. Silver & Co, the large conglomerate on the banks of the Thames that had managed Brock's 1870 Franco-Prussian War contract on behalf of the French government. George Eastman put photographic technology in the hands of millions with his inexpensive roll film camera, the Kodak. Light bulbs, electric irons, vacuum cleaners and typewriters were beginning to find their way into the wealthier homes, and Carl Benz was on the verge of unveiling the world's first motor car. Not many years around the corner were ballpoint pens, dishwashers, gramophones, moving film and Coca Cola.

Brock's Fireworks themselves were at the forefront of an iconic innovation when, in June 1892, they became the first manufacturing business in the world to advertise with flashing electric lights, sharing an 80ft × 60ft site on the side of the Cumberland Hotel in New York's Broadway with four other advertisers. Costing $10,000 to install (around £2,000 at the exchange rate of the time) the 1,457 green, yellow, red and white bulbs lit up alternately from dusk to midnight with the words: 'Buy homes on Long Island – Manhattan Beach swept by ocean breezes … Manhattan Hotel … Oriental Hotel … Gilmore's Band … Brock's Fireworks.'

With letters up to six feet high, this landmark advance in advertising was visible from Madison Square, Broadway and Fifth Avenue, and was one of the most compelling sights of New York in the early 1890s. Within ten years the Cumberland Hotel had been demolished to make way for one of the world's first and most photographed 'skyscrapers', the Flatiron Building, while the use of electronically lit advertisements in Manhattan had become so widespread

New York City 1891/2. Brock's takes part in the first ever electrical advertisement on Broadway and perhaps the first anywhere in the world.

that Broadway began to be named by the press as The Great White Way, a description that was to last for decades.

The success of the centennial celebrations in Philadelphia had already helped to make Brock's a household name in America. They quickly took offices in 192 Broadway (in 2015 designated a New York City Landmark), an office building developed by the 'robber baron' Austin Corbin. At about the time of their pioneering use of electric lights, Brock's was contracted to run a display on Brooklyn Bridge to mark the 400th anniversary of the landing of Christopher Columbus. The climax of this was a 'Niagara Falls' set-piece, over 500 feet long and over 130 feet high. The cataract of fire tumbling from the bridge covered an area of more than two acres, and inspired *The New York Times* to write:

> The multitude of onlookers saw a pyrotechnic display that was prodigal in quantity, in variety, and in colour. The heavens were simply gorgeous with brilliant fire effects, under the glare of which the bridge stood out in a beauty that made every citizen of the two great cities which it connects proud. While the discharge of fireworks from the bridge was at its height there began to fall from the entire span between the two towers a great stream of fire, so dense than it could not be seen through. It fell steadily, as if it were water. Its light illumined brilliantly all the boats in the river. The effect for the three or four minutes the fall of fire continued was superb.

In the Brock household in England, baby Frank's arrival in the world was equally a cause of much celebration. It was a foregone conclusion that one day he would take over the family business – the eighth generational Brock to do so – and from the start his childhood was steeped in fireworks. Days after his birth, his father chose the battle of Trafalgar as the subject of a spectacular pyrotechnical set-piece at the Crystal Palace. The portrayal in fireworks of

Brooklyn Bridge, New York City 1892. A Brock's display in 1892 to celebrate 400 years since Columbus sailed to America. The most spectacular item was the "Niagara of Fire" and it was estimated the spectators from New York, Brooklyn and New Jersey shores numbered fully a million.

Britain's greatest naval triumph, including a fiery depiction of the message 'England expects every man to do his duty', captured the joyous mood of a man who had just produced a son and heir.

By the standards of the day, 26-year-old Arthur was already extremely wealthy. His home in Enmore Park, South Norwood, on the outskirts of South London, was a detached three-storey villa with a tennis court, stables, greenhouses and a dovecote. He employed several domestic staff, including a uniformed housemaid, a gardener, and a nursemaid to look after young Frank. Conveniently, the house was just round the corner from the 15-acre Brock's Fireworks premises, opened in June 1877, which occupied a tree-fringed meadow owned by the Ecclesiastical Commissioners behind Birchangar Road. Here stood a sprawling collection of wooden, brick and corrugated-iron buildings redolent of a pioneer town in the Wild West. To minimise the damage in case of an explosion, the huts were set apart ('like the plums in a school pudding', as one visitor observed) and were connected

Arthur Brock seated on his horse with his family and servants at Stafford Villas, South Norwood
c. 1887. Frank is seated next to his mother and Alan Brock, the acclaimed historian and Frank's
younger brother, is in his nursemaid's arms.

to one another by tramways. Arthur – known to his employees as 'The Chief'
or Mr. Arthur – went there every day to oversee operations, sometimes on
foot, sometimes on horseback, and increasingly on one of the new safety
bicycles that were starting to replace the penny farthing.

Although the numbers were seasonal, some 200 people, including 70
women, worked at the factory, producing around 500 tons of fireworks
a year. Those who handled the black powder in the 'filling' sheds wore
black boiler-suits, while the packers and dispatchers wore white overalls.
Other products they turned out included flares and rockets to be used as
distress signals at sea. Security was tight at what was claimed to be the
biggest fireworks factory in the world. A Newfoundland dog patrolled
the yard, and every autumn the large numbers of temporary employees
who were taken on during the build-up to 5 November were led up to it
to be sniffed. So powerful was the dog's sense of smell that from then on
it always recognised their scent, so ensuring that only bone fide workers
gained access to the premises.

At an early age young Frank accompanied his father on visits to the
factory and was fascinated by the sights and smells to be found within its

unprepossessing sheds. The lure of black powder was as strong for him as it had been for his ancestors and would remain so for the rest of his life.

Victorian author John Corbet Anderson, who visited the site while writing a history of Norwood, was greatly impressed by the stringent safety precautions insisted on by Arthur. These included storing explosive material in floating hulks moored on the Thames 20 miles below London Bridge, guarding the premises at night with watchmen and dogs, and insisting that storage jars were made from papier maché rather than glass. He commended Arthur for the way he ran his business, 'the effects of which startle and delight equally the civilised and savage throughout the world.' Anderson went on:

> The interiors of the sheds are varnished, and the floors covered with lead or linoleum, fastened by copper nails. Any artificial light they may require is to be obtained only from gas jets, burning outside their windows. Throughout, the most scrupulous cleanliness is enforced, so as to avoid grit. Every precaution also is taken with the work-people. On entering the factory each person undergoes a search; and dons a non-inflammable guernsey, and over-shoes of brown leather without nails. Government regulations, exhibited by the door of each shed, indicate the number of persons allowed in it; and prescribe the kind of work, and quantity of composition, permitted. If the work people want anything they must hang out a red flag, and an attendant comes. Hydrants, and buckets of water, are in every direction. All is silent; save a low tapping sound, emanating from some of the sheds.

Frederick Willis, who regularly attended the Crystal Palace displays in the late 19th century, was equally impressed by the firm's commitment to safety, writing in *A Book of London Yesterdays*:

> Nothing ever went wrong at a Brock's display because it was conducted by experts. Some of the largest shells would scatter debris a quarter of a mile from the point of explosion, and there were set pieces an eighth of a mile in length which, of course, discharged great clouds of sparks. But I never heard of an accident.

In fact Arthur was not always as fastidious about safety as his reputation suggested, and in 1886 he was fined the then substantial sum of £161 by a Croydon court for seven contraventions of the Explosives Act, including the inadequate sweeping up of gunpowder particles from the shed floors. Other than that, his only other brush with the law was in 1888 when the High Court awarded a litigious lady named Mrs Whitby 25 shillings for damage caused to her dress and jacket by sparks at a Crystal Palace display.

Despite this enviable safety record, he met with resistance when he applied to expand his South Norwood premises in the mid-1880s. Sir William Grantham, a crusty barrister who was also the Conservative Member of Parliament for

MAKING CATHERINE WHEELS.

CHARGING SHELLS.

CHARGING HEAVY ROCKETS.

MAKING CRACKERS.

Brock's workers c. 1890s. (*The Strand Magazine*)

Croydon, led the attack, arguing that on top of the danger of explosions, 'the importation of young ladies needed to make the fireworks would seriously deteriorate the character of this superior residential neighbourhood.' The opposition quickly melted away in the face of widespread backing by local people. *The Croydon Advertiser* was also supportive:

> Of course some people are afraid of a firework factory. Some ladies are afraid of a mouse, and go into hysterics over the approach of a black beetle, but that is no reason why the Town Council should employ a staff of men to kill all mice and black beetles in the borough. Because a few silly people are afraid of a firework factory, and do not like to be shocked by the sight of a dirty face or a grimy hand, that is no reason why the Town Council should destroy a growing industry and ruthlessly drive thousands of pounds in hard cash out of the town. No, that won't wash at any price.

From the moment he took over the business, Arthur pulled out all the stops to ensure that Brock's Fireworks always kept several steps ahead of its competitors, not just where safety was concerned, but in terms of pageantry and drama. 'Not to progress is to retrogress,' he liked to remind his fellow directors at the company's monthly board meetings. One of his most successful innovations, which he patented in 1888, was the spectacle of so-called 'living fireworks'. To the wonderment of the Crystal Palace crowds, fireworks came to life in front of them in the shape of huge matchstick characters, dancing, sparring and gyrating of their own accord. These blazing figures included boxing kangaroos, sailors dancing 'The Hornpipe', fighting cats, snake charmers, trapeze artists, marionette skeletons, gymnasts turning over and over on a horizontal bar and, in due course, men and women looping the loop in flying motor cars. Most exotic of all was a Noah's Ark procession of animals, with a bear, a rhinoceros, a giraffe, a camel, an alligator and elephants spraying sparks from their trunks.

Arthur kept tight-lipped about his techniques ('so closely are most of the processes guarded that all I received was a sly wink,' observed an inquisitive newspaper reporter) and for a while no one could work out the secret of his living fireworks – or 'The Living Pyrograms' as he liked to call them. Various theories were advanced, including the use of complex automata. In fact the effect was achieved by using real people – 'living actors in fire' as the company later referred to them in its literature – clad in overalls of asbestos cloth. The brilliance of the background displays meant the actors themselves could not be seen by the crowds. All that was visible were the light wooden frameworks to which they were attached. The outlines of the frameworks were 'lanced' to depict the different characters, and often had moving parts such as arms and legs.

'The Fire King' Arthur Brock, 1858–1938, drawn c. 1888. (*The British Journal of Commerce*)

For young and old alike, the illusion never ceased to mesmerize and enthral. The Shah of Persia was 'particularly amused' by the fighting cocks and, as *The Strand Magazine* reported, the boxing men 'caused unbounded delight to the German emperor.' Particularly popular with children was a 'living' display introduced in 1890, which told the story of *Jack and the Beanstalk*. A pyrotechnic cow, an illuminated artful butcher, a giant bean-stalk and a firework-enveloped Jack all featured in the production. We can take it as read that Frank was taken to see it as a sixth birthday treat in June of that year, watching with a mixture of glee and terror from the directors' box at the Crystal Palace as the giant chased Jack across his fiery kingdom.

Forever turning his mind to new effects, Arthur also found a way of making shells burst in the air in the shape of a dome of dazzling white fire, an innovation which took him years to develop and which he unveiled before a delighted Shah of Persia. Keen to broaden the company's output beyond fireworks and marine flares, and having pioneered and patented the use of metals for brilliant illumination, he developed for British use in West Africa, a way of attaching flares to trip wires, so that soldiers or hunters camping in the wild could be warned of approaching animals or people. Known as the 'trip flare' it was an innovation that is still widely used by soldiers around the world to this day.

'Be Prepared' is, famously, the motto of the Scouts and in 1895/6 the man who was to found the Boy Scouts was one of the leaders of a small British military force generously equipped with Brock's fireworks in an extraordinary tale related in North American newspapers. The article was widely syndicated there under the headline 'England's Funny War, Attack on King Ashantee's Warriors with sky-rockets and fireworks', a raid which its writer noted was being completely ignored by the British press. Published in January 1896 the article described a British force, whose leaders included Robert Baden-Powell, famous for using subterfuge in his defence of Mafeking in the Boer War of 1899/1902, long before *Scouting For Boys* and his founding of the Boy Scout movement.

Camouflaged in rifle boxes, a huge display was carried out on a steamship *Angola* from Liverpool to the Gold Coast in December 1895. In early January the force cut its way through the jungle taking their hidden cargo 70 miles inland where it was fired at night over the main village of King Prempeh of the Ashantis, with exploding maroons, screaming shells, rockets and coloured fire, notably blue. The locals were well acquainted with firearms but fireworks were unknown and the next morning the king's delegation arrived suing for peace: we will sign any treaty you like, providing you kindly stop the black magic immediately! One condition of the treaty signed by King Prempeh was his exile in the Seychelles but, on return, he accepted Robert Baden-Powell's invitation to become Chief Scout for the Gold Coast, now Ghana. Ten years after the raid, in an interview in *Pearson's Magazine,* Arthur Brock appeared to confirm the main thrust of the story that had been so widely published in the United States.

None from either side are thought to have died in the raid of January 1896 but on the way home 18 British soldiers perished from fevers, including Queen Victoria's son-in-law, Prince Henry of Battenberg. He lies buried in the churchyard of St Mildred's Church, Whippingham on the Isle of Wight, an island off the south coast of England where, in a small coincidence of fate, Frank Brock's great granddaughter was married in the same church just over a century later.

Unsurprisingly, the press dubbed Arthur Brock 'The Fire King'. As *The Pall Mall Gazette* put it:

> Mr Brock's fame has penetrated to the jungles of India, and his Roman candles are as well known in Calcutta as in the City of London. The salt of the earth have at one time or another been fascinated by his arts, as have Czars and Shahs, Sultans and Viceroys, Mikados and Mandarins. We pay homage to the man who can lighten our November darkness.

The *Liverpool Weekly Mercury* summed up Arthur in one sentence: 'It is safe to say that Mr Brock knows more about fireworks than any other living man.'

Committed to having a contented workforce, Arthur organised works outings every summer. A typical excursion took place in September 1888. He hired four wagonettes to take 60 staff to the Swan Hotel at Walton-on-Thames in Surrey, with a stop on the way at Hampton Court for a tour of the palace and gardens. The party were treated to lunch and a concert in a marquee, and went boating on the Thames in the afternoon. In the evening the happy revellers watched the results of many hours of their labour go up in smoke when Arthur

Winifred Ashby, 1879–1975, Frank's 1st cousin. One of the first women to receive a PhD in the USA and a successful pioneering medical scientist working at the Mayo Clinic and later in Washington DC.

laid on the inevitable firework display. He also believed in helping charitable causes, and every Christmas he distributed boxes of Japanese lanterns to hospitals and workhouses 'to give them a festive appearance.'

Arthur's kindness also touched the lives of his favourite sister and her family, although somewhat hidden on this occasion. Mary Ann, known as 'Polly', had married George Ashby, whom Arthur had sent out to research the United States market in 1887 and again in 1892 to arrange a firework contract at the Chicago World Fair. In the US George had met several charming characters in New York City who had left him in no doubt they would support him in setting up business were he ever to move across the Atlantic. The following year, in 1893 and very much against the advice of his family and that of the Brocks, he did so with Polly and three children in tow. Sadly, on going to meet his erstwhile friends and supporters in New York, he was disappointed to learn that their previous generous encouragement and enthusiasm had disappeared.

To have admitted defeat and returned would have involved too painful a loss of face and so they struggled on in difficult circumstances. When Polly eventually disclosed to Arthur the extent of their discomfort he helped financially, perhaps known only to his sister. The family established itself and the two sons Holdon and Ralph had successful careers. Their unmarried sister, Winifred Ashby, another of Frank Brock's first cousins, became an eminent physician and research scientist said to have been responsible for saving many American lives during World War II. She was one of the first women in the United States to graduate with a PhD. She worked on children's health in the Philippines soon after the Americans' victory over Spain, one of the first American women to do so. Then as a teacher of physics and chemistry back in the States before joining the Mayo Clinic and subsequently St. Elizabeth's hospital, Washington DC. Working at the Mayo and against the sustained opposition of the established haematologists, Winifred proved that red blood cells have a life many times longer than had previously been thought and the Ashby Method of analysis she devised remained a stalwart of haematology for many decades. In one of her medical obituaries, it was suggested her work should have been considered for a Nobel Prize.

Another of Arthur's achievements was to break into the lucrative Australian market, helped by his brother Henry. He opened a factory in Adelaide in 1885 and put on shows in Sydney, Brisbane and Melbourne. Even in this most distant part of the empire he faced stiff competition from his chief British rivals, Pain's Fireworks. The two firms constantly tried to out-do each other, so much so that the journal *Australian Life* used them in a full-page cartoon to illustrate the border problems then existing between Germany and France. 'Herr Brock Bismarck' and 'Monsieur Pain Boulanger' were pictured facing each other from their respective stagings, flanked not by fireworks but by soldiers.

The *Melbourne Leader* newspaper also noted the fierce competition between the two firms after a consignment of Brock's Fireworks shipped out from England was delayed at sea, causing a show to be postponed. Pain's were quick to take advantage of Brock's misfortune by jumping in with two shows of their own. As *The Leader* observed:

> Pain's admirers say that their shows cannot be excelled, but supporters of Brock declare that it is but a box of vestas compared to what is coming. Under any circumstances the public will be the gainers, as, both being in possession of vast resources, the rival fireworkers will doubtless do their best and strive for the inevitable survival of the fittest.

Many of Brock's Australian displays were held at the Melbourne cricket ground on Monday nights, often to the accompaniment of martial music supplied by the intriguingly named Herr Plock's Military Band. They featured all the special effects pioneered at the Crystal Palace, and often required scores of actors and extras. On Boxing Day 1887, for instance, Duncan Gillies, the premier of Victoria, was the subject of what was billed as a 'monster fire picture', while a snake chasing a butterfly was the centre-piece of the 'living fireworks' section. The climax, which shamelessly exploited Australian paranoia about a possible Russian invasion, was a depiction of two Russian ironclads being torpedoed off Melbourne. 'The artillery men strove, by a well sustained fire of huge shot and shell, to repel the invaders,' ran a jingoistic report in the *Argos* newspaper. All this and more for an admission price of just one shilling. The crowds lapped it all up and demanded more.

To hammer home their claim that they were top pyrotechnical dog, Brock's advertised their Melbourne displays as 'eclipsing all previous shows in the city.' So successful were they at pulling in the crowds that other entertainment venues began to suffer. Irritated at losing patrons, the city's theatre managers grumbled to anyone who would listen that the cricket ground was being 'sublet for illegitimate purposes.' Someone – a disgruntled theatre manager, perhaps, or more likely an employee of Pain's – went so far as to write anonymously to *The Argos* complaining of 'delays, poor fireworks and sparks falling upon the spectators' at a Brock's display. The irate letter-writer claimed that a balloon with fireworks attached to it had caught fire and fallen into the crowd, and that 'had they not been standing up and therefore able to escape, I am certain it would have caused the deaths of four or five persons at least.' If the letter-writer's intention was to strike a blow at Brock's, he or she failed. No one apart from the unnamed correspondent appears to have been troubled by the incident, and the Brock's shows remained as popular as ever.

To even things out, supporters of Brock's regularly took pot shots at Pain's in the columns of the local newspapers. 'A huge swindle – a *Pain*-ful exhibition!'

Brock's display at the Association Ground, Sydney June 1887 for Queen Victoria's jubilee. 'Messrs. C. T. Brock & Co, whose recent achievements in Sydney, Melbourne and Adelaide have familiarised Australians with their reputation as the leading pyrotechnists of the day, show among their fireworks a huge bombshell, known as the "Jubilee", which is the largest ever constructed.'

was how an anonymous witness described one of Pain's Antipodean displays. One journal ran a strip cartoon depicting a small boy surreptitiously setting fire to some fireworks in his father's pocket. The ditty printed beneath it went:

> Ali Ben Hamid, his neighbours to shock,
> Had ordered some fireworks of Messieurs Brock
> His son, Ben Ali – the bad wicked boy!
> Soon put an end to his good father's joy.
> When their friends had picked up the pieces again
> They cried out, 'Alas! 'Stead of Brock there was Pain!'

In 1885 *The Melbourne Telegraph* printed an anecdote from one of its contributors which neatly illustrated Brock's world-wide fame.

> We remember, when far away up in the Queensland bush, discussing one night by the lonely camp fire the delights of the old country. 'What would you do, Ned, when you reached London?' 'I'd go down to the Crystal Palace to see Brock's fireworks.' The next night poor Ned was potted, or rather speared, by a villainous band of men who had been following us for a week. So his wish was never gratified. Poor Ned.

Poor Ned may not have made it to the Crystal Palace, but back in the 'old country' there was no let-up in the popularity of the Brock shows. More fireworks went up in smoke on Sydenham Hill in one season than in the whole of the rest of the United Kingdom put together. At the Crystal Palace on Thursday nights, pyrotechnical oarsmen in pyrotechnical lifeboats rescued pyrotechnical passengers from pyrotechnical ships foundering in savage pyrotechnical seas; firemen unrolled their hoses and extinguished house fires; trains ran in and out of alpine tunnels narrowly escaping avalanches; blacksmiths equipped with a forge, bellows and anvil shoed horses; sledgers dodged polar bears as they trekked across the ice; city policemen regulated bicycles, costers' barrows and hansom cabs; aerial huntsmen pursued aerial stags; cities were bombarded, and dreadnoughts shelled each other in great set-piece battles which the British always won. With their eclectic and unpredictable variety of stories, from thrilling adventures to quirky tales of romance, from tub-thumping historical dramas to portrayals of homespun domesticity, the Crystal Palace fireworks were in many ways a forerunner of the TV soaps and adventure series that would grip armchair-bound audiences a century later.

Not that the firm's British displays were confined to the Crystal Palace. Brock's went all over the United Kingdom to stage their shows, from South Shields to Southsea, from Rothesay to Whitstable, from Leeds to Weston-Super-Mare, from Buxton to Bristol. In late Victorian Britain it was a rare person who had never seen a Brock's firework light up the sky. In June 1888

Brock's Benefit at the Crystal Palace, 1890 – 'Voyage to the North Pole'. After several failed attempts to cross the Greenland inland ice, a Norwegian expedition was successful in 1889 to great international acclaim. Capitalising on the news, the Brock's artists, carpenters and fireworkers created a huge set piece to depict the human spirit triumphing over hardship. (*The Sporting and Dramatic News*, September 1890)

'The Sea of Ice'. A scene from the 1890 Artic expedition set piece. 'The display was on a splendid scale. It introduced the Aurora Borealis, reproduced the Arctic summer and the Polar sea, showed incidents of whaling, sledging, bear fights, and other features of Life in the Far North. The frontage of this piece was 600 feet by 100 feet and the quick-match (fuse) eight miles in length.' (*The Pall Mall Gazette,* September 1890)

Brock's held their first display in the North of Ireland at the Royal Botanic Gardens in Belfast. Across the Channel they laid on events in France, Germany, Belgium, Holland, Portugal, Spain and Italy. Further afield they ventured into Siam, Zanzibar and Dahomey.

During the 1880s the company also opened a fireworks shop at 109 Cheapside, near St Paul's Cathedral. It was one of the first businesses in the country to be connected to the telephone (it boasted the number London 211) and from the start it did a roaring trade. *The Pall Mall Gazette* enthused:

> Cast a look round Mr Brock's shop! Here are silver fountains, stars of dazzling brilliancy and of many colours, silver rain and dragonflies, fountains which pour out scintillating sprays of diamonds, or burning suns. Or do you prefer the coiling cobra with the gleaming eyes, the mine of serpents, the peacock's plumes, or the lilac blossom? Do you wish for explosives? There is the humble but startling cracker, the thundering maroon, or the twelve-inch shell. Again, you may purchase golden rain, equal to Jove's best, at a halfpenny, a Chinese tree for sixpence, a golden flower-pot for a shilling, or a fire balloon for half a crown. From the halfpenny squib to the ten guinea shell you pay your money and take your choice. All day long great vans arrive, padlocked boxes are carefully lifted out and carefully received. The window is stocked with all the products of the pyrotechnist's art, and is seldom deserted by groups of admirers and would be purchasers. But these are but dummies. The law forbids the exposure of fireworks in the window, and only allows the dealer to keep a stock not above 50lb in weight.

By now the company was selling some two million penny crackers, two million squibs and a million Catherine wheels every year. Arthur told *The Pall Mall Gazette*: 'The great change from the fireworks of forty years back is not so much in their form as in the multitude of colours. We produce every colour of the rainbow, shades ranging from the deepest purple to the lightest lilac, shades of blue, shades of red from pink to dark crimson of green and yellow, gold and amber.' Asked if his workforce was healthy, he joked: 'None more healthy than the firework maker. Everything is clean and tidy; there are no disagreeable fumes; he even eats the powder without fear of indigestion or explosion.' At least, one hopes he was joking.

By the year of Queen Victoria's Golden Jubilee in 1887, the company had notched up more than 500 Crystal Palace displays since their inception 22 years earlier, and the number of people who had flocked to Sydenham to enjoy the pyrotechnics there ran to many millions. In April of that year Arthur expanded his repertory company of special effects by unveiling his so-called transformation set-pieces, which involved floral designs changing into portraits. The first of these was of Benjamin Disraeli, and the floral design which preceded it featured primroses, the flowers with which the former Prime

Minister had for long been associated. The audience was captivated by the metamorphosis from flower to face.

Later in the year an enormous transformation picture, 200 feet long and 100 feet high, was fired at a Jubilee display. To the wonderment of the crowd, a floral design of roses, shamrocks and thistles remodelled itself into portraits of Queen Victoria, the Prince and Princess of Wales, and the Duke and Duchess of York, all picked out in magnesium light. A railway train, a motor car, a steamship and the Forth Bridge were also depicted to illustrate scientific progress during the queen's reign. In the wake of this success, Arthur's transformation scenes became ever more ambitious, reaching new heights of sophistication with 'The Seasons', which featured a rural scene changing from spring to summer, from summer to autumn, and finally to winter.

During that summer of celebration, Queen Victoria's daughter-in-law, the Princess of Wales, was one of the VIP guests at the Crystal Palace, and was accorded the honour of starting the firework display. As the *Daily Telegraph* reported: 'For the first time in her life, the princess became a pyrotechnist. Her Royal Highness, through merely touching a button, put an electric current in motion which set the whole piece on fire.' With justification the Brock's literature was able to boast:

> We have had the honour of showing the wonders of our art before Emperors, Empresses, Kings, Queens, Sultans, Shahs, Princes, Princesses and Members of almost every Royal Family, as well as other illustrious personages who have visited England, and from whom on many occasions the head of the firm has received personal congratulations.

Another innovation during this period was 'The World's Largest Firework Bombshell'. Going on later to hold this position in the Guinness Book of Records for many years, it was fired from a 25in mortar and created a canopy of coloured stars with a quarter of a mile radius on exploding. Weighing nearly 1.5 tons, and encased in a Krupp steel girdle to guard against shattering, it was used to spectacular effect at the wedding celebrations of the Crown Prince of Portugal in Lisbon in 1886, where its deafening boom was heard for miles around. Among other events at which it was showcased were the opening of the Lynton & Barnstaple Railway in 1898, the Tricentennial Celebrations in Quebec in 1908, and the official government London Victory Celebrations in 1946.

Meanwhile Arthur's celebrity status continued to soar. 'He is the Shakespeare of pyrotechnics, just as Shakespeare was the Brock of poets,' was how one newspaper hyperbolically described him. To others he was 'the Prince of Pyrotechnics' or simply 'The Professor.' Even the Prince of Wales counted him an acquaintance. 'Don't go giving me a green nose or a blue ear,' joked the future King Edward VII when Arthur explained to him how he made his portraits in fire. He was an expert at garnering publicity for Brock's, sending out press notices before each major display, spending hundreds of pounds annually on newspaper advertisements, and on one occasion entertaining 100 journalists to dinner at the Crystal Palace. *The Pall Mall Gazette* wrote jocularly of Arthur:

> Mr Brock has lived among fireworks all his life. His great-great-great-grandfather, his great-great-grandfather, his great-grandfather, his grandfather and his father made fireworks before him. He inherits the family secrets. He played with squibs in his cradle, he knew the component parts of a cracker before he could walk, a Roman Candle lighted him to his cot, he was advanced to shells before he cast off jackets. Nourished on powder and lampblack from his tenderest years, taking in the secrets of the magic art with his mother's milk, who can wonder that Mr Brock is an expert of experts?

Much the same could be said of young Frank's upbringing. By the time of the Jubilee year he was three years old and to all intents and purposes had been nourished by his father on powder and lampblack. From almost

Cast iron 25-inch mortar with Krupp steel girdle. The shell weighed 200 pounds and was shot to a height of 700 feet using a lifting charge of 7 pounds of gunpowder. For many years it featured in the *Guinness Book of Records* as the largest firework.

the moment he was born, fireworks were in his blood. Arthur made a point of bringing home all the company's latest innovations, such as the indoor 'Japanese Joke Bomb' which scattered a shower of presents round the room, or the outdoor 'Fiery Palm Tree loaded with Fairy Fruit.' If his family, the servants and especially Frank enjoyed them, he knew he was on to a winner. If they showed a lack of enthusiasm, Arthur would have another think. Young Frank did not even have to leave his bedroom to experience pyrotechnical thrills. Sydenham Hill was little more than a mile to the north of the family home in South Norwood, and on summer's nights he could see and hear his father's Crystal Palace exhibitions from his window.

Someone else, incidentally, who may have frequently seen and heard

Brock's Benefit at the Crystal Palace, September 1888. (*The Sporting and Dramatic News*, 15 September 1888). 'Over 50,000 watch an avalanche engulf a peaceful Alpine village, the scene reproducing the mountains, the Swiss chalets, the train emerging from the tunneled rock, and other accessories of an Alpine landscape, suddenly overwhelmed by the falling ruin.' (*The Observer*, 9 September 1888)

the displays from a South London bedroom window – that is when he was not at the Crystal Palace in person – was the Prince of Wales ('Edward the Caresser', as the writer Henry James christened him) who regularly 'took tea' in the 1880s with the voluptuous actress Lily Langtry, calling in on her whenever discretion allowed at her home on South Norwood Hill just up the road from the Brocks. Another near neighbour of the Brocks was Sir Arthur Conan Doyle, who lived round the corner in Tennison Road and wrote more than twenty Sherlock Holmes stories there, though not one of them featured fireworks.

Frank enjoyed an extremely happy middle-class childhood, devouring the great Victorian children's classics, enjoying rides on South Norwood's new-ly-introduced steam trams, learning to swim at the public baths in Birchanger Road, devising increasingly elaborate garden adventures with his growing band of younger siblings (in due course he would have five brothers and three sisters) and, above all, learning everything he could about fireworks. The heavy

Frank with two of his younger brothers, Alan and Bernard, c. 1890. As was the rule at the time, both younger boys are wearing dresses – they had not yet been 'breeched'.

bronze moulds used for making the hemispherical shell cases fascinated Frank. Pieces of brown paper were carefully glued, layer upon layer into the smooth concave shapes until there was a thickness ensuring structural strength. After they had dried, two hemispheres would be trimmed and stuck together, the whole wrapped and glued into a perfect ball. But if he was lucky enough to be present before they were finished, he could sometimes persuade a compassionate worker to let him have one of the larger, empty half-cases to take home. With its flanges not yet trimmed off, they strongly resembled what would become a British infantry helmet of WWI and were much appreciated by his growing platoon for favourite battle enactments.

As he became older Frank's visits to the factory were more frequent. He enjoyed watching the fireworks being tested for quality and meeting the chemists and engineers, the carpenters, firework makers and the talented artists, several of whom were said to have 'done credit to the walls of many exhibitions'. One of Arthur's leading managers 'was an honours man of two universities', with a previous training in journalism and was described as a pragmatist and 'the most prolific of contemporary musical librettists'. Above all Frank could not fail to notice the obvious way in which all he met showed their respect for the quiet, confident competence of his father.

Not only were there visits to the factory but increasingly he went to the Crystal Palace shows in person, taken there by his father, who wanted to educate him in the pyrotechnical arts and introduce him to the mysteries of the rayons d'argent, the jewelled cobras, the shower of pink pearls, the pyramids of iris wheels and jaxoons, the aerial wheat-sheaf and the flight of fiery pigeons. (On one occasion, to everyone's excitement, a fiery pigeon flew off too fast and too furiously and 'nested' in the set-piece, setting it off prematurely.) Almost certainly Frank was there when his father unveiled his biggest pyrotechnical crowd-pleaser to date – a 60ft-high mechanical depiction of the Victorian music-hall performer, Lottie Collins, singing the chorus of her famous song 'Ta-ra-ra-boom-de-ay' and giving a spirited kick of an automated leg each time the word 'boom' rang out.

In July 1891 Kaiser Wilhelm II of Germany was the guest of honour at another firm favourite with the Crystal Palace crowds – a lavish, 650ft-wide depiction of the battle of Trafalgar. According to another visitor that day, 16-year-old Winston Churchill, who happened to catch sight of him, Kaiser Bill was wearing 'a helmet of bright brass surmounted by a white eagle nearly six inches high, a polished steel cuirass and a perfectly white uniform with high boots'. At the end of the evening's entertainment, by which time he had exchanged his helmet for a more comfortable military cap, the Kaiser asked for Arthur Brock to be presented to him in the royal box. Having complimented him on the display, he mentioned that judging from a show he had recently seen in Amsterdam, the Dutch were clearly skilled pyrotechnists. 'I think if you had seen that display you would have admitted its excellence,' he added.

'Yes, your Majesty', Arthur replied with more than a hint of smugness. 'I admit it, without question. I supplied the display.'

It is tempting to think that seven-year-old Frank was present during this exchange, and briefly set eyes on the man whose war machine he would one day do so much to damage.

Another impressed visitor was the Chinese emperor's viceroy Li Hung Chang who was combining a tour of European capitals while attending the coronation of the new Russian czar. Arthur's international business acumen (he was importing special shells from Japan but also, over 100 tons of Chinese crackers a year at that time or, as he put it in a newspaper interview, 'some 2,616,500,000 bangs') is clear from their exchange. After attending a Crystal Palace show, Li Hung Chang told Arthur that the fireworks for which China had been famous for 1,000 years were completely eclipsed by the splendours of English pyrotechny.

He went so far as to suggest that Brock's should send a team to China to teach his countrymen how to produce such effects and to carry out large-scale displays. But as Arthur later recalled: 'Upon being questioned as to the amount he wished to spend he quickly changed the subject!' Li Hung Chang's awed reaction to the display was shared by his entourage. 'The Chinese visitors were delighted, and they could talk of nothing but the fireworks as they journeyed back to town,' reported the *Daily News*. The Shah of Persia, a devotee of Brock's

The German Emperor at the Crystal Palace, July 1891. 'Of the fireworks it can only be said that the display was marvelous … At the end of the display the Prince of Wales sent for Mr. Brock and presented him to the Emperor.' (*The Times*, July 1891)

since 1876, was another regular visitor. He told Arthur that 'the fireworks back home are not in the same street as Brock's.'

The firm was doing so well, and the Brock family was growing so fast, that in 1893 Arthur splashed out on a new and larger house half a mile away from Enmore Park – The Ivies in Selhurst Road. The property, which boasted every modern convenience, stood next to Holy Innocents Church and backed on to the local recreation ground. Norwood Junction railway station was close by. Arthur did not normally allow journalists to visit him at home, but a reporter from the *Star* newspaper who was allowed a brief glimpse inside described the house as a 'luxurious lair'.

During the latter years of the century, the firm began specialising in staging reconstructions of great news stories almost as soon as they had

Li Hung Chang, the Chinese Emperor's Viceroy, August 1896. (*The Daily Graphic*, 12 August 1896). 'Of all the numerous functions which China's great statesman has attended during his journeyings in Europe, none has given him more pleasure than the entertainment provided for him … at the Crystal Palace.'

happened. In this respect they were pyrotechnical forerunners of the cinema newsreels that started to become popular twenty years later. As the *Lee Journal* noted:

> Messrs C. T. Brock keep well ahead of events, and it is not too much to say anything happening in the world is very shortly afterwards to be seen reproduced in fireworks at the Crystal Palace.

Arthur Brock, his wife Annie and his nine children at The Ivies in Norwood, c. 1903. Frank (centre standing); Alan to Frank's left; Bernard to his right.

A case in point was the battle of Manila Bay, which took place during the Spanish-American war on 1 May 1898. Arthur instructed his staff to find out as much detail of the battle as possible, and staged a 690ft-wide re-enactment of the engagement at the Crystal Palace three weeks later. His literature boasted that it showed 'how the up-to-date armaments of the United States ships, the brilliant gunnery and seamanship of their crews, reduced the ships of Spain to battered, sinking vessels.'

These set-pieces were extraordinary in size and effect and are unknown today. Part of an article in the magazine *Tit Bits* in May 1898 described what was involved. See Appendix II for the full article:

> The set piece will be over 690 feet (over an eighth of a mile) in length and 70 feet in height. A tremendous amount of woodwork is required and the whole of the frames will extend to nearly 50,000 square feet. For the last five weeks 20 carpenters have been involved on these and another twenty have been engaged on filling up and fixing on the fireworks. Over 10 miles of quick-match (connecting fuse) will be used and nearly a million coloured lights

will be consumed. The fireworks burnt will weigh nearly 2000 pounds and over 30 different shades of colour will be shown.

Four months later Arthur staged a pyrotechnical re-enactment of the British victory at the battle of Omdurman (in which, incidentally, a young Winston Churchill had taken part) within days of it happening. The Crystal Palace crowds roared their approval. The battle of Tsushima Strait, fought between Russia and Japan during the Russo-Japanese War, also came in for the Brock treatment, and if it looked suspiciously like the battle of Manila Bay, no one seemed to mind.

Ever resourceful, Arthur managed to muscle in on great sporting events. The annual Oxford Cambridge Boat Race on the Thames was one such example. During the 1890s he won the agreement of the race organisers to fire maroons at the finish in Mortlake to let people for miles around know who had won. Five loud detonations, audible in Putney where the race had started, meant Oxford had won, and two detonations meant Cambridge were victors. It was yet another way of keeping Brock's in the limelight.

He expanded on this idea in October 1901 when he used 'bulletin bombs' to tell Londoners who was winning the America's Cup yacht race. Every fifteen minutes the progress of the yachts was cabled from Sandy Hook, New York, to the *Daily Express* in London. The newspaper telephoned the details to Brock's, who in turn sent up huge rockets, visible over most of the capital, from the Crystal Palace and Alexandra Palace. A green rocket meant the English challenger, *Shamrock II*, was ahead, and a red rocket meant the American yacht, *Colombia*, was in front. A combination of green and purple indicated that an accident had befallen *Shamrock*, and red and purple meant *Colombia* had come to grief. Three greens in quick succession meant a win for *Shamrock*, and three reds a win for *Colombia*. 'Cut out the signal code so that you will know what the Bulletin Bombs mean when you see them soaring skyward,' advised the *Daily Express*. This novel way of 'purveying the news pyrotechnically' ended, as far as Londoners were concerned, with an anti-climactic three reds.

There were many other walks of life in which the firm involved itself. It provided explosives to clear bakers' chimneys; smoke rockets to test drains; smoke-generating devices to deal with vermin; cartridges which fired coils over houses, enabling firemen to haul up their hoses; maroons to bring RNLI volunteers to lifeboat stations when they were needed; and portfires to light explosive charges in the South African mining industry. A less successful proposal was aimed at deterring sexual predators on railway trains. Carriages were often made up of unconnected single compartments, and assaults on lone women were all too common. Someone at Brock's came up with the idea of positioning a Roman candle by the window of every compartment to be lit in case of trouble and to act as a distress signal. Numerous practical problems, not least the temptation placed in the way of small boys, ensured that the scheme was not widely taken up.

Victoria's Diamond Jubilee in 1897 was an even busier time for Brock's than her Golden Jubilee. Victorian self-confidence was reaching its apotheosis, and in almost every town and city in Britain there were banquets, ox roasting, the lighting of beacons and, of course, firework displays, many of them organised by Brock's. 'Fireworks last night greatest success – everyone delighted – thousands present,' the Duke of Abercorn telegrammed to Arthur from Newtownstewart in Northern Ireland.

Fireworks to the value of £260,000 (around £26 million in today's money), including Brock's latest novelty 'Electric Rain,' (not intended as a bad pun for 'A Record Reign,' Arthur assured the press) were set off in the queen's honour across the empire. The logistics were formidable. One consignment of Brock's fireworks was sent to Blantyre in what was then British Central Africa, now Malawi. Complete with the obligatory portrait of the queen, it had to be transported more than 300 miles up the Zambesi in dug-out canoes, followed by a further 35 miles on the heads of porters through steeply-rising country, all the time covered in canvas to protect it from the searing heat. Once again, the Brock's team triumphed. The display, when it was finally held at the Blantyre Sports Club, went off without a hitch.

Not that the business of making fireworks was all plain sailing. In some explosion or other, never spoken of by Arthur and not recorded in the firm's archives, he lost his right eye. The accident was variously described as an accidental childhood encounter with a stick, with a cock's beak or with an explosion but whatever the cause it was not as severe as the ones which destroyed his grandfather's premises in Whitechapel, nor which killed his four-times great-grandfather. But for the rest of his life he was self-conscious to the point of mortification about his disfigurement. Like his acquaintance Kaiser Bill, who was discomfited by – and went to great lengths to conceal – his dwarfish left arm, Arthur grew a striking moustache as a form of compensation. In almost every photograph taken of him over the next half a century or more, including family portraits, Arthur never faced the camera but invariably looked unsmilingly to one side, leaving the right side of his face always hidden.

Whatever You Are, Be Brave Boys!

During the Jubilee year of 1897, Frank, now aged 13, became a day boy at the fee-paying Dulwich College, a flourishing public school set in 65 acres of rolling green fields, chestnut-lined avenues and cricket pitches three miles to the north of the Brock family home in South Norwood. The college had been established in 1619, and although it could not count itself in the 'top drawer' alongside the likes of Eton and Winchester, catering as it did for the sons of civil servants, solicitors and bankers rather than for the heirs of the aristocracy, it was high up in the second rank, and was widely regarded as a suitable establishment for educating children of the empire. 'If you go east,' noted one observer, 'you seem to fall over Dulwich boys at every turn.'

Frank's day was a long one. Pupil Number 5083, as he was ranked in the school list, had to leave home soon after seven o'clock each morning to catch a train from Norwood Junction to West Dulwich, boarding a carriage usually packed with other Dulwich boys. (Although the school accepted boarders, most of the 680 pupils were day boys like Frank and many lived in the South London suburbs.) The 15-minute journey took him past the Crystal Palace, and on summer and autumn Thursdays he would peer out of the window in the hope of spotting his father's workforce putting the finishing touches to a new display. The Eton collar and black coat of his school uniform, adorned by a cornflower on Founder's Day, at first seemed a little like fancy dress, and sometimes he found himself running the gauntlet of local lads during the walk from West Dulwich station to the school, but he was a confident, well-built boy and was more than capable of looking after himself.

Like one of his fellow pupils, P. G. Wodehouse, who looked back on his time at the school as 'six years of unbroken bliss', Frank thrived at Dulwich, shining in both the classroom and on the sports field. Wodehouse was not the only successful author the school spawned during the late 19th and early

Boys in front of New College Dulwich, a Royal Institution of British Architects' Gold Medal winning design by Charles Barry Junior, son of the architect of the Houses of Parliament. (Dulwich College)

20th centuries. Another of Frank's contemporaries was the future detective fiction writer Raymond Chandler, whose mother had brought him over from America specifically so that he could receive the best possible education. The 1890s later became known as Dulwich's 'Golden Decade', not least in terms of the boys who went on to achieve eminence. Frank was high up on that list, being described nearly a century later in the school history as 'one of the most famous sons of Dulwich'.

Some Dulwich parents tended to look down on families like the Brocks because they were 'in trade', but not so the boys, who delighted in having a member of the famous fireworks clan in their midst. Three decades earlier Charles Brock had been hired to put on a spectacular display at the college to celebrate the laying of the first stone of new buildings, and on fine summer evenings it was possible to see the flashes of the fireworks at the Crystal Palace from the school grounds. One old boy, recalling his time at the school during the final years of the Victorian era, told Dulwich College historian Sheila Hodges:

> I remember when I first went to the college that there were traces of a snobbish prejudice against people who were 'in trade': it was silly and quite unreasonable, because our prosperity depended on our world-wide trade. I don't think we boys ever took this view at all – on the

contrary, I think we found it rather intriguing to be rubbing shoulders with well-known manufacturers such as Epps [cocoa], Johnson [Bovril], and above all Brock.

Frank's imaginative exuberance and delight in wild notions assured him of popularity among his peers. Unsurprisingly, he quickly became known as 'Fireworks', a nickname that was to stick with him into adulthood. He more than lived up to his sobriquet – and achieved lasting folk status among his fellow pupils in the process when he managed to blow up a stove in his classroom during a pyrotechnical experiment. As the school register records:

'Old Fireworks' blew up the stove in the 3rd Engineers Form Room with powdered fire and was sent up to the Old Man, who let him off (presumably a beating) as he was so fond of fireworks.

It was an event that was remembered with admiration at the school for years afterwards.

His school day started at eight o'clock with prayers in the 17th-century chapel, after which he went straight into lessons. In his first year he received a solid grounding in the classics, acquainting himself with Livy and Ovid in Latin, and Euripides and Thucydides ('Thick-sides' in public school slang) in Greek. The school curriculum drew inspiration not only from Athens and Rome but from the Bible and the British Empire. English subjects involved a term learning about Africa and a term on Australia with the aim of instilling in the boys a sense of British imperial superiority and destiny. One by-product of learning about a diverse range of countries was that Frank developed a keen interest in stamp-collecting. He also began nurturing an ambition to travel the world.

Lessons continued until lunchtime, with a 15-minute break for milk and a jam or chocolate 'split' in the school buttery. In the afternoon, lessons continued from two until four, after which the boys ran to the sports fields for two hours of games – rugby in the autumn and winter terms, and cricket in the summer. Fascinated by firearms (when he was just four years old he had posed

Frank Brock aged four with his rifle.

with a toy rifle for a studio photograph in London's Bayswater) Frank joined the school shooting team, excelling at both 200 and 500 yards in competitions against other schools. At six o'clock, armed with his homework, he was free to go home.

He was already an avid reader and at West Dulwich station there was a bookstall where he could buy magazines containing the latest instalments of thrilling serials by authors like Sir Arthur Conan Doyle and Jules Verne. A publication called *Pluck* was especially popular. Its masthead informed readers that it contained 'the daring deeds of plucky sailors, plucky soldiers, plucky firemen, plucky explorers, plucky detectives, plucky railwaymen, plucky boys and plucky girls and all sorts of conditions of British heroes.' Another favourite was *The Boys' Own Paper* which carried articles such as 'From Powder Monkey to Admiral', or the 'Stirring Days of the British Navy' and included advice on 'The Right Way to Carry a Boa Constrictor' and 'How to Make an Exploding Spider'. Robert Baden-Powell, the founder of the Scout movement, was a regular columnist, exhorting his young readers 'to live clean, manly and Christian lives.' The paper frequently carried poems which summed up not only its own ethos but neatly captured the over-riding philosophy of Dulwich College.

Whatever you are, be brave boys!
The liar's a coward and slave, boys!
Though clever at ruses,
And sharp at excuses,
He's a sneaking and pitiful knave, boys.

The Master of Dulwich during Frank's time was the devout Arthur Gilkes, whose dedication to teaching and to the moral welfare of his charges did much to boost the school's reputation during the closing years of the 19th century. At six-feet five-inches tall and weighing 18 stone, he was a giant of a man who sported a tawny mane of hair and a flowing white beard. (The boys wondered if he slept with the beard inside or outside the bedclothes.) To his charges he was a god-like figure, and his imposing frame, invariably clad either in cap and gown or in frock coat and top hat, struck terror into the hearts of many of the younger boys, especially if they failed to live up to his terrifyingly high moral principles. According to one contemporary, he was driven by a moral purpose 'more marked than in any other man I have ever known'. A painting in the school library of Sir Galahad, one of the knights of the Round Table in Arthurian legend, reminded everyone that courage, gentleness, courtesy and chivalry were qualities to which they should all aspire. To Gilkes, fair play, patriotism and Englishness were more important than intellect.

Arthur Herman Gilkes, 1849–1922, a noted educationalist and Frank's headmaster at Dulwich College. (Dulwich College)

The atmosphere at the college was unusually benign for a public school of the late Victoria era. Gilkes was sparing in his use of corporal punishment as can be seen from his treatment of Frank after the stove explosion, and bullying was rare. Tormenting smaller boys was certainly not part of Frank's ethos, or of the Brock family generally, although two of his brothers once dangled a fellow pupil's feet out of a carriage window on the train journey home for no better reason than that they took exception to his brightly coloured socks.

Gilkes was not without his foibles. In the year Frank joined the school, he replaced the biennial play with an annual concert – an unpopular move, for the boys were proud of the college's dramatic tradition. (The school's founder, Edward Alleyn, had been an important figure in Elizabethan theatre.) The change was made partly because Gilkes felt the play took up too much time which should be devoted to work, but also because he took a dim view of boys acting female parts, believing that this introduced an unwholesome element into school life. Boy trebles were banned for the same reason, as was any music he regarded as enfeebling or decadent (Chopin fell into this category). The only music he tolerated was that which he judged to be virile and good. He even barred certain passages from Shakespeare and the Bible from being read out in class or during Assembly, although it was generally impossible to work out what he found offensive about them.

Concerned that his pupils should be made aware of the misery and deprivation in which less privileged people lived, Gilkes created the Dulwich College Mission in a slum area of Camberwell to help destitute orphans, and he enlisted the boys to raise funds to support it. He encouraged team games, distrusted individualism (to such an extent that he banned tennis, which he considered 'unmanly') and instituted the prefect system. The son of a chemist, he introduced engineering and science into the curriculum, an innovation perfectly suited to a boy of Frank's background and aptitude. He used magic lanterns to enliven meetings of the Science Society, established photographic and astronomical societies, appointed a meteorological observer whose findings were posted on the school board, and encouraged the boys to make natural history collections. Frank absorbed everything the school could give him. He was especially fascinated by an experimental steam engine, described as a 'Horizontal Fixed Engine of 6 Nominal Horsepower with separate Jet Condenser and Boiler for 80lbs pressure of steam', which lived in the engineering workshop, and was one of only six or seven in Great Britain at that time.

Above all, Gilkes believed in service to country, and every lunchtime he led the boys in a toast 'to my country, right or wrong'. During Frank's time many Old Alleynians (as old boys from the school were called) were fighting in the Boer War. Frank, like pretty well everyone else at the school, followed the campaign closely, avidly reading the despatches of war correspondents like Rudyard Kipling. In May 1900, at the height of the war, Gilkes organised a day of celebrations to mark the Relief of Mafeking. Frank was one of 200 members of the school corps who paraded in front of him, sang 'God Save the Queen' and gave three cheers for the defender of the South African town, Robert Baden-Powell. In the evening there was a huge bonfire and firework display. It was laid on, naturally, by Brock's. Gilkes wrote of the occasion: 'It is not possible to speak too highly of the demeanour of the school, loyal, sound and enthusiastic, without the least trace of anything disagreeable.'

In due course no fewer than 2,000 boys from this most patriotic of schools enlisted for active service in World War I. Five won VCs, and a horrifyingly large proportion were killed in action.

Gilkes's moral effect on the school was sometimes compared to Thomas Arnold's at Rugby. With his ideals of selflessness, service, sportsmanship and teamwork, he had an enormous influence on Frank during his formative schoolboy years. He discussed his essays with him during individual tutorials and personally guided him through his confirmation classes. Under Gilkes's guidance, Frank acquired a greater knowledge of the Bible than almost any other boy in the school, and took to carrying a pocket edition of the New Testament with him wherever he went. An avid reader, he took a keen interest in old prints and books, especially those of a pyrotechnical nature. As with the other boys, his termly reports concentrated on character rather than achievement. It was not surprising that he developed at Dulwich a deep sense of patriotism and a love of competitive sport. 'Stocks managed to pass the ball to Brock, who planted it firmly over the line,' ran a typical report in the school magazine, *The Alleynian*, in March 1901.

Blessed with a remarkable memory, he was an able and enthusiastic scholar with a rich palette of interests and talents, and a moral compass that pointed due north. The wrecked classroom stove apart, he must have been the source of considerable pride to his headmaster. It is not hard to see why, like Tom Brown before him, he went out into the world, no longer a boy but a gentleman, and, above all, an Englishman, the very distillation of the Victorian faith in masculine virtue and muscular Christianity.

With this ethos firmly embedded in him, Frank left Dulwich College soon after his 17th birthday in 1901. All five of his brothers followed him to the school, the last not leaving until 1915. With his formidable intellect, Frank could easily have won a place at one of the country's leading universities, but a more exciting future beckoned, and he went immediately to work for the family firm, which had now out-grown its South Norwood premises and had moved to a larger site in Sutton, Surrey. Queen Victoria had died at the beginning of the year, and the firm was gearing up for its most intense period of activity yet in the shape of Edward VII's forthcoming coronation.

Frank cut his pyrotechnical teeth by helping out with the big set-piece exhibition at the Crystal Palace that summer. Its theme was an old favourite – 'The Revenge and the Fifty-Three' – a depiction in fireworks of Drake's flagship routing the Spanish Armada. Among those who saw the display was a contingent of 40 British soldiers who had distinguished themselves during the most recent Ashanti War in the Gold Coast of Africa. During their visit to London they were presented to the new king at Marlborough House, attended a review of the Household Troops, and were given grandstand seats at the Royal Tournament in Islington. Asked to name their lasting impressions of London, they were unanimous in their verdict: what they would remember most, they said, were a performing elephant playing the piano at the Alhambra Theatre in Leicester Square and the firework display at the Crystal Palace. Brock's fireworks had evidently lost none of their magic.

With this successful debut as a pyrotechnist under his belt, Frank looked to extend his horizons beyond Sydenham. In the time-honoured tradition of Dulwich College, the time had come to head east.

CHAPTER 6

Pomp and Circumstance

The new Brock's premises in Sutton dwarfed the previous site at South Norwood. They covered an area of more than 200 acres, and consisted of around 160 buildings, connected by three miles of tramways. Nearly 600 men and women were employed there, and at any given time the storage sheds might hold up to 500 tons of completed fireworks, ranging from farthing squibs to £1,500 set-pieces an eighth of a mile long.

At the time Frank began working there, almost all the company's efforts were being directed towards the forthcoming coronation, originally set for 26 June 1902, but postponed to 9 August after the new monarch was struck down by appendicitis. In a studio on the site, several artists, led by the principal designer, Philip George, were already working on numerous sketches for the 'firework portraits' which would form the centrepieces of hundreds of displays. These included likenesses of King Edward VII and Queen Alexandra, as well as of the new Prince and Princess of Wales (the future King George V and Queen Mary). One image of the king, 40ft in diameter, was to be the largest firework portrait ever made.

Pyrotechnic mottoes such as 'God Save the King' and 'Peace to King and Empire' were also being prepared, along with a sheet of flowing fire called the 'Coronation Cascade', which measured 60,000 square feet, or almost one and a half acres. Another item was 'The Curtain of Crown Jewels', described by the firm as 'a fiery curtain of falling colours, 400 feet in length, decked with lustrous jewels of every colour, which lose their delicate tints and change to brilliance of dazzling splendour.'

In the months before the coronation, orders came in for no fewer than 11 million Roman candles, and for 50,000 'bombshells' which would be fired into the air to signal the lighting of bonfires all over the country. Novelty fireworks devised by the firm for the occasion included 'The Alexandra' and

Part of Brock's factory in Sutton. It was used by the company between 1901 and 1933. Probably the largest firework factory in the world at the time, in excess of 200 acres and 150 buildings plus storage sheds, explosives magazines and three miles of tramways. It employed up to 500/600 people but this number exceeded 2000 during WWI.

the patriotic 'Red, White and Blue'. Production of more than 1,000 miles of 'quick-match' for the big set-pieces was also underway. To fulfil its orders the firm had acquired, among other materials, 60 tons of gunpowder, 25 tons of paper, five tons of flour to make paste, five tons of glue, half a ton of pins, and countless tons of wood to make rocket sticks. With an estimated £600,000-worth of material due to go up in smoke in England alone (about £60 million in today's money) pyrotechnists had never had it so good.

Despite the king's playboy lifestyle ('I never can, or shall, look at him without a shudder,' his own mother had said of him) his gross corpulence (his waist measurement was 48 inches), and his age (at nearly 60 he was one of the oldest monarchs to have ascended the throne), Edward was extremely popular both in Britain and in the empire as a whole, and genuine coronation fever gripped the country. It was not just in towns and cities that his loyal subjects pushed the boat out. There was hardly a village in the country that was not determined to play its part in ushering in the

Magnesium shell showing the 64,000 crowd at the Crystal Palace, 1901. Brock's pioneered the use of magnesium and aluminium in entertainment and military illuminating pyrotechnics. The picture shows how effective it was. The royal box, seen in several of these images, is visible in the centre of the palace.

Edwardian era. Expenses incurred by the parish of Wateringbury in Kent were a typical example:

> 456 teas – £11 8s.
> 15 bushels of cherries – £8 11s.
> West Kent Band – £12 15s.
> Nemo's Punch and Ventriloquist – £7 10s.
> Prizes – £7 7s. 7d.
> Brock's Fireworks – £10 10s.

The coronation expenses of Wavendon in Buckinghamshire went along similar lines:

> Band – £7
> Roundabouts – £5
> Sweets and medals – £1 3s 7d
> Bread & cakes – £5 14s
> Tea & sugar – £1 3s 8d
> Brock's Fireworks – £5

By the end of the summer the Brock's balance sheet had never looked healthier, and the firm's reputation had never been greater. For young Frank, however, the real excitement was only just beginning. To educate him more fully in the workings of the business, Arthur asked him to join him on a trip to India to help with the pyrotechnics for the coronation celebrations to be held there in January 1903. The opening of the Suez Canal in the 1860s had revolutionised travel to the Eastern Empire, and the tedious four-month voyage via Cape Town was a thing of the past. It was now possible to travel to India in fewer than three weeks and, given Brock's enormous profits, father and son were able to enjoy the comfort of first-class cabins at £100 apiece. Accompanied by a team of Brock's operators, they arrived in Bombay in December, and from there they made the gruelling 900-mile journey by train to Delhi.

The logistics of the operation were fraught with difficulty. Planning had begun shortly after the death of Queen Victoria when a senior Brock's representative, J. H. Sharpe, travelled to India to secure bookings for displays at all the country's major cities. So influential was the firm that he was immediately granted an interview with the Viceroy, Lord Curzon, who enthused about the fireworks he had seen at the Crystal Palace and gave the go-ahead for a Brock's display to be held in Delhi.

Sharpe spent the next six months travelling from city to city winning approval for further displays. While in Calcutta he discovered to his annoyance that a man named Schoenberg, who represented Brock's chief rivals, James Pain & Sons, was also intent on winning orders for the coronation festivities. Sharpe befriended him and challenged him to a game of billiards in a city hotel. They stayed up until 11.00 pm at which point Sharpe suggested they should stop for the night and continue the game at 10.30 am the next day. While Schoenberg slumbered, Sharpe rose at 5.00 am and within the hour he had boarded a boat sailing for his next port of call, Rangoon. He arrived there a week ahead of the unfortunate Schoenberg, who not only lost out on the Rangoon display but contracted malaria and died soon afterwards without having won a single order. Such was the ruthless competition between the rival fireworks firms of those days.

With a full order book in the bag, the fireworks had to be prepared in Sutton and sent to India – another massive exercise in logistics. A merchant ship was contracted to take out 70 tons of material from England but got no further than the Thames estuary. The consignment was transferred to another vessel, which broke down in Port Said. The shipment arrived many days late in Bombay, drastically curtailing the time allowed for preparation, but Arthur and his team overcame the problems and the displays went off without a hitch.

British Imperial India was now at its apogee – 'the brightest jewel in the Imperial diadem' – and for the Brock family to have been chosen to play a central role in this unprecedented show of spectacle and fanfare was an enormous honour. Ceremony and pomp were the means by which a small British contingent kept in submission a population of 315 million with 147 languages and 2,380 castes. The presence of Arthur and Frank at the festivities confirmed Brock's Fireworks' place at the heart of the imperial machine.

Soon after their arrival in India, Arthur and Frank were given news of a shocking accident in New York's Madison Square Garden, yards from the spot where the ground-breaking Brock's advertisement had once lit up the side of the now demolished Cumberland Hotel. Some 30,000 people had gathered in the park to watch a firework display financed by the newspaper tycoon William Randolph Hearst to celebrate his return to Congress. The show was

Calcutta, the royal firework display for the Coronation, 1903. 'It was agreed on every hand that the Fireworks for which the well-known firm of C. T. Brock & Co., the world famous Pyrotechnists were responsible, made far and away the finest display ever witnessed in the City.' (*Empress*)

Delhi, 'A Night Scene After The Durbar', the day after the Durbar in front of the Jumma (now known as Jama) Musjid. 'Great Britain stands pre-eminent and unchallenged in her possession of the "Fire King" of the world, for Brock's is the acknowledged pioneer and inventor of the higher class of Pyrotechnic Art'. (*Indian Daily News,* 3 January 1903)

about to begin when the premature explosion of a bomb shattered the cast-iron mortar from which it was being discharged. The sparks fired a whole battery of similar missiles, sending shrapnel flying into the crowd and, as the *New York Times* described it, 'transforming in an instant the entire east side of the park into a scene of death and carnage which a battlefield could scarcely have surpassed in its horror.'

Nineteen people were killed in the disaster, including a policeman and several children, and more than 80 were injured. It was a nightmare for the organisers, Pain's Fireworks, and in the immediate aftermath of the tragedy, when feelings were inevitably running high, ten Pain's employees were arrested and charged with homicide. The charges were later dropped, but some of the victims and their families sued the company for more than $500,000, and the American side of Pain's business was effectively wrecked. Much of the public anger was directed at Hearst, who tried to distance himself from the disaster by leaving New York the following day and instructing his newspapers to bury the story on their inside pages.

Arthur and Frank had the accident very much in mind as they prepared the ground for their Indian displays. In particular, they ensured that the mortars to be used were almost completely buried in the ground, so that they could only discharge their shells vertically. Their meticulous planning ensured that the shows they put on in Delhi, Bombay, Calcutta and several other locations were resounding successes

The Delhi celebration, or Durbar as it was called, lasted a full two weeks. Frank took time off to join the vast throngs who lined the streets to watch the processions of maharajas, ambassadors, bejewelled princes and boy kings ride past on painted elephants, camels and tasselled horses, or in howdahs and gilded carriages. His voice added to the cheers that went up for the Viceroy, Lord Curzon, who was perched high on a richly caparisoned elephant alongside his beautiful young wife, Mary, described by the Indian poet Ram Sharma as 'a rose of roses bright, a vision of embodied light'. Frank found the whole experience fascinating. He loved exploring the markets, trying out the exotic foods and taking rickshaw rides down the teeming streets. Through this visit he developed a lifelong love of Rudyard Kipling's stories and poems about life in British India, relishing the tale of 'Rikki-Tikki-Tavi' and thrilling to the gallantry and sacrifice of 'Gunga Din'.

In a letter written to his sister Gwenlian (difficult for her young siblings to say, so the family nicknamed her 'Cissy') on New Year's Eve 1902, the 18-year-old Frank, giving his address as Delhi Reformatory, Delhi finished his letter:

> Last Monday we saw the Delhi elephant procession. It lasted 80 minutes passing elephants with solid silver howdahs as big as broughams (horse drawn carriages) and one with a gold one, all covered in silk with ropes of real pearls hanging from their tusks, which are decorated with bands of gold inlaid with jewels. And all of them trained to brush the flies off their riders with a brush carried in their trunks. 11 o'clock and I am very tired. Goodnight old girl. Your affectionate brother, Frank.

The Delhi fireworks laid on by Brock's cost some £1,500 (the equivalent today of £150,000) and featured portraits of the new king and queen beneath glittering crowns of Roman candles, as well as of Lord and Lady Curzon, and Lord Kitchener, the Commander-in-Chief of the army in India. During the event – held in the same park on Burari Road where Arthur had helped organise the 1876 display for the then Prince of Wales – fireworks were fired from gas balloons at a height of several thousand feet and could be seen from 50 miles away. 'It was one of Brock's finest pyrotechnic efforts, and its result was beautiful beyond comparison,' declared the *Indian Daily News*. The *Adelaide Advertiser*'s special correspondent in Delhi, Lady Brown, enthused:

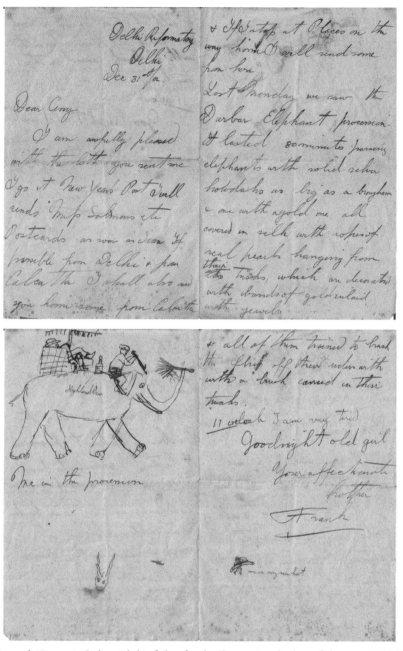

Frank, aged 18, was in India with his father for the Coronation displays of the great 1903 Delhi Durbar. On 31 December 1902 he wrote home to his sister Gwenlian whose family nickname was Cissy. Notice the cartoon drawing of his pith helmet and observe the pith helmets being worn in the next picture taken three days later.

Preparing the great Coronation Durbar display in front of the Jumma Musjid in Delhi, 3 January 1903. Frank's pith helmet is shading him from the sun.

> A 101-rocket salute commenced the display; effective, indeed, but terribly brain-racking for heads already somewhat in a whirl with so much gaiety in so short a time. Needless to say, the whole display of fireworks was worthy of the occasion, the showers of gold and silver, and the wheat-sheaf, being really splendid.

At the end of January, after another gruelling 900-mile train journey, Arthur and Frank arrived in Calcutta, where they put on a display at the racecourse watched by half a million people. 'It was agreed on every hand that the Fireworks for which the well-known firm of C. T. Brock & Co., the world-famous Pyrotechnists were responsible, made far and away the finest display ever witnessed in the city,' went one report of the show. *The Times* of India commented:

> The reputation of Messrs C. T. Brock & Co, the famous pyrotechnists, who have made the fame of Crystal Palace unapproachable in all the world, did not suffer one iota by the great show they gave…one might rhapsodize all night and still fall short of reality.

In Bombay they staged a display in the 22-acre Oval Maidan recreational ground, an event so well attended that a British reporter observed that 'there wasn't even room to slide a sheet of tissue paper between two natives.' The same reporter added that the Bombay crowd was more dignified than at Delhi, being 'charmed but impassive.' The *Indian Daily News* summed up the general feeling:

Great Britain stands pre-eminent and unchallenged in her possession of the 'Fire King' of the world, for Brock is the acknowledged pioneer and inventor of the higher class of Pyrotechnic Art.

Still only 18, Frank arrived back in England at the end of March having more than proved his value to the firm. To his father's delight he had turned out to be a 'natural'. Such was Arthur's confidence in him that a month later he put him in sole charge of a display in Hungary. The state festival of which Frank's display was the centrepiece was held on the Danube in front of Emperor Franz Joseph I. It was one of the most elaborate events staged in Europe for more than half a century. Frank's contribution was to lay on a magnificent 'volcanic eruption' on the crest of a hill high above Budapest, lighting up the royal palace, the riverside boulevards and the city's bridges. The emperor, it was reported, was 'astonished', while a local journalist enthused:

As night fell over the beautiful Danube and the glorious blaze of English fire burst into the sky with a roar which shook the towering Blochsberg, the multitudes lining the river on either side swayed in the vivid light. From venerable emperor to poorest workman, all Budapest came forth to see the beautiful city clothed in a sheen of borrowed light; they gazed in wonder, and in imagination visited the London Crystal Palace of world renown.

Frank returned to Sutton a hero. He had shown himself to be far more than a safe pair of hands. Despite his youth, he had demonstrated that he possessed the flair, the technical skills, the showmanship and the sheer bravado to handle a large-scale assignment. For his father there was the added satisfaction of knowing that when the time came, he would be more than capable of taking over the reins of the firm. The future of Brock's had never looked more assured.

In the wake of his Budapest success, Frank was sent off again, this time to supervise the fireworks for a visit to Ireland by King Edward VII and Queen Alexandra, accompanied by their daughter, Princess Victoria. The royal visitors stayed at Kilkenny Castle and at Waterford, and were entertained at both venues by magnificent displays, supervised by Frank, which 'bathed both cities in brilliant light.' The special effects included a portrait in fire of the royal party's host, Sir James Power, a motto in fire 'Prosperity to Waterford', and a 'hot-off-the-presses' depiction of the Japanese bombardment of the Russian fleet, which had taken place two months earlier at Port Arthur in Manchuria. 'The battle between the Russian and Japanese navies was lurid enough to satisfy the most bloodthirsty tastes,' commented a local newspaper. For Frank, it was yet another triumphant notch in his pyrotechnical belt.

Frank directed the Budapest displays in 1903 after his return from India. 'A Colossal display fired from the crest of the Blochsberg mountain and including the illuminations of the royal palace, the riverside boulevards and the bridges ... one of the most elaborate fêtes to be staged in Europe since the palmy days of Napoleon III.' (Alan Brock, *A History of Fireworks*)

A comprehensive record of all the trips he undertook for the firm following these assignments does not exist, but it is known that he travelled extensively in subsequent years. He may well have had a hand in many of the numerous Brock's displays held on continental Europe during the rest of that decade – Liege in 1905, Milan and Marseilles in 1906, Malaga and Nice in 1907. He is believed to have travelled to Russia, Patagonia and Spitzbergen, and it is on record that he went to Brazil in 1908 to supervise displays at the Rio de Janeiro National Exhibition, an event which attracted more than one million visitors. In 1909 he supervised the fireworks at Jersey's annual Battle of Flowers festival, laying on a spectacular one-hour show which included a 'Depiction of the Aurora Borealis', 'A Huge New Device – the Kaleidoscopic Wheel', and a humorous item entitled 'Performing Monkeys'.

Rio De Janeiro, 1908. Frank directed the displays accompanying the exhibition of 1908. 'Brock's wonderful fireworks and pretty illuminations have firmly caught the public taste; the crowd again last night was enormous and enthusiastic.' (*Jornal do Brasil*)

Back in England Frank was kept equally busy. In August 1905 he directed a dazzling display at Spithead to mark the 'entente cordiale' visit of the French fleet. Fireworks were set off from 58 British warships in front of the king, with a full 6,000 men taking part in the spectacle. In a summer season when the Crystal Palace paid £100 on each occasion and most of the operator-fired displays supplied to fêtes, regattas and aristocratic coming-of-age parties cost between £10 and £25, the Foreign Office was prepared to pay Brock's £2,532 9s/1d to help strengthen the alliance. The accolade *The Times* gave the event could not have been bettered:

> It is scarcely possible to convey by description any adequate idea of the scene presented last night by the illumination of the combined fleets and the display of fireworks by the Channel Fleet. The epithets 'magnificent', 'brilliant', 'imposing', 'effective,' 'successful', are all summed up in one word: 'unprecedented'.

Review of the fleet at Spithead, August 1905. Frank arranged and directed this 'Colossal Naval Firework Display' during the Entente-Cordiale on the occasion of the French Fleet's visit to Portsmouth. It was fired from 58 warships and 6,000 men took part.

The *Morning Leader* newspaper said simply: 'Messrs Brock out-Brocked Brock!'

A proud Arthur described the Spithead extravaganza to the *Evening News* as 'the most important firework display which has taken place in England since the peace celebrations in Hyde Park in 1856 to mark the end of the Crimean War.' He went on: 'It was the biggest display we have ever made and was carried out without a single hitch. I represent the seventh generation of the family and I see no reason to doubt that the business will still be in the family's possession for many years to come.' He was so impressed by what Frank had achieved that he asked him to reproduce the display at the Crystal Palace the following month.

All this when Frank had only just turned 21.

The following year he was part of a Brock's team which provided a pyrotechnic commentary on the 1906 general election results. Every time a seat changed hands, huge rockets were sent up from the Crystal Palace, Shooters Hill in

South-East London, and the Hotel Cecil on the Thames embankment. A team from Pain's Fireworks did the same from Hampstead Heath, the Alexandra Palace and Chelsea Power Station. A red rocket announced a Liberal gain and a blue rocket was intended to announce a Conservative gain. As it turned out, the blue rockets were surplus to requirements, for the Conservatives failed to gain a single seat. The skies over London turned red all evening as Henry Campbell-Bannerman led the Liberals to a landslide victory.

In 1910 the amount paid by the public to see the Crystal Palace fireworks since their inception in 1865 was calculated at £2,250,000, or almost a quarter of a billion pounds in today's money. That same year the Brock's displays at Sydenham went into abeyance when new promoters took control of operations and awarded the fireworks contract to arch-rivals Pain's. Much to Arthur's fury, Pain's promptly began using the 'Crystal Palace Fireworks' trademark in their advertising. He won a high court injunction to stop them doing this and secured the backing of the Master of the Rolls, Sir Herbert Cozens-Hardy, when the case went to the appeal court. Like pretty well everyone else in the country, Sir Herbert had been to a Brock's display at the Crystal Palace and had a soft spot for the firm. In his summing up, he ruled:

> Brock's have got a high reputation for the great displays which most of us have seen at the Crystal Palace in years gone by. They are entitled to use those words to distinguish their goods.

As it turned out, the Pain's association with the Crystal Palace lasted barely 12 months. In the wake of nearly 60 years of financial problems, the Palace went bankrupt in 1911. With the added disruption of World War I, it would be ten years before firework displays – organised by Brock's – were held there again. The temporary loss of business did not worry Arthur unduly. He and the king had helped build the Empire together and having worked closely with him around the world and at the Crystal Palace for many decades, Arthur was saddened by the death of King Edward VII in the spring of 1910 but it meant another coronation was looming and his order books would stay full. Not only that, but Brock's had also won contracts to hold firework displays at the Alexandra Palace in North London and the White City stadium, recently built in West London for the 1908 Olympic Games.

Possibly smarting from having lost the Crystal Palace contract, Arthur put much effort into the White City Coronation Exhibition displays of 1911. The beautiful colour poster the company produced shows magnificent portraits of the new monarchs with huge set-pieces depicting erupting volcanoes, airships fighting aeroplanes and naval battles between Super Dreadnoughts. One new effect Arthur had been working to perfect for some time, born from the

Brocks' deep knowledge of pyrotechnic illumination, was what he called the 'Shimmer Light'. In a speech to the directors and the press in June 1911, he introduced it:

> The recent developments in the pyroforic alloys of magnesium, aluminium and chromium, and our experiments in the auto-galvanic compounds, have enabled us to produce some marvelously pretty and brilliant effects hitherto unknown in pyrotechny …

The established connection between Brock's and the military, a connection that was to play a crucial role in Frank's life, was alluded to in subsequent press reports. *The Wakefield Herald* commented on the Shimmer that summer: 'It is a light of extraordinary brilliance and power, and is capable of enormous developments. Its evolution from a single light has been watched by scientists and the War Office experts with the greatest interest.'

The firm had numerous other sidelines, including supplying Christmas crackers to the British royal family and being official pyrotechnists to the King of Spain. With an annual turnover in the region of £500,000, Arthur was able to boast with good reason that Brock's were 'the leading flame-manipulating artists of the world and never intend to stand still.' In explaining the degree to which Brock's fame and market reach had extended across the world, in words and sentiments that are no longer acceptable, *Pearson's Weekly* enthused: 'They have shed coloured light on "darkest Africa", they have shaken the Moor out of his habitual calm; the Cingalee has prostrated himself in adoration; the stolid Turk has been keenly interested at Constantinople; the noble Sikh has impressively salted the "fire portrait" of his Empress.'

Frank was by now on the board of Brock's. He owned 500 shares in the firm and was effectively second-in-command. Anything to do with pyrotechnics fascinated him, and he built up a substantial collection of books on the subject. Among his most treasured possessions was a rare first edition of *A True and Perfect Relation of the Whole Proceedings against the late most barbarous Traitors*. Published in 1606, it was the first written account of the gunpowder plot.

He still lived with his parents – who were now residing at the palatial Haredon House in Sutton – but was seldom to be found at home. When he was not travelling, attending board meetings, or dropping in on the factory, he devoted as much time as possible to sport. He played rugby for Richmond, already established as one of the country's leading clubs, and was a keen amateur boxer, as happy to receive a punch as to land one. One of his frequent destinations was Eastbourne on the Sussex coast, a resort he came to know well when Brock's replaced Pain's as 'park pyrotechnicians' at the town's main recreational centre, Devonshire Park, in 1907. Frank's displays there, according to the *Eastbourne Gazette*, were 'better than anything that had come before' and included 'exceptionally brilliant set-pieces'.

Frank came to love the town, and almost every weekend, fireworks or not, he booked himself into the Alexandra Hotel on the seafront before seeking out his good friend Edgar Allan Brown, Devonshire Park's managing director. After a Sunday morning swim in the park's baths, followed by a hearty lunch, they played tennis or golf or, if the weather was bad, they honed their combat skills with a wrestling match in the park's gym. Like Frank, Brown was a keen rugby player, and the two men helped to establish the Devonshire Park Rugby Football Club.

There is every likelihood that Frank was at Devonshire Park on Easter Saturday, 1911, when it was the scene of Britain's first known plane crash. The holiday crowds on Eastbourne promenade that morning were excited by the appearance of a Bleriot biplane, which proceeded to perform graceful loops beyond the pier. The pilot, Captain Oscar Morison, then headed inland and attempted to land in the grounds of the park. He failed to notice some electric wiring, with the result that the plane clipped the branches of a tree, struck a lamppost and dropped heavily on to some chairs. A crowd of people, most of whom had never seen a plane before, let alone seen one crash, gathered round excitedly. Morison, who was unhurt, was helped out of his wrecked machine and good-humouredly signed autographs while waiting for a lorry to tow away the mangled remains.

Even if Frank did not actually witness the accident, his natural curiosity would have drawn him to the scene, and one might reasonably speculate that it helped to spark his own interest in aviation. Here, in the shape of Oscar Morison, was the very epitome of one of those fabled magnificent men with his (albeit pranged) flying machine. A tall, nonchalant figure with impeccable manners and a neat moustache, Morison had been born in Dulwich in the same year as Frank. In many ways he was a mirror image of Frank himself, or at least the type of man that Frank aspired to be – a daredevil gentleman adventurer who was prepared to take risks and to push the boundaries, while never showing an ounce of fear. In true swashbuckling style, Morison walked away unscathed and unperturbed from two more 'prangs' the following month, the first when he struck a fence while landing in the grounds of Roedean Ladies' College on the Sussex coast, and the second when he hit trees after his engine cut out at Hayward's Heath. He went on to serve with distinction in the Royal Naval Air Service during World War I. Frank, as it turned out, would do exactly the same, and in years to come would display the same nonchalance in the face of danger as Morison.

The Devonshire Park crash may also have been the inspiration for a new Brock's product launched the following year – aviation 'smoke rockets'. These devices, cooked up by Arthur, were ignited on the ground to help guide aviators to a designated landing spot, and could certainly have saved Oscar Morison from his little spot of bother in Eastbourne. In the event the first person to benefit from them was another larger-than-life figure, the Wild West showman and air pioneer Samuel Cody, who used them during a trail-blazing flight from London to Manchester.

In December 1911 Frank undertook his biggest assignment yet for Brock's when he returned to India (this time without his father) to oversee displays for the Delhi Durbar to mark the coronation of King George V as 'King-Emperor' of India. Billed as the most spectacular ceremony in the history of the British Empire, it was the only Durbar to be attended in person by the reigning monarch. Costing at least £1 million to stage, it attracted more than 200,000 people, including 400 ruling chiefs and princes, maharajas and rajas.

The Durbar was not without incident, especially for Frank. Some saw it as a bad omen when a magnificent pavilion on silver poles, built for the king's reception, burnt down before the start of the festivities. Then, during the rehearsal for the king's arrival, Frank himself was at the centre of a minor drama when a large store of fireworks, stockpiled beside the Yamuna river for the 'people's fete', apparently self-ignited, destroying the building in which they were stored. Whether or not this was an act of sabotage by anti-British rebels was never established, but in any event Frank was more than equal to the task of ensuring the display went ahead as scheduled. As it happened, he was also able to provide invaluable assistance in the wake of a much more serious incident a few days later.

As one of the state processions was moving slowly through the centre of Delhi, a bomb was thrown at the silver-encrusted howdah on which the Viceroy, Lord Hardinge, was riding with his wife on top of an elephant. It exploded in the face of one of the native fan-bearers sitting behind them, killing the man instantly. At first the Viceroy appeared to be unhurt, but shortly afterwards he fainted from loss of blood and a fragment of metal from the howdah was found embedded in his shoulder. Hardinge duly recovered, but the rumour mill went into full swing and for a time it was believed that the king himself had been assassinated.

Knowing that in Frank they had on hand one of the world's foremost experts on explosives, the Delhi police asked him to examine the bomb fragments. He analysed the yellow deposits left by the blast on the silver casing and was able to identify the type of explosive used in the bomb's manufacture as a mixture of potassium chlorate and arsenic sulphide. He presented his evidence to the investigators, and it was used not only in the successful prosecution of the man who threw the bomb, Vasant Kumar Vishwas, but also to track down his co-conspirators, who had used the same compound in previous attacks. This was perhaps the first time that Frank's extensive scientific knowledge was utilised in the interests of state security, and it would not be the last. Word was beginning to spread about this remarkable young man's abilities, and it may well have been his work for the Delhi police that sparked the interest of the desk-bound wallahs back home in Whitehall. Before long they would be employing him in many different ways to help protect Britain's interests at home and abroad.

Frank was by now showing a keen interest in politics and was passionate about the Irish question. He was vehemently opposed to the Liberal Government's efforts to introduce Home Rule to Ireland, and was an ardent supporter of the Protestants in the North who were prepared to resort to armed struggle to stop any attempt to sever or dilute Ulster's attachment to the United Kingdom. His strong views may have been the result of friendships he formed while organising firework displays in Ireland, but he was probably also influenced by his literary hero, Rudyard Kipling, who published a poem in 1912 – 'Ulster' – which powerfully urged the Protestant cause.

> We know the war prepared
> On every peaceful home,
> We know the hells declared
> For such as serve not Rome

In September 1913 Frank took the unusual step for an Englishman of enrolling as a volunteer in the British League for the Support of Ulster and the Union. This was a shadowy organisation whose stated aim was to assist the Ulster loyalists in their struggle to remain under the British Crown. It was strongly suspected of attempting to smuggle arms into Ulster from the mainland and questions were asked in the Westminster Parliament about its activities, along with calls for its founders to be indicted for conspiracy. In April 1914 the Ulster Volunteer Force, to which the League was affiliated, managed to ship 24,000 rifles and three million rounds of ammunition into Ulster in a well-organised, clandestine operation. Whether Frank had the time to be involved in this and other gun-running escapades is not known but his membership of the League means it was a distinct possibility. As it turned out, the weapons were not needed. International events intervened when Britain declared war on Germany later that year, and the Irish problem went into abeyance.

CHAPTER 7

A Carpet of Violets

Even in a life as crowded as Frank's, there was time for romance, and towards the end of 1913 he met a darkly beautiful woman, Gladys Grosvenor Albert, who was to become the love of his life. She was known to all her friends as G (she loathed the name Gladys), and very unusually for the times she ran a high society hat shop in the West End of London, a few doors away from the haute couture business of her younger sister, Leila. Their childhood had not been easy. When she was eight years old, her mother Ellen had given birth to her youngest son, Tom, and mother and child had not survived.

Unable to raise his children by himself, her father had sent G and three of her siblings, including three-year-old Pitt, to a no-nonsense boarding school in North London. Here they stayed for several years. On one occasion, in order to save Pitt's seat of glory from a sound thrashing, G distinguished herself by claiming responsibility for his overnight raid on a large apple pie that was intended for Sunday lunch. They spent several years here before G and Leila were sent to a girls' boarding school opposite the Broad Walk in Kensington Gardens, London. Years later G liked to recall the Saturday morning readings of the school rules by the headmistress – in particular rule five: 'No hair combings to be put in the grates because great damage will be done to the drains.'

G as a child aged around 11/12.

G did not let this unpromising start in life stand in her way, and the Albert sisters' high fashion businesses in and around New Bond Street very quickly became the first port of call for large numbers of their friends and upper-crust women seeking to impress their fellow silk stockings. As part of their work, the two enterprising sisters travelled to Paris at least twice a year to select designs from the latest collections for their wealthy clientele, bringing these back to London to be turned into the finished product by their milliners and seamstresses.

Socially, G had the character and looks to have a most enjoyable life but the time and energy she invested in her successful young business, the high standards she applied to any potential suitor and the consequent lack of a husband led her father, with concerns founded in the mid-19th century when he had been a young man, to frustration and worry. 'You'll walk through the wood and [in the end] choose a crooked stick [worthless fellow] my girl' was one of his not infrequent complaints which amused G and her siblings, entertaining her but in truth, simultaneously causing concern.

G was indeed highly sociable and had the type of warm personality that encouraged her clients and friends to confide in her. At a time when few women would venture outside without a hat, one of the benefits of being her customer lay in her knowledge of which parties and functions they were all attending so as to avoid any embarrassing wardrobe clashes.

One of her customers and close friends was Joy Coverdale, whose brother went to Dulwich College and whose husband Harry played rugby for England and Blackheath. The Coverdales in turn knew Frank (Harry had played rugby with him) and Joy decided that here was an excellent opportunity for some match-making.

Her chosen method of playing Cupid was to set up a blind date. Her plan was for the four of them – herself, Harry, Frank and G – to meet for dinner at a restaurant one Saturday night and to see how things progressed. But fate intervened. Sadly, Harry was injured on the pitch that afternoon and the meal had to be cancelled. Having been shown a photograph of G, and having heard so much about her, Frank decided that he could not allow matters to rest there. He acquired her telephone number from Joy, took the plunge and rang her that evening.

Her warm, beguiling voice enchanted him, and he was thrilled when she mentioned in passing that she was an avid reader of Rudyard Kipling. By the time he had hung up – much, much later – he was smitten. During the course of the conversation he asked her to name her favourite flower. Caught

G in her late 20s, a photograph given to Frank after their friendship developed.

Frank gave this photo to G after they met. It is signed on the back 'Frank Arthur Brock' and on the front 'Jan 20th 1914' with musical notes added giving an approximation of the song, popularized the previous year by the singer Al Jolson, 'You Made Me Love You'.

by surprise, and slightly flustered, she volunteered the first thing that came into her head – violets.

The following Monday evening, when she returned from work to her apartment at Lauderdale Mansions in Maida Vale, she found the entire landing outside her door covered with violets. Born in 1879, G was five years older than Frank, but the age gap was of no relevance to either of them. The arrival of the violets set in motion a whirlwind romance.

To help things along they exchanged photographs and Frank sent his, which he had arranged to be taken by a Sutton portrait photographer. Dated 20 January 1914 he marked it 'YHTB + wood' – his private acronym for 'Your Husband To Be' and an allusion to her father's frequently voiced wood-land metaphor of frustration. Beneath the inscription he drew some musical notes based loosely on a popular song of the day, 'You Made me Love You – I didn't Want to do it', which had been written for the hit Broadway musical *The Honeymoon Express* in 1913, and was recorded by Al Jolson the same year. The lyrics speak of a man who has known the agonies of love, but is besotted none the less.

The same year the heir to the German throne, Crown Prince Wilhelm – son of Arthur's helmeted Crystal Palace acquaintance – had published a book, *Germany in Arms*, which enthused about the prospect of war in Europe and argued that peace was not advantageous to his country. The Kaiser himself believed that a war in which Britain was one of Germany's opponents was inevitable. Not many people in England took much notice of this Teutonic posturing. To the public at large, the likelihood of war seemed remote. The *Daily Telegraph* declared soothingly in its main leader on 1 January 1914: 'Our foreign relations are such as to cause no sort of uneasiness and there has been a steady improvement in the tone and temper of our intercourse with Germany.'

Certainly the prospect of war was one of the last things on the minds of Frank and G as the weeks passed and their love grew. It was the year in which Charlie Chaplin made his film debut in *Making A Living*, George Bernard Shaw's play *Pygmalion* opened to rave reviews, and *Tarzan Of The Apes* first appeared in bookshops. King George V became the first monarch to attend the FA Cup Final at Wembley (he saw Burnley beat Liverpool) and, to Frank's delight, England won the Five Nations Championship. At the Queen's Hall in London, Arthur Brock was the guest of honour when Stravinsky staged a private performance of his orchestral production of *Fireworks*. To Stravinsky's great pleasure, the 'Shakespeare of Pyrotechnics' declared afterwards that he had found the work to be 'graphic and pictorial'. He was grateful to Stravinsky, he said, 'for being the first musical composer to recognise the absorbing beauties of the pyrotechnic art as a theme for his compositions.'

On sunny evenings in Surrey, of which there were many in that long, hot summer of 1914, courting couples like Frank and G attended tennis parties and stole time together on country walks or at the weekend house parties where they had both arranged to be individually invited by their friends. The world seemed a happy place, and only to a superstitious few did the blood-red evening skies portend a cataclysm. As the author Lesley N. Smith wrote:

> In retrospect, the moment before a storm breaks is found to have been heavy, lurid, pregnant with foreboding. So it is with the summer of 1914, which seems to have been lived in a breathless pause before the storm. Actually at the time it was like every other summer there ever had been or ever would be.

By now the rise of Germany's military might was causing some trepidation at Westminster, but the threat did not seem immediate. On Sunday 28 June, one of the few things that mattered to large numbers of Londoners was the result of the Grand Prix de Paris horse race. When a teleprinter stuttered into life at the Reuter's news agency near the Bank of England, an eager young editor started typing out what he thought was the result: '1. Sarajevo; 2. Ferdinand; 3. Assassiné'. Fortunately for the agency's reputation, an alert senior editor stopped the transmission just in time, although for most people in the United

Kingdom the assassination of Archduke Ferdinand of Austria and his wife in Sarajevo was only marginally more interesting than Sardanapale's victory at the Longchamp racecourse.

As in most of the rest of Europe, news of the shooting was received with equanimity, and was generally dismissed as a characteristic example of Balkan savagery. Out of respect, a Buckingham Palace Court Ball scheduled for 29 June was postponed until July. The popular novelist, Sarah Macnaughtan, recalled:

> We felt deeply for a great family who had known many tragedies, and we said sorrowfully that here was another awful happening to an ill-fated house. But the murder was an historic event and not a personal one, and after a time it was forgotten or left undiscussed.

Even those at Westminster who feared that the events in Sarajevo might lead to war did not think it would involve Britain. The Prime Minister Herbert Asquith wrote in his diary: 'There seems to be no reason why we should be anything more than spectators.'

But like burning quick-match at a Crystal Palace firework display, the spark had been lit. A month after the assassination, Austria invaded Serbia, an action which led to the mobilisation of the Russian and German armies. When Germany over-ran Belgium on 4 August, as a means of reaching Paris, Britain had little option but to declare war. Even then, for a while at least, it was 'business as usual.' County cricket continued, and Jack Hobbs led Surrey to their first championship. The Football Association decided to carry on as normal, as did the horse racing authorities. 'We hope,' declared *The Field*, 'that as little sport as possible will be abandoned in these islands during the bitter weeks to come; for it will help not only the body but the mind.'

The overall mood was buoyant. 'This war will be more than a tonic, it will be a TEUtonic,' went the popular joke. Only Lord Kitchener appeared to think the hostilities would last much beyond the end of 1914, and he started to prepare an army of millions for a war he expected to last for years.

The Germans were buoyant too. Confident of a rapid victory, the Kaiser told troops departing for the front: 'You will be home before the leaves have fallen from the trees.' The newspaper *Kolnische Zeitung* declared:

> There will be no such country as Great Britain at the end of the war. In its place we shall have Little Britain, a narrow strip of island territory peopled by loutish football kickers, living on the crumbs that Germany will deign to throw them. The once-mighty Empire, with her naval strength represented by the few old tubs which Germany will have left her, will become the laughing stock of nations, the scarecrow at which children will point their fingers in disdainful glee.

A month later, after the British Expeditionary Force had been sent packing at Mons, many people in England started to wonder if there was more to Germany's braggadocio than mere swagger. In October, two of Frank's distant cousins, Eleanor and Millicent Brock, arrived back in England after a four-month stay in Heidelberg. The Germans had allowed them safe passage home, seeing them as a useful propaganda tool. Stressing that they had been neither 'molested nor insulted' while in Germany, the young sisters brought with them dire warnings about the possibility of a Zeppelin invasion. Parroting the words of their German hosts, they told newspaper reporters:

> There is not the least doubt that they mean to visit London, and they are straining every nerve to increase the Zeppelin fleet. From what we were told, there are now about forty Zeppelins in the country, and they are said to be turning out one every fortnight. Large numbers of men have been taken from business firms solely for the purpose of assisting in the construction of Zeppelin engines. The Zeppelins can fly 1,000 miles and stay up for thirty-six hours, so that they assert that the destruction of London is possible and will be attempted.

By now the popular press in Britain was awash with tales of alleged German atrocities. The *Daily Mail* declared:

> In Belgium the Germans have treated the villages where any resistance has been offered to their attack with something like savagery. Peasants have been shot; houses have been wantonly burnt; hostages have been seized and maltreated, or forced to march in front of the German troops where they would have been most exposed to German fire.

Anti-German sentiment was reflected on Guy Fawkes Day when effigies of Kaiser Bill were burned on bonfires up and down the country. Selfridge's department store sold sixpenny 'Guy-ser' puppets to be thrown on the flames, and amateur poets penned appropriate ditties:

> We all will remember
> This Fifth of November
> By Wilhelm's infernal plot
> We see no reason
> Why Germany's treason
> Should ever be forgot!

Frank had mixed feelings about Germany. On the one hand his family business had carried out displays there over many years for patrons from the German royal family downwards. He and his family had often visited the country to organise these, and to negotiate new contracts. As a result he was not without affection for the country. At the same time, like many others around the world, he was extremely concerned about the long rise of German military expansionism. He vowed at an early stage to play an active role in the war, and even before the outbreak of hostilities he had conceived the idea of developing an explosive bullet that could be used to destroy the Zeppelins his cousins had warned about in the press. True to the words of his old headmaster – 'For country, right or wrong' – he enlisted almost as soon as war was declared and was commissioned as a temporary lieutenant in the Royal Artillery on 6 October. His father, in generous mood, insisted that for the duration of the war he should receive a £500-a-year allowance from Brock's on top of his services pay and the family gathered for a final photograph together, this time with G sitting in front of Frank and his brother Alan's new wife Dorothy looking lovingly towards her son James who sat on his grandmother's lap.

War or not, nothing was going to stop him marrying G. The likelihood of an imminent and lengthy separation meant there was no time to waste, and he proposed to her a day or two after the start of hostilities. Although Frank was deeply religious, he and G ruled out a grand church wedding, which

The Brock family at home in Sutton as it prepares for war, autumn 1914. Standing L to R: Frank showing his Royal Artillery Lt.'s insignia on his cuffs, a cigar between his fingers; Harold; Roy; Sylvia; Christopher; Bernard. Sitting R to L: Alan; his wife Dorothy; Arthur; Annie with Alan's son James; Margaret aka Nora; Gwenlian aka 'Cissy'; G.

would have taken months to organise. Instead, like many other war-time couples, they married as quickly as time allowed. The brief civil ceremony took place on Saturday 24 October at Paddington Register Office, a couple of miles from G's mansion block. As it turned out, they were not even able to spend their wedding night together. They barely had time to celebrate with a handful of relatives over a glass of champagne before Frank said his goodbyes and departed that afternoon for France on a hazardous and top-secret mission. His bride remained as stoical as she could in the circumstances, but was left wondering if she would ever see him again.

CHAPTER 8

Monsters of the Skies

After fireworks, one of the biggest crowd-pullers at the Crystal Palace during the second half of the 19th century were the balloon ascents by William Duncan Dale. A watchmaker by trade, Dale had been fascinated by ballooning all his adult life, and was appointed 'aeronaut to the Crystal Palace' in 1875. Over the next 15 years he made more than 200 ascents there, often in front of tens of thousands of awe-struck spectators. He hated not giving value for money, and on one occasion, when his balloon stubbornly failed to lift off, he unhitched the basket and ascended on the balloon's hoop, carrying a bag of ballast on his lap.

Ballooning was a dangerous business. On his first ascent from the Crystal Palace, Dale received a nasty crack on the head from the hoop securing the basket. On another occasion, while ballooning in Scotland, he lost his way in mist and touched down in the Firth of Forth. He and his two passengers, who included his wife, were dragged across the water in the basket for the best part of two miles until a steamer came to their rescue. Disaster struck again in 1885 when he and two others nearly drowned after their balloon crash-landed in the English Channel.

Dale's ascents at the Crystal Palace were usually the prelude to a Brock's firework display in the evening, and there must have been many occasions when the young Frank saw the renowned balloonist in action, either at the Crystal Palace itself, or from the garden of the Brock home in South Norwood. So began his life-long interest in aeronautics.

The lifespan of balloonists in Victorian times tended to be short, and Dale died as he had lived. On 29 July 1892 the main event at the Crystal Palace was a choral festival, and he was hired as additional entertainment. He and his three passengers, who included his son, had reached a height of 1,000 feet when a large tear appeared in the balloon's fabric. As the craft deflated, the four occupants frantically threw anything of weight over the side of the basket, even ripping the metal buttons from their jackets, but their efforts were to no avail. The crowds – which included Dale's horrified wife – saw the balloon 'fall like a rag' and hit the ground with a sickening thud. Dale's son, though badly hurt, survived the crash, but Dale himself and one of the other passengers were killed.

The incident was the talk of the crowds at the Crystal Palace for days afterwards. If eight-year-old Frank did not actually see the incident he must have heard about it, and no doubt it gave him food for thought. In the fullness of time his interest in aeronautics, and in particular the vulnerability of airborne craft, would play a critical role in World War I, for it was through his endeavours that men intent on doing harm to Britain would come crashing to earth like the ill-starred William Dale.

The evolution from balloons to airships began in earnest the year before Frank was born. France was first off the mark when, in 1883, Gaston Tissandier fitted a Siemens electric motor to a dirigible, so creating the first electric-powered flight. The following year a French airship made the first fully controlled flight when it landed on the exact spot from which it had taken off 23 minutes earlier. Germany was close behind. Count Ferdinand Graf von Zeppelin began working on designs for a rigid airship in the 1890s, housing his prototypes in a floating hangar so that they could be aligned with the wind. In 1900 his first airship successfully dragged its bloated frame across Lake Constance near Friedrichshafen in southern Germany at a height of 1,300 feet. The 420ft, cigar-shaped craft had a 16-horsepower engine and was kept afloat by hydrogen gas.

The British had their own plans for airships, envisaging them as a low-cost means of punishing unruly natives in far-flung colonies, but they were slow off the mark compared to France and Germany. It was not until 1902 that the first British airship flew the 30 miles from the Crystal Palace to Ruislip in West London, carrying an advertisement for Mellins baby food. Before long the army and the Royal Navy began taking an interest. All over Europe, as Frank grew up, the skies were becoming busier. Even Frank's favourite author, Rudyard Kipling, joined the craze, penning a short story, 'With the Night Mail', which foresaw a future in which air transportation was dependent on airships.

Whether Frank himself ever went up in a balloon or an airship is not known, but given that Brock's often deployed huge gas balloons in their firework displays, and given that airships regularly docked at the Crystal Palace, it is more than possible. One way or another, he followed Count Zeppelin's pioneering work in Germany with interest, and later with concern. In time he would become one of the most dedicated enemies of the huge German airships.

Contrary to British legend, the German government did not spend limitless funds developing the Zeppelin. The invention was a purely private affair. Count Zeppelin first became interested in lighter-than-air travel in 1863 when, as a military observer in the American Civil War, he made several ascents in Union observation balloons. In 1891 he retired from the Prussian army to devote his time to the building of motor-driven dirigibles, funding his work with his own money. At one stage he sold his horses and carriages and dismissed most of his servants in order to support his experiments.

German officialdom at first showed little interest. The Balloon Division of the army was lukewarm, and the Marine Office, while conceding that the craft might be useful for naval reconnaissance, was not prepared to stump up much in the way of funds for further development. Abroad there was ridicule. The *New York Times* predicted: 'The gigantic gasbag of the Zeppelin passenger ship will not survive – it is too much at the mercy of the elements and of human destroyers.' The project was kept alive by donations, a public lottery and a mortgage on Count von Zeppelin's wife's estate. The inventor persevered, and although progress was punctuated by accidents and disasters, the machines he sired grew increasingly viable. By 1908 the German army was prepared to commit to its first vessel.

Everything about the Zeppelins was formidable. Each ship was kept in the air by nearly 800,000 cubic feet of purified hydrogen contained in 18 separate gas cells or bags. These in turn were enclosed within an envelope covering a rigid metal frame. The gas bags were made from the same tough membrane of a cows' intestines used for sausage skins. The membranes, each the size of a pocket handkerchief, were obtained from Argentinian slaughterhouses and were bound to a supporting cloth with isinglass cement. Highly skilled German women built them up one at a time until they had a strong, gas-tight sheet. Since it took 15 skins to make one square metre of fabric, the guts of more than 250,000 cows were required to complete a single Zeppelin, making the airships extremely expensive to produce. Each one represented up to 33 million sausage skins sacrificed to the Kaiser's imperialist ambitions. For a time, when Argentina was unable to supply enough membranes, the making of sausages was outlawed in Germany and in areas under German control so that more Zeppelins could be built.

The airships quickly captured the imagination of the German public. The newspaper *Thüringer Zeitung* observed:

> Whenever one of the airships flew over a village, or whenever she flew over a lonely field on which some peasants were working, a tremendous shout of joy rose up on the air towards Count Zeppelin's miracle ship which, in the imagination of all those who saw her, suggested some supernatural creature.

There was considerable excitement in 1908 when a German magazine published an illustration showing how Zeppelins might be used to drop sticks of dynamite on ships of the Royal Navy. Warming to this theme, a German privy councillor, Rudolf Martin, told a public meeting in Berlin that in the event of war a fleet of 10,000 Zeppelins, each carrying 20 soldiers, would 'land and capture the sleeping Britons before they could realise what was taking place.' He went on to predict that the British fleet 'would abandon the coasts when the airships came into view so that they could avoid the shells that might be dropped on them from the skies.' His German audience thought his apocalyptic scenario too far-fetched to be taken seriously (at a realistic rate of production it would take 500 years and the guts of five billion cows to build 10,000 Zeppelins) but a large number of *Daily Mail* readers were aghast when his comments were reported in the paper a day or two later.

As if Martin's flights of fancy were not alarming enough, the Kaiser himself was reported in 1908 to have told a secret meeting of the German High Command in Potsdam:

> I have given orders for the hurried construction of more airships of the improved Zeppelin type, and when these are ready we shall destroy England's North Sea, Channel, and Atlantic Fleets, after which nothing on earth can prevent the landing of our army on British soil, and its triumphant march to London.

In truth the Kaiser probably never spoke these words, but that was irrelevant. What mattered was that they were reported in the British press and were duly believed and taken on board by worried readers. The following year the American periodical *McClure's Magazine* predicted the end of all armies within a decade owing to the inability of ground troops to survive aerial bombardment by Zeppelins.

Stirred up by an excited press, the British public became fearful to the point of paranoia. The fact that their reaction was wholly out of proportion to reality, and ignored the many limitations of Zeppelins, not least that there were very few of them and that they were vulnerable to bad weather and mechanical failure, did nothing to reduce the hysteria. H. G. Wells drew on these anxieties in his 1908 novella *The War in the Air* in which he imagined a fleet of German dirigibles destroying the American naval fleet in the Atlantic before 'pouring death and destruction' on New York. Using language calculated to shatter the illusion of cosy security enjoyed until then by Edwardian Britain, he wrote:

> That huge herd of airships rising one after another had an effect of strange, portentous monsters breaking into an altogether unfamiliar world … New York they had left behind to the south-eastward, a darkened city with one hideous red scar of flames … and now the whole fabric of civilisation was bending and giving, and dropping to pieces and melting in the furnace of the war.

Up and down the country, people began looking to the sky in trepidation and saw – or thought they saw – plenty to worry them. In March 1909, Police Constable James Kettle was walking his beat on Cromwell Road in Peterborough, Cambridgeshire, when 'the steady buzz of a high-powered engine' caused him to look up and he saw a 'bright light attached to a long oblong body outlined against the stars as it crossed the sky at high speed.' His superiors, anxious to avoid a panic, played down Kettle's account, but soon mystery airships were being sighted all over the country. By May of that year British newspapers had carried reports of 49 sightings, including one by the royal servants at Sandringham, and another by a Welsh Punch and Judy showman who claimed to have seen a landed airship and its foreign crew near the top of Caerphilly Mountain. A Zeppelin was even reported over Ireland, where, according to the *Belfast Telegraph*, 'the aerial visitant was thousands of feet high, and came steadily in the direction of the city.'

In every walk of society there was now speculation that Britain might be vulnerable to invasion from the air. More than a century had passed since Admiral Lord St. Vincent, writing to the Board of Admiralty about the threat of invasion, made his famous remark: 'I do not say, my Lords, that the French will not come. I say only they will not come by sea.' Suddenly his pithy maxim, of comfort to generations of Britons, seemed worryingly out-dated.

Brock's Fireworks did their patriotic best to try to allay the 'scareship' hysteria although, as artists and entertainers, they naturally connected to the latest fashion. The poster on the dustcover, showing cannon or field guns turned 90 degrees to fire vertically, was produced to promote displays at the Crystal Palace in 1909, the year immediately following the publication of *The War in the Air*. But another poster two years later from the 1911 season of summer displays at the recently built White City stadium in London, shows that ideas had moved on with more sophisticated air-war concepts and most importantly, marauding Zeppelins being attacked by British aircraft in a shell-studded sky. In these pyrotechnical fantasies, devised and overseen by Frank and his family, the British naturally came out on top, as they always did in any Brock's portrayal of international conflict. The audiences clapped and cheered, burst into patriotic singing and threw their caps skywards. But when it came to the real thing they were far less confident, and with good reason.

By the time war broke out, the latest models coming off Count Zeppelin's production line in Friedrichshafen were capable of climbing to 20,000 feet. They carried bomb loads of between 3,000lb and 5,000lb, and were equipped with machine-guns to protect themselves. With three engines and four propellers, they could reach a speed of 47 mph, travel more than 1,000 miles, and stay aloft for 36 hours. Quiet, and frequently invisible, they were the stealth bombers of their time.

Most daunting of all, these models of Teutonic thoroughness and Prussian efficiency were all but invulnerable to attack. It was all very well for the First Lord of the Admiralty, Winston Churchill, to dismiss them as 'enormous bladders of combustible and explosive gas', but the science and art of air warfare was in its infancy, and there was no reliable way of shooting them down. At the beginning of World War I they could fly higher and further than any aircraft of the day, and could remain far out of reach of land-based or ship-based artillery, which was ineffective above 3,000 feet. Even if an aircraft could get close enough to take a pot shot (the first fixed armament on an aeroplane was a sawn-off Lee Enfield rifle screwed to the upper wing of a biplane and fired by pulling a piece of string), solid bullets would only make small holes. These presented no threat and could be quickly repaired by the dedicated sailmakers who were usually part of a Zeppelin crew.

One man had given the problem a lot of thought. Frank's mission to help eliminate the German airborne threat began months before the outbreak of hostilities. Although he did not officially join HM Forces until October 1914, his pre-war work involved more than being a director of Brock's Fireworks. Unknown even to his close friends, he was already moving in a shadowy world of espionage and derring-do. One clue to his undercover activities was the minutes of a Brock's board meeting which recorded his resignation as a director of the firm on 23 October 1914, the day before he married G and headed off to France. The minutes added intriguingly that Frank had resigned verbally five weeks previously on 14 September, 'but that he had disappeared on Government service without confirming this in writing.'

The phrase 'disappeared on Government service' has an intriguing James Bond whiff to it, and one might reasonably ask if he was working for the newly created Secret Service Bureau, the forerunner of MI5. The Bureau, established in 1909, was a joint initiative of the Admiralty and the War Office to control secret intelligence operations both in the UK and overseas, with a particular brief to concentrate on the military ambitions of the Germans.

No proof exists that Frank was an SSB agent, but we have it on the authority of his brother Alan, writing in 1922, that he was carrying out secret work for the Admiralty during the pre-war period, specifically in connection with the production of smoke to provide cover during naval operations. (He was already looking into the use of smoke for commercial purposes, such as insecticides.) By 1915 he was in charge of air intelligence for the Royal Naval Air Service, suggesting he had a background in top secret work. The likelihood is that he had been 'talent-spotted' by the navy while putting on a display for them – perhaps at the exhibition he staged in 1905 during the French navy's visit to Spithead. The event had been masterminded by Admiral of the Fleet Sir Arthur Wilson – known as 'Old 'Ard 'Art' because of his refusal to consider the cares and comforts of officers and men. Wilson may well have mentioned Frank to his long-term friend and colleague Jacky Fisher, the First Sea Lord. Fisher, as we shall see, became a friend and great admirer of Frank. He made considerable use of his expertise during World War I, and probably did so in the years leading up to it.

Hush-hush though Frank's experiments with smoke screens were, they would hardly have required him to 'disappear', and it is clear that in addition to his work with smoke he was sent on pre-war covert missions by Naval Intelligence to gather information about Zeppelins. The Admiralty, like the public, had every reason to be worried about the German airships. Not only did their ability to spy at sea threaten to negate Britain's naval supremacy, but there was a lurking fear that a fleet of Zeppelins might appear out of nowhere and launch a crippling attack against the Royal Navy at anchor.

Since Zeppelins flying above 3,000 feet were pretty well invincible, it followed that in the event of war the only way to strike a mortal blow at them would be to attack them on the ground at their sheds in Germany, in particular at Count Zeppelin's Friedrichshafen base. Or, as Churchill was to put it, 'you get rid of hornets by destroying their nest.' If such a plan were to be put into action, it would be necessary to find out as much as possible in advance about the Friedrichshafen site, in particular its layout and its ability to defend itself. This was where Frank came in.

As a director of Brock's Fireworks, he was unusually well suited to the task of helping his friends in the Navy to obtain such information. As late as the early days of July 1914 – one month before Britain declared war on Germany – Brock's were negotiating to win the contract for firework displays at a trade exhibition in Dusseldorf (where there also happened to be some

Zeppelin sheds) enabling Frank to be in Germany without arousing suspicion. Certainly he was in an excellent position to find out about – and perhaps photograph – the Dusseldorf sheds.

And Friedrichshafen? During that pre-war summer a smartly dressed young man in civilian clothes turned up at Count Zeppelin's base beside Lake Constance. Speaking in an American accent, he said he was a tourist and asked if he could look round. He had read much about these magnificent airships in the American newspapers and would appreciate the chance to see one at first hand. The Germans were not averse to showing off their achievements at Friedrichshafen. Their Zeppelins were a source of great national pride, and they happily assisted the charming visitor. After all, what was the harm? Neither they nor anyone else at that time envisaged that America would be drawn into a European conflict, and they preened at the prospect of the glowing description of Teutonic prowess the visitor would take back to the States. They gave the man a tour of the factory and took him into one of the sheds to see a newly-completed Zeppelin. Professing he was impressed by what he had seen, the man thanked his hosts and went on his way.

The 'American' was Frank. Although he talked little about his undercover visit afterwards, he confided some of the details to G and to his brother Alan, and evidently gleaned some useful information about the layout of the factory. It seems likely he had detoured to Friedrichshafen from Dusseldorf, and to safeguard his cover as an American tourist he would have needed a false passport and a plausible back story or 'legend'. These were presumably supplied by the Secret Service Bureau or by Naval Intelligence.

This peace-time escapade was not without its risks (at the very least exposure would have resulted in a serious diplomatic incident) but it was child's play compared to what came later. On the second known occasion that Frank 'dropped in' on Friedrichshafen the circumstances were far more dangerous. This time the war had already begun, and had he been caught he would have been shot as a spy.

The background to his second visit was Churchill's decision in October 1914 to give the green light to the world's first strategic bombing campaign. Reluctantly acknowledging the threat posed by Count Zeppelin's invention, the First Lord of the Admiralty ordered the destruction of the airship sheds at Dusseldorf and Cologne, and the elimination of the Zeppelin base at Friedrichshafen. Captain Murray Sueter, director of the newly created Royal Naval Air Service (the air arm of the Royal Navy) was tasked with making this happen.

Sueter wasted no time. The war was less than three weeks old when, just after dawn on 22 September, four RNAS planes took off from Antwerp in Belgium and flew 200 miles into Germany. Thick cloud and mist thwarted the two aircraft heading for Cologne, but one of the Dusseldorf raiders – Charles Colett, a contemporary of Frank at Dulwich College – found his target and dropped two 20lb bombs from 400 feet on the Zeppelin shed. His pinpoint accuracy may well have been thanks to information supplied by Frank earlier in the year. Several men on the ground were injured and a good deal of glass was broken. Other than that, little damage was done, but despite the raid's limited operational success it had considerable propaganda value. It proved that bombing missions were possible and it came as a shock to the Germans to discover that their airships on the ground were vulnerable to attack.

Sueter now turned his attention to the far more difficult problem of attacking Friedrichshafen itself. The only way to approach Count Zeppelin's lair without violating Swiss neutrality was from eastern France, and he concluded that the best place from which to launch the attack was a French airship station at Belfort, 12 miles north of Switzerland and 125 miles from Friedrichshafen.

To this end, Sueter began putting together a small team of trusted men to organise and carry out the raid. One of those he selected was Frank, not least because he was one of the few people in Britain who had actually been to Friedrichshafen and had seen a Zeppelin close up. Although Frank had yet to learn to fly, Sueter believed he could be extremely useful in laying the groundwork of the operation and in running the team of air mechanics who would be needed to service the planes. The two had met previously to discuss Frank's ideas for destroying Zeppelins with explosive bullets. Sueter, who had long recognised the threat posed by the German airships, was impressed by this dedicated and talented young man, and would later describe him as one of the best officers who had ever worked for him.

The man Sueter chose to work alongside Frank, and whom he placed in overall charge of the operation, was Noel Pemberton Billing, a raffish former soldier who was well-known in the worlds of motor racing, boating and aviation. Before the war Pemberton Billing had tried to persuade Sueter to place orders for a flying boat he had designed and built. Sueter was not interested in the flying boat but he took a shine to the man himself, marking him out as a daring and resourceful maverick with excellent organisational skills. Arranging for him to be granted a temporary commission in the Royal Naval Volunteer Reserves, he told him to link up with Frank and head for Belfort to sort out the logistics of the bombing operation.

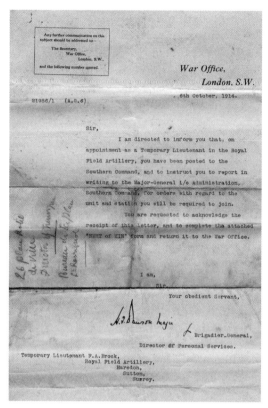

Frank's orders for the Friedrichshafen Raid, given to him shortly after he had joined the Royal Artillery. He was lent to the Navy for the raid. Following this he joined the Royal Naval Air Service before finally being transferred to the Royal Air Force when it was created on 1 April 1918. It appears he may have remained in all branches concurrently.

And so, on the day of his wedding, Frank left his bride in London and headed for the south coast. There he met Pemberton Billing and crossed the Channel with him to France. At this stage they were the only people other than Sueter and Churchill to know about the planned attack on Friedrichshafen. The two travelling companions were very similar in temperament. Both were inventors, entrepreneurs and adventurers, both had boundless energy and enthusiasm, and each was intensely patriotic. In typically flamboyant style, Pemberton Billing brought with him his ostentatious white sports car, a spanking new Brooklands Napier 'Mercury' known to his friends as 'The Birdcage', which he ordained would be their means of transport throughout the mission.

Their first stop was Paris, where the British Consul General, Sir Walter Risley Hearn supplied them with false passports (Frank's described him as

On 24 October 1914, his wedding day, Frank left for France and a few days later was given a false passport by the British consul in Paris. It was true that Frank was an engineer but not at that moment!

an 'engineer') to enable them, when the time came, to cross the border into Switzerland on a reconnaissance sortie. Then, dressed in civilian clothes, they drove east through Chalons and Nancy at speeds worthy of Toad of Toad Hall, making an eye-catching sight wherever they went, particularly in the remoter parts of rural France where motor-cars, especially eye-catching models like 'The Birdcage', were still a rarity.

Having struggled their way through a seemingly interminable series of French sentry posts, they reached Belfort in the southern foothills of the Vosges mountains after a journey of some four hundred miles. There they made themselves known to their opposite numbers at the airship base. At first it was touch and go whether the French would agree to Belfort being used for the raid. The Franco-German front in that area had been quiet until now, and the French wanted it to stay that way. With good reason, they feared a retaliatory strike should the base be used for an attack on German territory. In the face of this resistance, the two Englishmen had to deploy all their powers of charm and persuasion, but they eventually won their case, and the French agreed to the plan on condition that every effort was made to maintain secrecy.

This, as it happened was not a problem. Belfort, being an airship base, had no runway. This meant that the aircraft selected to take part in the raid – four Avro 504 biplanes – would have to be crated and transported across France by train. Boxing them up in this way, and assembling them in a closed hangar at Belfort, would minimise the risk of the plan being exposed. Once the French had agreed on the principles of the operation, they proved generous with their time and resources.

Having made arrangements for the arrival of the aircraft and their pilots at Belfort the following month, Pemberton Billing and Frank, still in plain clothes, set off again in 'The Birdcage'. This time their objective was to find out all they could about the current lay-out at Friedrichshafen, and if necessary to go behind enemy lines. Armed with a stash of Swiss banknotes and gold sovereigns, they drove 50 miles to the Swiss border and used their false passports to bluff their way across the frontier near Basel posing as commercial travellers. They were taking a big gamble. As serving officers on active duty, they faced internment by the determinedly neutral Swiss if caught. Continuing their journey, they motored due east along the Rhine for a hundred miles, passing through Schaffhausen and the Swiss farming communities of Altnau, Guttingen, Kesswil and Utwill, before arriving at Romanshorn on the southern shore of Lake Constance. From here, looking north across the lake to Germany, they could see Friedrichshafen seven miles away.

A language teacher in Romanshorn, who was friendly to the British cause, had been primed to help them and provide them with a base. They bought maps of the area and kept their field glasses trained on the Zeppelin installation in the far distance. Their presence in the village inevitably attracted the attention of local people, some of whom clearly wondered why these young Englishmen were not fighting for their country in France or Belgium. They were not challenged at the time, but several weeks later the German press suggested that the British envoy to Switzerland, Sir Evelyn Grant Duff, and a 'younger' man had been in Romanshorn attempting to spy on Friedrichshafen. The two had reportedly been seen together looking out over Lake Constance from the tower of the Roman Catholic church at the water's edge. Grant Duff's vehement denials were accepted by the Swiss, and in hindsight it seems almost certain that it was Pemberton Billing and Frank who had aroused suspicion.

After a day or so the two men decided they needed to get closer to the Zeppelin base. They befriended some local fishermen in Romanshorn, and bribed one of them to row them across the lake. They made the crossing by night, beaching in a secluded area just north of Friedrichshafen. Frank then rowed back to Romanshorn with the fisherman, having arranged to return to the same spot the following night. Pemberton Billing, meanwhile, headed off by foot for a close-up look at the base. He walked round Friedrichshafen marking key areas of the installation on his map, but aroused the suspicions of guards at the base and had to hide in an empty house for the rest of the day. He was about to leave when he saw three German officers approach the front door. Climbing through a back window, he slipped round the side of the house and knocked the officers' driver unconscious with an ornamental lion he had seized from the mantelpiece. Dragging the driver from the car, he drove off towards the lakeside rendezvous followed by a fusillade of shots.

Frank had not let him down. As agreed, he was waiting at the pick-up point with the fisherman. The gunfire and shouting in the distance alerted him to trouble, but he held his nerve and ensured that the apprehensive fisherman stayed put until Pemberton Billing had re-joined them and scrambled into the boat. Extremely relieved, the men rowed back in the darkness to Romanshorn. Armed with the information they had gleaned, they drove back along ice-bound roads to France at top speed. Mission accomplished.

Things now moved quickly. Briefed by Sueter on the arrangements made at Belfort, and on the intelligence gathered at Friedrichshafen, Churchill gave the final go-ahead for the raid. The aircraft components were shipped across the Channel, and Frank was put in charge of laying on a special train to transport them from Le Havre to Belfort. The crates containing the parts, marked with Russian lettering to confuse prying eyes, duly arrived at the base under cover of darkness on 13 November. Under Frank's watchful eye a team of mechanics opened the crates and began assembling the planes in one of the sheds. They worked through the night to have them ready by morning.

The four RNAS pilots, Edward Briggs, Sidney Sippe, John Babington and Roland Cannon, arrived separately by train and by car. To preserve secrecy, no one was allowed to set foot outside the shed in daytime, although the pilots were later allowed to move into a hotel. The rest of the team, including Frank, ate, slept and worked in the shed, stealing out after dark to remove stones from the rough ground to create a primitive runway. The planes were equipped with a bomb rack beneath the fuselage, which released its load when a wire was pulled in the cockpit. Each plane was limited to four small bombs.

For the pilots it was a daunting mission. Some had not flown an Avro 504 before, and none had dropped a bomb. The need for secrecy meant there could be no trial flights. The round trip of 250 miles would test them and their planes to the limits of their endurance. To add to their problems, the French

Three British RNAS pilots attack the Zeppelin Works with Hales bombs in Avro 504 aeroplanes. Two managed to return to the French airfield at Belfort: Flt. Commander J. T. Babington and Flt. Lt. S. V. Sippe. Their fellow RNAS pilot, Squadron Commander E. F. Briggs was wounded over Friedrichshafen, shot down and imprisoned.

insisted they should not carry maps which could reveal they had flown from France (although it was hard to see from where else the Germans might have thought they had come) and this meant they had to memorise large sections of the route. After a wait of several days for suitable weather, the raid took place on 21 November. At 9.30 am the hangar doors were opened, the planes were wheeled out, and the ground crew swung the propellers round by hand to start the engines. Briggs, Babington and Sippe took off successfully at three-minute intervals, but Cannon damaged his aircraft on the rough ground and to his frustration he had to abort. Still, three had made it into the air, and Frank and Pemberton Billing watched with satisfaction as the tiny planes vanished into the eastern sky.

Briggs was the first to arrive at the target at a few minutes before midday. He released his bombs, but his plane was hit by anti-aircraft fire and his engine failed. Wounded in the head, he was forced to land in front of the sheds, where he was arrested and taken to hospital under armed guard. Despite coming under heavy fire, Sippe and Babington both managed to release their bombs and make it back to Belfort. Frank subsequently 'liberated' the

Part of the rudder from Flt. Lt. Sippe's Avro 504 brought back by Frank from Belfort. There is a bullet hole in the rudder's canvas hinge.

bullet-damaged tail of Sippe's Avro 504, and on his return to England he had it mounted on a plaque as a memento of the mission. It remains in the family to this day.

The actual damage caused by the raid was slight, and in operational terms the mission yielded little more than a satisfying sense of theatre. No Zeppelins were hit, and only one workshop was slightly damaged, but in terms of propaganda the operation was a resounding success. Fuelled by Churchill's exaggerated claims, the story went round the world as an example of the enterprise and pioneering spirit of the RNAS and the character and calibre of the men who belonged to it. The *New York Times* reported that all the bombs reached their objective, and that 'serious damage was done to the Zeppelin airship factory.' The *Sacramento Union* headlined its story: 'Churchill Declares English Birdmen Drop Bombs Effectively at Friedrichshafen.' French newspapers went further and claimed that a newly built Zeppelin had been completely destroyed.

Regardless of the embroidery and the overblown claims, the operation was indisputably a compelling story of *Boys' Own* heroism. In that it helped to diminish the aura of invincibility of Zeppelins, and therefore reduce public anxiety about them, it was well worth the time and effort expended on it. A by-product was that it tied up some 4,000 German soldiers who were sent to Friedrichshafen in the wake of the raid to defend the Zeppelin factory against possible further attacks.

The pilots themselves, having hoped the raid would do more physical damage than it did, experienced a sense of anti-climax, but they were nonetheless widely feted. The French awarded them the Legion d'Honneur (Sippe and Babington were given their medals at a parade in the Belfort hangar at which Frank was present) and they were awarded the Distinguished Service Order on their return to the United Kingdom.

The British pilots line up with their French hosts at Belfort before the Friedrichshafen Raid. L to R: Frank, Flt. Lt. Sidney Sippe, Squadron Commander Philip Shepherd; Capt, R. Seyrig; Flight Commander Noel Pemberton Billings (centre); Squadron Commander Edward Briggs; C. Renault; Lt. John Babington; Flt. Commander Roland Cannon.

Everyone involved in the historic raid went their separate ways afterwards. Frank later confided to his family that on his return to England he was presented to Winston Churchill and took the opportunity to ask for a transfer from the Royal Artillery to the Royal Naval Air Service, where he believed he would be in a better position to carry on the fight against Zeppelins. His request was granted and he was made a flight lieutenant in the RNAS on New Year's Day 1915.

Greatly impressed by what Churchill and Sueter had seen and heard, they decided to take him off intelligence field work and ordered him to establish, commission and command a secret RNAS Experimental Station in Stratford, east London, very close to where the Olympic stadium was to be built nearly a century later. In this new role Frank resolved to deal the monsters of the sky a devastating blow that would see them off for good.

CHAPTER 9

Seeking the Holy Grail

'Do you burn or do you jump?' Kapitanleutnant Heinrich Mathy, one of his country's most celebrated 'knights of the sky', was asked the question by a German reporter early on in the war. 'Your airship is on fire, you see death and have seconds to decide … burn or jump, what will you do?'

At 32 years old, the dashing Mathy was rated Germany's ablest airship commander. So daring and audacious were his raids during the 'Zeppelin Scourge' of 1915 and 1916 that he was one of the few Germans whose names were household words in Britain. He was feared and respected in equal measure. The British shuddered at his name. German women sent him perfumed letters. Like all the Zeppelin commanders, he was motivated, disciplined, brave and derided the use of parachutes. Although parachutes were available, airship crews almost invariably discarded them to keep loads to a minimum. To burn or to jump? Renowned for speaking short, staccato-like sentences, Mathy looked the reporter in the eye and replied tersely: 'I won't know until it happens.'

At the time he gave the interview, there had been little or no effective retaliation against the Zeppelins, and Mathy was reasonably confident that the reporter's question was of academic interest only. With any luck he would never have to make the choice. But as the war dragged on, his confidence started to drain away to the point where the 'burn or jump' question invaded his thoughts day and night. 'It is only a question of time,' he told a reporter. 'Any moment we may be plunged below, a shapeless mass of wreckage and human bodies shattered beyond recognition.' His flight engineer, Pitt Klein, was gripped by the same cold fear. 'Everyone admits that they feel it,' he wrote. 'Our nerves are ruined by mistreatment. If anyone should say that he was not haunted by visions of burning airships, then he would be a braggart.'

One man above all others was responsible for sapping the spirits of the Zeppelin crews in this way. That man was Frank Brock, and it would not be long before his ingenuity and inventiveness forced Heinrich Mathy and many others to make the terrible 'burn or jump' decision.

It was actually a biplane dropping a bomb on Tommy Terson's cabbage patch in Dover on Christmas Eve 1914 which represented the first attack on mainland Britain for centuries. Zeppelins were close behind. The first airship raid was planned for 13 January 1915 but was abandoned due to bad weather. But it was only a matter of time. People knew the lumbering monsters were coming, and all along the east coast of England anxious faces looked towards the North Sea. Ten Belgian civilians had been killed during a Zeppelin attack on Antwerp the previous August. Everyone knew that Britain would not come off so lightly. On 15 January, Alice Cubitt, the 50-year-old wife of a Gorleston-on-Sea bank manager, died when a primitive air raid shelter she was helping a neighbour to build collapsed on top of her. She was arguably the new terror's first fatality.

Four days later, on the evening of 19 January, two Zeppelins of the Imperial Germany Navy, *L3* and *L4*, each carrying eight 110lb explosive bombs and ten 25lb incendiary bombs, took off from their base at Fuhlsbüttel near Hamburg. Their arrival over the Norfolk coast nine hours later led to a phrase appearing on death certificates never before seen for British mainland fatalities – 'from the effects of the acts of the king's enemies'.

The intended targets of *L3* and *L4* had been military and industrial installations on Humberside, but strong winds forced them south. In the night sky their navigation lights looked like stars, but the low drone of their engines alerted people on the ground to expect trouble. As they drew closer, they made an astonishing sight. Bigger than ocean liners, they floated majestically through the high, thin air. They were beautiful, graceful … and terrifying. Imaginations ran riot. Some claimed they could see men walking around in the airships' gondolas. Others reported that one of the craft travelled so low over Cromer that it nearly became caught up in the pinnacles of the church tower.

L3, under the control of Kapitanleutnant Johann Fritz, made for the herring-packing town of Great Yarmouth and began its bomb run at 8.25 pm. During an attack that lasted for about ten minutes, one of its high explosive bombs landed on the St Peter's Plain district. Samuel Smith, aged 53, a shoemaker, was standing outside his shop watching the raider when he was struck by shrapnel and killed instantly. Not far away, spinster Martha Taylor, aged 72, was walking home from a trip to the grocer's when she too sustained fatal shrapnel injuries. They were the first British civilians to be killed by aerial bombardment. The same bomb knocked several other people off their feet, including Mr W. J. Sayers and his 11-year-old son, Louis. 'We went down like a pair of shot rabbits,' reported Mr Sayers.

Meanwhile *L4*'s commander, Kapitanleutnant Count Magnus von Platen-Hallermund, was hopelessly lost. Convinced he was still on course for the Humber, he crossed the coast near Bacton and muddled his way along the Norfolk coast, blindly dropping bombs wherever he saw lights on the ground. His subsequent combat report would describe a remarkably adventurous mission, with fierce battles over heavily fortified towns, during which the crew was dazzled by searchlights amid furious barrages of anti-aircraft fire. It was pure quixotic fantasy. There were no guns or searchlights, and not a shot was fired. His bombs fell relatively harmlessly on a handful of remote farms and coastal villages – Brancaster, Sheringham, Holme-next-the-Sea, Heacham, Snettisham and Dersingham – until finally he chanced upon King's Lynn. Spotting the lights of what he described in his report as an 'unidentified big city', he followed the railway line into town. Bentinck Street, a densely packed Victorian terrace, bore the brunt of his salvo of bombs. Alice Gazley, aged 26, whose husband had been killed three months earlier on the Western Front, ran into the street in panic as a bomb exploded. She died instantly. The same bomb destroyed the home of fitter's mate John Goate. He and his wife were injured, and their 14-year-old son, Percy, was killed.

Although the *Manchester Guardian* reported that 'Yarmouth has taken the visitation with remarkable calm and cheerfulness,' the general reaction to the raids was a combination of disgust and impotent rage. The Great Yarmouth coroner said of the deaths of Samuel Smith and Martha Taylor: 'The unfortunate man and woman were victims of so-called warfare – but I do not call it so. It is the offspring of German culture.' At King's Lynn, the foreman of the jury returned a verdict that Mrs Gazley and Percy Goate had died from the effects of the acts of the king's enemies, adding tersely: 'Murder'.

On top of the anger, there was widespread disappointment that British aircraft had not engaged the Zeppelins. The RNAS squadron at Lowestoft had decided not to respond to the alert because only three airplanes were combat ready and these were of low performance. Added to which it was dark and the weather was poor.

The British press was predictably strident, branding the Zeppelins 'baby killers' and forecasting that recruiting offices would be busier than ever as a result of the raids. 'Every German bomb means another British battalion!' was a typical headline. *Punch* ran a cartoon depicting John Bull glancing up at a Zeppelin and saying: 'Ah, here he comes again – my best recruiter.' A correspondent for the *Daily Mirror* commented drily:

> I have just received a private telegram from Berlin which describes the people's joy at the success of the Zeppelin attack as being widely enthusiastic. I have an intuitive feeling that the joy could not have been greater even if Dr Barnardo's Homes had been destroyed.

Readers seeking more emotion were offered the bombast of *The War Illustrated*: 'The loathsome, blood-mad fiends who could do this foul work and rejoice stirred every Briton's heart to sterner resolve to crush that degraded nation whose war methods are more savage than those lowest races known to anthropology.' Feelings also ran high in America. The *New York Herald Tribune* called the attacks 'a disgrace to civilisation'. The *New York World* commented that 'the wanton slaughter of women arouses a world-wide resentment against Germany.'

By contrast, the German press was euphoric. Glossing over the fact that the victims of the raids were an elderly woman, a war widow, a schoolboy and a middle-aged cobbler, they declared that the terrified English were now in the grip of 'Zeppelinitis', and that further 'iron thunderstorms' would 'reduce the whole of England to ruins.' It was only a matter of time, they prophesied, before Zeppelins delivered the killer blow. The *Berliner Lokalanzeiger* claimed that the inhabitants of Great Yarmouth had gone 'shrieking into their houses' and hid in their cellars after the first bomb fell. The *Kolnische Zeitung* asserted:

> It has come to pass, that which the English have long feared and repeatedly have contemplated with terror. The most modern air weapon, a triumph of German inventiveness, has shown itself capable of crossing the sea and carrying the war to the soil of old England.

And there was more. The German navy discovered to its delight that during his blind manoeuvrings along the Norfolk coast in *L4*, Platen-Hallermund had unwittingly passed over Sandringham. This inspired the *Hamburger Nachrichten* to write: 'Sandringham, the present residence of King George, was not overlooked. Bombs fell in the neighbourhood of Sandringham and a loud crash notified the King of England that the Germans were not far off. Our Zeppelins have shown that they could find the hidden royal residence.' It was all nonsense. Platten-Hallermund had no idea he was over Sandringham, besides which neither the king nor any of his family were staying there at the time.

The crews of *L3* and *L4* were all awarded Iron Crosses, and Count Zeppelin became a national hero. Schoolchildren were encouraged to sing a new song:

Zeppelin, flieg,	Zeppelin, fly,
Hiff uns in krieg,	Help us win the war,
Flieg nach England.	Fly against England,
England wird abgebrannt,	England will be burned,
Zeppelin, Flieg.	Zeppelin, fly.

At a military base in Kent, a hundred miles south of King's Lynn, Frank – now sporting a neat, military moustache – sought out every scrap of information he could about the air raids in East Anglia. His forces career had taken a sharp upward turn since the raid on Friedrichshafen. Soon after his return from Belfort, Murray Sueter put him in charge of air intelligence for the Royal Naval Air Service. The director of the RNAS was greatly taken with this able and enterprising young officer. 'I was very much struck by Brock's keenness,' Sueter wrote after the war. He was all the more impressed when Frank told him he was trying to develop a .45 inch calibre explosive bullet which would destroy Zeppelins, a far more complicated challenge than it might at first sound. Sueter told him to press ahead but asked him to produce a .303 version instead, this being the standard military calibre.

Frank was pleased to have Sueter's blessing for the project, but raised a nagging worry with him: would an incendiary or explosive bullet contravene the international laws of war? Explosive bullets, developed half a century earlier by the Russians to blow up powder magazines and ammunition wagons, caused gaping wounds if they struck a man. As long ago as 1868, Britain had signed the St Petersburg Convention, which outlawed such bullets on humanitarian grounds. Its successor, the Hague Convention, which was ratified by all the major powers in 1899, confirmed the ban. It also prohibited projectiles dropped from balloons and projectiles intended to spread asphyxiating fumes. Sueter was unsure how the law would view an explosive bullet designed solely to bring down an airship, and not intended specifically to hit men. He told Frank he was inclined to think that such a bullet would not be deemed illegal, but he advised him to look up the full text of the Convention 'as we have to be careful.'

The legality or otherwise of the bullet was not the only complicating factor. Sueter was obsessively concerned about Navy budgets, to the point where he had written a memo lambasting officers who used petty cash to buy rubber stamps and pads when they could be obtained more cheaply through official channels. No fewer than 28 Naval Air officers had been obliged to study and sign off this time-wasting exercise. Sueter viewed Frank's bullet in the same musty light. Why should the Navy cough up for a device that might not work? All he would agree to for now was to provide the necessary facilities for its testing. The cost of the invention itself was not part of the deal. Frank had no alternative but to accept this painful condition and he agreed to pay for the development of the bullet out of his own pocket.

Despite this stricture, he was in his element. For several months, he had devoted much of his spare time to exploring ways of shooting down his bête noire in flames. He had obtained permission from his father to use the Brock's Fireworks' premises in Sutton for many of his experiments, and workers there often saw him leaning against a shed door with a rifle and firing off round after round at specially constructed targets, each shot ringing out over the factory site like a squib on firework night. Now he was being given the navy's official blessing to continue with work which he rightly regarded as supremely important and to which he was uniquely suited.

For much of the next few months he located himself at the 57-acre Kingsnorth Airship Station on the southern shore of the Hoo Peninsula in Kent. The RNAS used the station as a base for observation balloons. Spotters on these tethered aerial platforms watched for submarines which threatened allied shipping in the Thames Estuary, the North Sea and the Channel. To Frank the balloons looked like bloated yellow slugs asleep in the clouds. They were ungainly and voluminous compared to the sleek German airships raining terror on England's east coast – and far less interesting. Here, on this lonely finger of marshy, mosquito-infested land separating the estuaries of the Thames and the Medway, he fine-tuned and put to the test his ideas for destroying Zeppelins.

Explosive bullets were not new to the British top brass. A New Zealand engineer, John Pomeroy, had invented one using nitro-glycerine in 1902, but the country's military leaders, though impressed, had not taken it up. A dispirited Pomeroy went to Australia where he worked on numerous other inventions, including a hat fastener, a process for taking the bitterness out of oranges, a headlight dimmer and a painless rabbit-trap. Later he turned up in England where he submitted his designs for explosive bullets as a means of destroying Zeppelins to the War Office in 1914. Early tests of the Pomeroy on tethered balloons were disappointing. Its principal problem was that it lacked sensitivity. This meant it had to hit a solid object, such as a girder, to work successfully and explode. Crucially, it did not function effectively on the actual fabric. It created a small hole but did not ignite the hydrogen.

Another bullet, the Buckingham, also had its problems. Invented by a Coventry engineer, James Buckingham, in 1914, this was an incendiary projectile filled with phosphorus. Three holes in its jacket were plugged by a solder with a relatively low melting point. The friction caused by the rifling on the gun-barrel melted away these plugs, allowing the phosphorus to escape and ignite in the air. The bullets were often referred to as 'smoke tracers' because they left a trail of blue smoke. Their chief drawback was that the range was limited by the time it took for the phosphorus to burn itself out. In other words, the miserly parcelling out of the incendiary material over many hundreds of feet of travel meant it would almost certainly be depleted before it hit the airship unless fired from a position so close that the Zeppelin's machine guns would almost certainly destroy the attacking British plane.

Frank's goal was to come up with the Holy Grail of bullets – one that retained its explosive element until impact and which was sensitive enough to detonate the moment it touched the fabric of a Zeppelin. He told an RNAS gunnery officer and friend, Flight Commander Peregrine Fellowes, who witnessed many of his experiments at Kingsnorth: 'I will produce a bullet which will act on the matchbox principle' – in other words a bullet that would blow a hole in the fabric of a Zeppelin and flare up for long enough to ignite the escaping gas. Fellowes watched him sketch his ideas on a piece of paper before replying dubiously: 'If you can do that – it sounds to me impossible – so much the better.' He believed Frank had set himself an insoluble problem but, as he stated after the war, he was greatly impressed by his 'tremendous energy and persistence'.

For Frank, the task he had set himself went beyond being an engrossing scientific challenge. The war was starting to become personal, not least because of the continuous appearance on the casualty lists of friends from his Alma Mater, Dulwich College. One of his contemporaries, Captain Francis Townend, fell victim to a German shell on the Western Front in March 1915 which blew off both his legs. He died an hour or so later, having apologised to his dressers for the trouble he was causing and joking that he thought he would probably give up football next year. The ambulance driver who took him to hospital spoke of 'such courage as I've never seen before and hardly imagined.' Later that year, nine more former Dulwich College pupils died on a single day at the battle of Loos. Another 73 would die at the Somme during the second half of 1916. By the end of the war, more than 500 of the school's old boys had lost their lives while on active service. Frank mourned the loss of so many young men he had known, and saw the Brock bullet as a means of avenging some of those deaths.

The oratory of his hero, Rudyard Kipling, was another spur to landing a crushing blow on the Germans. Kipling told a recruiting rally that summer:

> However the world pretends to divide itself, there are only two divisions in the world to-day – human beings and Germans. And the German knows it. Human beings have long ago sickened of him and everything connected with him, with all he does, says, thinks, or believes. From the ends of the earth human beings desire nothing more keenly than that this unclean monster should be thrust out from membership and the memory of the nations of the earth.

Frank was not the only member of the Brock clan to be roused to action by words such as these. By the end of 1915 three of his five brothers, mindful of

Kipling's exhortations, had also volunteered for active service. Alan, the next eldest after Frank, had followed him into the Royal Navy Air Service and was attached to the Anti-Aircraft Corps. Harold had enlisted with the Honourable Artillery Company, and Christopher with the Middlesex Regiment. Roy would join the newly created Tank Corps the following year and a fifth brother Bernard joined the City of London Yeomanry although his main responsibility was to help his father run the factory where Arthur too was very much part of the war machine. Under his stewardship, Brock's were kept busy throughout the war with numerous military contracts, including the production of hand grenades known as Mills bombs.

Frank's quest to eradicate the Zeppelin menace dovetailed neatly with his new role as head of the Air Intelligence section. If he learned of an air raid he dropped everything and drove to the scene to collect details from eye-witnesses about the interloper's height, speed and methods of operation. If he was in luck he might be able to collect some booty in the shape of a German incendiary bomb, about half of which failed to ignite when dropped. He would take these back to be dismantled and examined. A friend commented: 'He was without fear … during air raids he dashed about in a car, intent on discovering all he could of the explosives employed by the Hun.'

During this period Frank also learned to fly, probably on Sopwiths at the Naval Flying School in Eastchurch on the Isle of Sheppey. Acquiring the necessary instruction and knowledge to acquire a licence was not always a lengthy business. His former colleague Noel Pemberton Billing, a man he greatly admired at the beginning of the war, had won a bet that he could manage it in a day. Training accidents were common, and for most of the war they accounted for more fatalities – 8,000 in all – than losses in combat. Kingsnorth's commanding officer, Neville Usborne, a friend of Frank, was killed in a flying accident in early 1916. Frank took to heart the maxim – true even of new-fangled, comparatively primitive machines – that the gravest dangers were not mechanical but human, and that there was little risk of an aircraft dropping out of the sky unless the pilot made a mistake.

There is no evidence that Frank took part in combat missions. In his intelligence role, one of his chief interests lay in the relatively new art of aerial reconnaissance and to this end he tested out various cameras in different atmospheric conditions. The challenges were great. Subtle atmospheric anomalies invisible to the aircrew could corrupt images. So could poor camera stability, shutter speeds and lens quality. These were all areas in which Frank sought improvements. Flying also enabled him to experience the kind of conditions that pilots might face when they attacked a Zeppelin. He was described by those who knew him as an 'expert' and 'intrepid' flier. Henry Major Tomlinson, one of the army's official war correspondents, called him 'a first-rate pilot'.

Another more controversial field in which Frank became involved was in the development of poisonous and asphyxiating gases. Like explosive bullets, the use of poison gas in warfare violated the Hague Convention, but the pact had started to unravel almost as soon as hostilities broke out. The French used tear gas as early as August 1914, though in such small quantities that it was not detected by the Germans. Two months later German troops fired fragmentation shells filled with a chemical irritant against British positions at Neuve Chapelle. Again, their use was barely noticed. In January 1915 the Germans upped the ante by firing 18,000 artillery shells containing tear gas on Russian positions west of Warsaw.

For a time the British remained implacably hostile towards the use of gas. Sir John French, the commander of the British Expeditionary Force, called it 'a cynical and barbarous disregard of the well-known usages of civilised war'. They felt compelled to change their attitude when the Germans used poison gas – in this instance chlorine – against French colonial troops (*Zouaves*) at the start of the second battle of Ypres on 22 April. Anthony R. Hossack of Canada's Queen Victoria Rifles witnessed the ensuing panic:

> Plainly something terrible was happening. What was it? Officers, and Staff Officers too, stood gazing at the scene, awestruck and dumbfounded; for in the northerly breeze there came a pungent nauseating smell that tickled the throat and made our eyes smart. One man came stumbling through our lines. An officer of ours held him up with levelled revolver, 'What's the matter, you bloody lot of cowards?' says he. The Zouave was frothing at the mouth, his eyes started from their sockets, and he fell writhing at the officer's feet.

A fortnight later, again during the battle of Ypres, the Germans used gas against British troops for the first time, killing 90 men. To be able to hit back like for like was now considered essential, and the British launched their first gas attack the following September. They did so reluctantly, and one of the most disliked duties was the carrying of gas cylinders for installation in front-line trenches. Such was the stigma attached to the new weapon that even using the word 'gas' during a field operation carried the risk of punishment. The guidance given to generals by the government was to limit the scope of the gas war as much as possible without harming Britain's chances of victory.

With his wealth of scientific knowledge, Frank was immediately called for and instructed to manage the development of a British retaliatory weapon. He played an important role in this area, and recognized the potential value of gas in helping to bring the war to an early end. As well as advising on counter-measures, such as the use of appropriate masks, respirators, goggles and, in the case of ships at sea, electrically-driven pressure fans to disperse toxic clouds, he experimented with numerous different chemicals at Kingsnorth and Stratford, including potassium cyanide, arsenic sulphide, hydrocyanic acid or prussic acid. In the event he chose the latter, mixing it with chloroform and cellulose acetate to act as a thickener and during the summer of 1915 he developed a gas he named Jellite because of the jelly-like consistency during manufacture.

In September 1915, at a time when he was already fully occupied, including seeking a solution to the Zeppelin problem, Frank supervised its batch production in Stratford and in 1916 the UK authorized its use on the battlefield. But by the time it was ready for use, the Germans had started using more deadly substances and it is said that Jellite, thought insufficiently lethal, was never used by the British forces.

The trials Frank carried out were often dangerous and did not always go smoothly. On one occasion he was taken ill after an experiment with phosphorus pentoxide, and was forced to miss a meeting with the Fourth Sea Lord, Rear Admiral Sir Lionel Halsey, and other naval chiefs to discuss progress. It was typical of his robust and positive attitude to all his work that he saw only the benefits of this mishap. In a note explaining his absence he pointed out that the 'small quantity I inhaled' went to show how effective it was.

After the war the Cambridge Professor of Chemistry, Sir William Pope assessed Frank's work with Jellite:

> [Pope] had been associated as a casual scientific adviser on the production of toxic prussic acid mixtures, the manufacture of which was undertaken at the Stratford factory designed and built by this officer. The Brock mixture, Jellite, and its developments proved as efficient as the French mixture, Vinconnite, but of course the later developments in chemical warfare rendered them both obsolete. It ought to be realized that large scale working with prussic acid was attended with the utmost danger and it is greatly to Brock's credit that he understood this dangerous work and so organized the factory routine that no serious accidents occurred.

Although he worked long hours, not infrequently for 36-hour shifts, he knew how to unwind. He was not averse to slipping away in the evening to enjoy the song-and-dance acts at Barnard's Palace of Varieties in Chatham or to down a few beers at one of Hoo's public houses. Patriot though he was, he was never tempted to follow the example of King George V and forgo all alcohol until the end of the war. One of his party tricks was to sink a pint of beer in one go to the cheers of fellow officers. Experienced wrestler that he was, he probably also took part in the organised wrestling matches held regularly in the Wardroom at Kingsnorth. These bouts often turned into free-for-alls. Captain T. B. Williams in his book *Airship Pilot No 28* wrote of one such fight at Kingsnorth in which a well-built officer 'seized me by my ankles and swung me round his head. Tired of knocking down opponents with my poor body he made one more swing and let me go, straight for a window, through which I went, taking the frame with me.' Was he perhaps describing Frank?

Repeated Zeppelin attacks in the east of England provided Frank with a further incentive to perfect his bullet. In the spring of 1915 six people were killed in raids on Southend, Ipswich, Bury St Edmunds, Ramsgate and Dover. During one of these, Major Erich Linnarz, the commander of *LZ-38*, scribbled a note on an engraved calling card, attached it to a lead weight and threw it overboard. It landed in Rayleigh Road, Southend, where it was picked up by local people. The message, which was designed to infuriate and intimidate, had a 'you'll never catch me' ring to it.

> You English! We have come,
> and we will come again soon,
> to kill or cure. German.

As the summer approached, the Germans turned their sights on London. The Kaiser, fearing for the safety of his royal cousins in Buckingham Palace, and still hoping to wage a noble war, had initially banned attacks on the capital, but he now saw Zeppelin bombing as a means of forcing a despairing Britain to sue for peace through mass hysteria and public disorder. Linnarz was the first to attack the city on the night of 31 May. In a hyperbolic account written after the war, he described how he mounted the bombing platform of his craft 10,000 feet above North London:

> My finger hovered on the button that electronically operated the bombing apparatus. Then I pressed it. We waited. Minutes seemed to pass before, above the humming song of the engines, there arose a shattering roar. Was it fancy that there also leaped from far below the faint cries of tortured souls? I pressed again. A cascade of orange sparks shot upwards, and a billow of incandescent smoke drifted slowly away to reveal a red gash of raging fire on the face of the wounded city.

A Blackheath teacher, Hugh Orde, who had signed up as a special constable, was guarding the water reservoir at Woolwich Academy when he saw 'the long, luminous cigar-shaped outline' of the Zeppelin passing overhead. He wrote later that it was 'a strange thought to realize that we were watching the first time London had been attacked since the time of the Danes.'

The first of Linnarz's bombs fell on railway clerk Albert Lovell's house in Alkham Road, Stoke Newington, shortly after 11.00 pm, setting the property ablaze but causing no injuries. It was the first aerial bomb ever to be dropped on the capital. A few minutes later an incendiary bomb set fire to a second-floor bedroom in Cooper Road where Samuel Leggatt's five children were asleep. Leggatt pulled four of them to safety, but in the confusion three-year-old Elsie was left behind. A policeman later discovered her burned body under the bed where she had crawled to hide – the first person in London to die in a Zeppelin raid. Her 11-year-old sister May died in hospital of burns a few days later. Six other people, including an eight-year-old boy, were killed in the same bombing raid.

To the disquiet of Britain's political and military leaders, not a single defensive shot had been fired at Linnarz's Zeppelin. Fifteen sorties were flown against the intruder, but only one pilot made visual contact and then only fleetingly. Londoners were aghast to learn that the 'baby killers' could roam the skies above them at will, impeded only by the weather. Their anger increased when the airships continued to target the capital with impunity during the following weeks and months. Those on the receiving end of what *The Times* called 'the most savage instincts of primitive humanity' were not professional soldiers but British civilians, including mothers and children. That their country was incapable of protecting them brought a sense of shame and failure. It reached the point where British pilots deemed it prudent to avoid being seen in public in their uniforms during air raids.

Civil defence was at best amateurish. People were alerted to raids by policemen blowing whistles and ringing bicycle bells, and later by boy scout buglers. The Germans, convinced that bringing the fight to the doorsteps of ordinary people would induce enough fear to force Britain out of the war, gleefully published cartoons depicting Londoners fleeing in panic from marauding Zeppelins. A cartoon in the *Lustige Blatter* showed Nelson climbing down from his column in Trafalgar Square and telling a policeman: 'Well, just you spend some time up there with the threat of a Zeppelin!'

Amid fears that Zeppelins might start dropping asphyxiating gas, a wide range of ideas, mainly fanciful, were mooted for combatting them. 'Why cannot we meet Zeppelins with Zeppelins?' asked the author Sir Henry Rider Haggard in exasperation. 'Airships of the right sort could rise when warned of the approach of Zeppelins and wait aloft to attack them when they came.' Neville Usborne, Frank's commanding officer at Kingsnorth, looked at a plan for sending up scores of balloonists armed with Davis guns every time a Zeppelin approached London, but the idea was quickly ruled out as hopelessly impractical. So were the myriad of other suggestions put forward by the various branches of the armed forces. Murray Sueter's Air Department suggested establishing a mobile defence force by mounting machine guns on 'the cars of gentlemen in towns and large villages'. By firing at the airships, the theory went, the 'gentlemen' volunteers would stop them from hovering at low altitudes and so prevent accurate bombing. The concept of the Lord of the Manor perched at the back of his Roller, urging on his chauffeur to greater exertions as, through monocled eye-glass, he waited for a Zepp to cross his sights, had a certain quixotic charm, but it was quickly discarded as foolhardy. So too was an idea to launch fighter planes from balloons at a height of 12,000 feet to save them having to make the long and arduous climb to reach their prey. Another suggestion, to create aerial minefields by attaching shells to grappling hooks and dangling them from balloons, went the same way.

The most extreme proposal came from the First Sea Lord, Lord Fisher. He called for German prisoners to be executed in a tit-for-tat reprisal for every Zeppelin attack. Even the pugnacious Churchill recoiled at this suggestion, although he could offer no deterrent of his own. He admitted privately to his newspaper magnate friend George Riddell: 'These raids by airships will be frequent and the chances of coping with them are small.'

Matters became so desperate that suicide missions against marauding airships were seriously mooted. 'Any pilot who met a Zeppelin and failed to bring it down by firing at it, would be expected to take other measures, that is to say, charge it,' Squadron Leader Charles Burke of the Royal Flying Corps wrote in his diary in 1915. A headline in the *New York Times* proclaimed: 'British Airmen All Ready To Die – pledge themselves to dash machines through Zeppelins if London is invaded.' In reality, there were no recorded cases of airmen ramming Zeppelins, either in Britain or elsewhere, but Zeppelin crews were aware of the possibility. Major Erich Linnarz wrote after the war: 'We went in dread since your pilots had orders that if they failed to reach us with the machine-gun fire they were to climb above us and ram our gas-bags with their machines.'

In the autumn of 1915, a mother, son and daughter were killed when their house in Stretton Road, South Norwood was destroyed by a bomb dropped from a Zeppelin. The tragedy happened just up the road from Frank's childhood home. During the same raid three brothers, Brian, Gordon and Roy Currie, aged 10, 14 and 15, were killed when a bomb fell on their home in Beech House Road, Croydon. All over the country the anti-German climate was growing. Postcards depicting survivors and damaged buildings heightened the mood through a best-selling series entitled 'Horrid Crimes of the Boche Pirates'. An Englishwoman married to a German was foolish enough to say within earshot of others that 'Count Zeppelin is a gentleman.' For that and for not registering as an alien she was fined £25.

Feelings were running so high that when engine trouble forced a Zeppelin into the North Sea after a bombing raid, a British fishing crew refused to go the aid of the 16 surviving airmen, all of whom perished in the freezing waters. The Bishop of London attracted the fury of the German press by backing the fishermen's decision.

In a letter to a friend, the writer D. H. Lawrence declared that the advent of Zeppelins meant the world as everyone had known it was over. The pre-war suffragette Sylvia Pankhurst wrote of 'that terrific burst of noise; those awful bangs, the roar of falling buildings, the rattle of shrapnel'. George Bernard Shaw professed himself amazed at the 'impunity and audacity' with which the Zeppelins operated, but confessed to being fascinated by them. In a letter to Beatrice and Sidney Webb, he wrote:

> The Zeppelin manoeuvred over the Welwyn Valley for about half an hour before it came round and passed Londonwards with the nicest precision over our house. It made a magnificent noise the whole time; and not a searchlight touched it. What is hardly credible, but true, is that the sound of the Zepp's engines was so fine, and its voyage through the stars so enchanting, that I positively caught myself hoping next night there would be another raid.

An entry in the diary of Mrs Ethel Bilbrough from Chislehurst, Kent, was less forgiving: 'These most vile implements of modern warfare have been rife lately and rarely a month – or even a week – passes without a barbarous raid on some perfectly peaceful town or village. In modern slang, it's simply not cricket.' Talking of which, the great cricketer, W. G. Grace, was so angry whenever he heard Zeppelins above his home near the Crystal Palace that he went outside and shook his fist at them. When fellow England batsman H. D. G. Leveson-Gower pointed out that he had not allowed fast bowlers to unsettle him, Grace retorted: 'I could see those beggars; I can't see these.'

Rumours abounded. Some claimed the Zeppelins were dropping poisoned sweets in the hope that children would eat them. A story did the rounds that a one-eyed saboteur had been lowered to the ground in a basket by a Zeppelin hovering above Hackney Marshes. British traitors and German spies were alleged to be plotting bomb routes, and there was talk of mysterious figures painting luminous arrows on the ground to guide the Zeppelins to their targets. In an incident that typified the growing paranoia, Arthur Brock was contacted by the War Office at his Sutton factory and asked to carry out tests on ash left on the roof of the Holborn Viaduct Hotel in London by two men suspected of signalling to enemy airships with coloured fire. It turned out they were vagrants trying to keep warm.

Others wondered at the ability of the huge craft to travel all the way from Germany and back. 'Don't you believe it,' charwoman Annie Bolster assured her employer, Mary MacDonagh, the wife of *The Times* journalist Michael MacDonagh. 'We know in Battersea that these 'ere Zeppelins are hidden away in the back yards of German bakers!' A persistent rumour of a Zeppelin operating from a clandestine base near Grasmere was dispelled only after Lieutenant Bentfield Hucks of the Royal Flying Corps made repeated reconnaissance sorties over the Lake District in a Blériot monoplane. Scottish police were said to be searching for a Zeppelin base in the remote Highlands.

Up and down the country, people were on edge. In some areas any street-lamps left burning during and after raids were smashed by fearful residents. A whining dog or a restless cat could spark unease, since it was widely believed that household pets sensed the approach of Zeppelins up to an hour before they arrived. Reacting to the anxieties, Joseph Cowen, owner of the *Newcastle Daily Chronicle*, offered £500 'to the crew of the first aircraft to bring down a Zeppelin in the British Isles.' There seemed precious little hope of anyone claiming the reward.

The editor of the *Daily Express*, R. D. Blumenfeld, wrote in his diary in February 1916: 'I actually met a man this week who confessed that the raids made him feel so much afraid that he had decided to go and live far inland.' What people wanted was some kind of indication that the long shadowy monsters – the 'monstrum horrendum' as some called them – were not as invulnerable as they appeared. Thanks to Frank's efforts at Kingsnorth they would not have long to wait.

CHAPTER 10

The Magic Bullet

The term 'Brock's Benefit' was by now one of the most commonly used phrases in the trenches and at sea. Asked to describe his experiences in Flanders, a London infantryman arriving back on leave at the end of August 1914 told the *Portsmouth Evening News*: 'The shells burst right over us – thousands of them every hour. Talk about Brock's Benefit!' Writing to his mother from front-line trenches near the French village of La Cauchie in September 1915, Private Roland Mountfort wrote: 'The flames rose higher than ever illuminating the scene brilliantly & sending Brock's Benefits of sparks all over the village.' A captain who saw action at the Somme (where, incidentally, a key artillery observation post was named 'Brock's Benefit') told war reporter Philip Gibbs: 'When we popped over the parapet we advanced into the middle of the Brock's Benefit.' A Royal Navy officer describing a sea battle in the Dardanelles in 1915 wrote: 'It was a proper show, regular Brock's Benefit, beat the Crystal Palace for fireworks hands down.' The term also made its way into war poetry, such as Edmund Blunden's *Trench Nomenclature*.

> Thence Brock's Benefit commanded endless fireworks by two nations,
> Yet some voices there were raised against the rival coruscations.

Long after the end of hostilities the phrase continued to be used in war literature. In *Realities of War,* published in 1920, Philip Gibbs wrote: 'They discovered the bomb store and opened such a Brock's Benefit that the enemy must have been shocked with surprise.' Ian Hay wrote in his novel *The Willing Horse,* published in 1921: 'The Germans were furnished with bombs which exploded on impact; ours were of the Brock's Benefit type, and had to be lit with a match.' In 1936 *The History of the 12th Battalion of the East Surrey Regiment* recorded that 'the star shells and bursting shrapnel gave the Salient the appearance of a Brock's Benefit on a tremendous scale.' Such was the fame of the Brock name.

Heinrich Mathy, being a well-informed man, had probably heard of the phrase. Frank had certainly heard of Mathy – and he had him in his sights. On 8 September 1915 the infamous Zeppelin commander carried out the deadliest attack so far on London. He passed over the dome of St. Paul's at a height of 8,500 feet (he later took credit for having spared the cathedral itself) before unloading a *Liebsgabe* (a 'love-gift' from the bomb factory to the Zeppelin) on the Aldersgate area of the city. At 660lb, this was by far the largest bomb yet dropped on English soil. Mathy watched from the airship's gondola as it exploded far beneath him, and wrote in his report of a whole row of lights vanishing in one stroke.

An American reporter, William Shepherd, who witnessed the bomb run along the narrow streets surrounding the Guildhall, wrote:

> Among the autumn stars floats a long, gaunt Zeppelin. It is dull yellow – the colour of the harvest moon. The long fingers of searchlights, reaching up from the roofs of the city are touching all sides of the death messenger with their white tips. Great booming sounds shake the city. They are Zeppelin bombs – falling – killing – burning. Suddenly you realise that the biggest city in the world has become the night battlefield in which seven million harmless men, women, and children live.

By the time Mathy had finished his evening's work, 22 civilians, including six children, were dead. Never had the term 'baby killers' seemed more appropriate. The raid sparked increased calls for better protection and led to anti-aircraft defences being diverted from the front lines in France and positioned around the capital. The lake in St James's Park was emptied to prevent its night-time glitter from directing Zeppelins to Buckingham Palace, and the government released a morale-building propaganda film – *Zepped* – which featured Charlie Chaplin bringing down an airship. Much good it did. The Zeppelins kept coming, and for the moment the very idea of shooting one down belonged in the world of fantasy.

The pilots charged with taking on the aerial bandits had the odds stacked against them. Their aircraft were primitive affairs made of wood, wire and canvas, and were powered by small, unreliable engines. Night-time navigation was next to impossible, and often involved trying to read a map in a dark cockpit. Sky and earth were indistinguishable in this pitch-black world. The airmen had no sure way to communicate with the ground and had to rely on spotting the Zeppelins themselves or following the tell-tale splashes of anti-aircraft fire and searchlights. It could take them an hour or more to claw their way up to the altitudes at which the airships operated, and by then their ghostly prey had usually moved on. As one pilot described it: 'The darkness deprives the air pilot of all senses of direction and of locality, greatly hampers him in the manoeuvring of his craft and renders unpleasantly possible a collision with another aeroplane.'

Even if a Zeppelin were successfully intercepted, there appeared to be no way of shooting it down. Early attempts to fly above the airships and drop one of Frank's explosive bomblets or darts on them usually proved hopelessly inaccurate. Hitting them with bullets was difficult if not impossible in the dark. Vickers machine guns, which weighed around 40lb, were too heavy for most aircraft to carry. Holland & Holland, makers of bespoke sporting guns for the aristocracy, came up with the novel concept of 'Zeppelin Shotguns'. These 'weapons of the nobility' were mounted on the wings of RNAS planes from 1915 onwards firing balls held together with wires, but were no more successful than the Lee Enfield rifles they replaced. On the rare occasions that bullets found their mark, they passed harmlessly through the airship's hull. The small tears they made, comparable in size but not effect to a pinprick hole in a child's balloon, could be quickly repaired by the Zeppelin crew before any significant amount of gas had escaped. It was hardly surprising that many Royal Flying Corps commanders were reluctant to send pilots on night-time sorties which achieved nothing more than putting them at grave risk.

In the east end of London and on the quaggy Hoo Peninsula one man believed he now had the answer to the scourge. Frank had known from the start that merely puncturing the gas-impermeable sacs enclosed within the Zeppelin's rigid canvas shell with ordinary bullets was not enough. Hydrogen needs access to a suitable volume of oxygen before a spark will ignite it. What was needed was a bullet capable of rupturing the sacs on a grand enough scale to mix the gases into a pyrotechnic cocktail. To achieve this, the bullet needed to be sensitive enough to explode immediately on making contact with the Zeppelin's skin, rather than to pass straight through it as was the case with the Pomeroy bullet.

The main composition of Frank's bullet was potassium chlorate, with a priming charge of potassium chlorate and mercury sulphocyanide. The priming charge protruded through the envelope and was covered by orange varnish. The impact of the bullet served to force the relatively inert explosive material in its nose rearwards, setting off the fuse or igniter. This in turn ignited the explosive material. The effect – or so Frank hoped – would be to launch a burning chemical spray into the Zeppelin's hydrogen gasbag and set fire to it.

Creating a bullet which was sensitive enough to trigger when it touched the light fabric of the Zeppelin's envelope, but which would not explode from the shock of being fired from the gun, required exceptional engineering ingenuity. The key to success was the sensitivity of the fuse, and Frank made numerous modifications to it in his quest for perfection. Inevitably some bullets went off prematurely during testing. As protection against this, Frank had shields fitted to the trays of the Lewis machine guns from which the bullets would be fired during combat missions. (The Lewis gun was little more than half the weight of the Vickers and had become the weapon of choice of many pilots.) No injuries or serious damage were reported during the course of the trials.

Among those whom Frank regularly consulted was Sir William Pope, Professor of Chemistry at Cambridge University, and a fellow member of the Board of Invention and Research for the Admiralty. Pope, who thought Frank 'brilliant', later described the challenges involved:

> I quickly formed the opinion that the Brock bullet would be a much more effective instrument than the Pomeroy bullet for the destruction of Zeppelins. What was required was a bullet which moved with the velocity of several thousand feet a second, and which would fire and blow a hole in the fabric of perhaps a foot in diameter immediately it struck the fabric. This was essential if you were to get a rapid issue of gas from the Zeppelin. If the bullet pierces the fabric and explodes afterwards, comparatively little damage is done, because a hole of a quarter of an inch or so in diameter only is made, and no considerable escape of gas can take place. So the bullet was required to fire on hitting the surface of the fabric. Now, it was quite clear that a bullet of that kind must be an extremely sensitive thing. You need to imagine a bullet proceeding at several thousand feet a second, and firing as it passes through a piece of fabric which is no thicker than a pocket handkerchief.

In October 1915 the Brock bullet underwent its first full trials with the RNAS. Shots were fired from an army service rifle at a number of steel and wooden aeroplane struts stuck in the ground on a range at Kingsnorth. One of those who witnessed the proceedings, RNAS squadron leader Lord Edward Grosvenor, reported that the trial was 'a great success' and that the struts were all shattered by the explosion of the bullets.

During the next test, conducted at Shoeburyness in Essex, a Winchester rifle was used to fire numerous rounds from 200 yards at a large balloon filled with hydrogen to represent a Zeppelin. The first two rounds failed to ignite the balloon, but this had been expected as the right mixture of hydrogen and oxygen had yet to be achieved. At the third or fourth rounds the balloon burst into flames and was destroyed. Grosvenor reported: 'I am convinced that there is currently no bullet of any make which could compete with or surpass the Brock bullet.' Peregrine Fellowes, the officer who believed Frank had set himself an impossible task, reported: 'I saw his bullets in a stream strike and ignite the hydrogen…he deserves the entire credit for this bullet.'

Needless to say, with each successful test, there were admiring comments from the witnesses. 'Every shot a coconut!' was one. 'Talk about a Brock's Benefit!' was inevitably another.

Impressed by the trials, Murray Sueter asked for further work to be carried out as soon as possible. Frank increased the sensitivity of the bullet's fuse yet further, and in subsequent tests with a Lewis machine gun a balloon was destroyed at a distance of 800 yards. In numerous further trials between then and July 1916, the target balloon never failed to ignite. Many thousands of rounds were used during these tests, the cost of which was met entirely by Frank.

Only when the trials had been successfully concluded did a new obstacle arise. It was the one Frank had foreseen all along. On being informed of the bullet's existence, senior figures on the newly created Air Board, chaired by Lord Curzon, voiced their opposition on the grounds that it contravened the Hague Convention. They quoted a recent ruling by the Lord Chancellor, R. B. Haldane: 'It is no doubt true that the signatories were not thinking of aerial warfare, but … there is no escape.'

For a time it looked as if their negative view of Frank's invention might win out, but Sueter was able to argue convincingly that their concerns were out-dated. Doubts about the bullet's legality were far less compelling now that so many civilians had died in Zeppelin attacks. The discovery that the Austrians were using an explosive bullet of their own provided a further excuse to give Frank's invention the green light. In the face of these arguments, the Air Board withdrew their objections, but stipulated that the Brock bullet should be used only for attacking airships. It also insisted that the bullet should not be sent for use in France or other friendly countries in case it fell into enemy hands.

Admiral Richard Bowles Farquhar, Vice-President of the Ordnance Board, had no qualms about Frank's invention. He concluded that it was 'a very remarkable bullet' and on his advice the Admiralty placed an order for 105,000 rounds. The Brock's factory in Sutton was contracted to fulfil the order, filling ordinary .303 bullets with the correct explosive mixture at a cost of 25 shillings (£1.25) for a hundred. Frank decided to forego his £500-a year allowance from the company because he did not think it right that, as a serving officer, he should receive payments from a firm which was turning out government orders. He did, however, retain his 500 Brock's shares.

Unsure which of the three anti-Zeppelin bullets in production to back, the Ministry of Munitions ruled that the drums of the Lewis guns fitted to fighter aircraft should generally be loaded with a mixture of ammunition – the Brock and the Pomeroy to puncture the Zeppelin's fabric and ignite the gas, and the Buckingham to be used as a tracer to show the direction of flight. A Colonel Forbes gave this order on the principle that there would be a better chance of success if more than one type of bullet was deployed, even though he had seen for himself that the Brock bullet invariably worked during trials. His decision caused pilots to joke that 'if one of the bullets doesn't blow up in your face, the other one will.'

At 11.08 pm on Saturday, 2 September 1916, 21-year-old Lieutenant William Leefe Robinson took off from Sutton's Farm airfield in Essex on a routine 'search and find' operation. His BE2c 2963 aircraft was armed with three drums of Brock and Pomeroy bullets. Far beneath him, many of the civilian population were in a state of high alarm. Zeppelin raids were on the increase, and tonight's was the biggest yet, involving 16 airships carrying a total of 32 tons of bombs. There were warnings of even worse to come. Newspapers were predicting 'a gigantic raid on London' by no fewer than 80 airships before the end of the month. General Sir John Monash, writing home to Australia a few days earlier, had provided a graphic portrait of a city in dread:

> The Zeppelin scare is just as if the whole place was in imminent fear of an earthquake. At night the whole of London is in absolute darkness, every window heavily screened, no street lamps, no lamps on vehicles, all trains with windows closed and blinds drawn, constant street accidents and traffic blocks, and a bewildering pandemonium of confusion in the streets.

After two and a half hours in the air Leefe Robinson saw an airship caught in the bright glare of searchlights 12,500 feet above Finsbury in North London. Closing in on the target, he riddled its entire length with bullets. For a while the airship flew on unhindered, apparently indestructible. To the thousands of fascinated spectators who had gathered below, Leefe Robinson's plane looked like a tiny insect fluttering around a great lamp.

The young pilot had one drum of ammunition left, and precious little fuel. Taking up a position behind the airship, he dived down and poured the last of his bullets at the twin rudders. His first indication of success was a dull pink glow from within the rear of the ship. Seconds later the entire hull went up in flames as thousands of cubic feet of hydrogen ignited with a brilliance which turned the night sky into day. To ecstatic cheering from the ground – the drama was visible up to 50 miles away – the airship plunged from the sky and crashed into a field in Cuffley, Hertfordshire, where it burned furiously for two hours.

A local police constable, having no idea of the full significance of his words, told reporters: 'It was a magnificent spectacle, and seemed almost like a brilliant firework display at the Crystal Palace on Brock's Benefit night.' Lewis Freeman, an American journalist who was watching from central London, wrote: 'Never before has so huge a number of people been suddenly and intensely stirred by a single event.' The novelist John Galsworthy, observing the burning vessel from his flat in the Strand, took a more sombre view. He wrote: 'Glad to say that enthusiasm did not quite prevent feeling for the thirty men roasting in the air.'

The airship's demise was witnessed by most of the other attacking Zeppelins, and what they saw effectively killed the raid. They turned tail and made for home. For many people it was the finest moment yet of the war, and the day was immediately christened 'Zepp Sunday'. As it turned out, Leefe Robinson had shot down not a Zeppelin but one of the German army's wooden-frame Schütte-Lanz machines, the *SL-11*, but the technicality was lost on the thrilled British public. Photographs of the pilot appeared in newspapers and magazines and he became instantly recognised all over the country. Barely 48 hours after the event he was awarded the Victoria Cross.

At the Admiralty, Murray Sueter sent for Frank and asked him which bullet – Brock or Pomeroy – had shot down the airship. 'Mine, sir,' replied Frank.

The nose cone of a downed Zeppelin – the photograph illustrates their immense size.

'I have just been congratulated by Leefe Robinson's commanding officer.' Sueter drove to Hertfordshire to see the wreck of the airship for himself. While there, he was told by one of the Royal Flying Corps officers on the scene that 'Brock's bullet had done the trick.' For Frank, as for so many members of the public, it was a high point of the war, but the top-secret nature of his work meant that unlike Leefe Robinson he could receive no public recognition. Indeed, the very existence of the Brock bullet was not revealed outside military circles until after the war, and even then the details of its composition remained classified.

News of *SL-11*'s loss reached Heinrich Mathy while he was waiting for repairs to be made to his own ship in Germany. He was filled with a sense of foreboding, as were the others in his crew. His Chief Machinist Mate, Viktor Woellert, wrote in his diary: 'I dream constantly of falling Zeppelins. There's something in me I can't describe. It's as if I saw a strange darkness before me, into which I must go.'

Three weeks later Second Lieutenant Frederick Sowrey shot down one of the new, larger 'Super-Zeppelins', *L32*, over Billericay, after what the press called 'a spirited chase and a ding-dong battle'. Like Leefe Robinson he used a combination of Brock and Pomeroy bullets. A pilot who witnessed the action, Lieutenant Alfred de Bathe Brandon, noted in his official report: 'I could see the Brock bullets bursting. Two drums were fired, I should say. Just after the last one the Zepp looked as if it were on fire internally in about a dozen places and it fell in flames.' (Frank later obtained a fragment of metal from the downed airship and presented it to a proud Arthur.) Again there were no survivors, and the bodies of the aircrew were found charred and burned on farmland. 'This airship, although it looked bigger, did not give us such a Brock's Benefit as the one at Cuffley,' a Sheffield man told reporters, again unaware of the significance of his words. On the same night another German airship was damaged by gunfire from both ground and air. It landed near Chelmsford and its crew was captured. Mathy himself witnessed the destruction of *L32* from his own airship several miles away, and there was no doubting the traumatic and demoralising effect it had on him and his crew. He wrote:

> First the bow burned, and then the flames tongued over the whole envelope. The aft gondola broke off, and the wing cars followed. For eighteen terrible seconds the blazing ball hung like a fateful planet in the sky; then it burst asunder.

Disaster seemed to be beckoning Mathy with a bony finger. Though he tried to behave normally at his base in Nordholz, his men noticed the change: his manner grew more serious, his facial features became more sharply defined.

In the privacy of his quarters, he wrote of his fears to his young wife, Hertha, at home nursing a new baby:

> Peterson is dead, Böcker a prisoner. Hertha, the war is becoming a serious matter … During these days, when you lay our little daughter down to sleep, a good angel will see you and will read what is in your heart, and he will hasten to guard my ship against the dangers which throng the air everywhere about her.

The implacable gods of probability claimed him a few nights later, just as they had come for the hapless William Dale at the Crystal Palace all those years ago. On the evening of 1 October he headed for London in the *L31*. His craft came in over the Suffolk coast near Lowestoft at about 8.00 pm. Searchlights lanced the darkness and caught the airship in their beams as it approached Chelmsford. Normally Mathy would have ploughed on, but on this occasion he abandoned the raid on the capital and made a wide, sweeping detour to the north-west, passing Harlow, Stevenage and Hatfield. The supreme self-confidence for which he was famed had apparently deserted him. At around 11.30 pm, as he approached Cheshunt, he was again picked up by searchlights and began attracting anti aircraft gun fire.

Off to the south, a pilot of No. 39 Squadron, Second Lieutenant Wulstan Tempest, was two hours into his patrol, having spent much of the time climbing to around 14,500 feet in his BE2c plane. From this height he could see searchlights converging upon a distant, silvery, cigar-shaped object, and he headed to the area at top speed. As he passed through the beam of a searchlight, he was spotted by the Zeppelin's crew. Mathy immediately ordered the release of 24 High Explosive bombs and 26 incendiary bombs in an attempt to gain height (the bombs landed on Cheshunt, damaging houses but causing no loss of life). His evasive action came too late and he was unable to shake off Tempest's plane.

Flying straight at the Zeppelin, Tempest flew under its belly, firing off a short burst of Brock and Pomeroy bullets. He turned and released another volley, drawing machine-gun fire from the German crew. He banked, sat under the airship's tail and, in his own words, 'pumped lead into her for all I was worth.' His account of the action went on:

> As I was firing I noticed her begin to get red inside like an enormous Chinese lantern and then a flame shot out of the front part of her and I realised she was on fire. She then shot up about 200 feet, paused, and came roaring down straight on to me before I had time to get out of the way. I nose-dived for all I was worth, with the Zepp tearing after me, and expected every minute to be engulfed in the flames. I put my machine into a spin, and just managed to corkscrew out of the way as she shot past me, roaring like a furnace.

Jubilant crowds in London sang the National Anthem as they watched the drama high above them, and ships on the Thames sounded their sirens. The noise was louder than on New Year's Eve. Beyond question the Zeppelin menace now was a bugbear in eclipse. *The Times* reporter Michael MacDonagh was walking home from work when he witnessed *L31*'s death throes from Blackfriars Bridge:

> The searchlights were turned off and the Zeppelin drifted perpendicularly in the darkened sky, a gigantic pyramid of flames, red and orange, like a ruined star falling slowly to earth. When at last the doomed airship vanished from sight there arose a shout the like of which I never heard in London before – a hoarse shout of mingled execration, triumph and joy; a swelling shout that appeared to be rising from all parts of the metropolis, ever increasing in force and intensity. It was London's Te Deum for another crowning deliverance.

As the Zeppelin plummeted downwards like a freight train, Mathy had to make his choice – jump or burn? Like most other members of his crew, he chose to jump, although he left it to the last possible moment. He wrapped a thick scarf (a present from his wife) around his head and leaped from the gondola above a field in Potter's Bar. As his blazing ship smashed into an oak tree, he hit the ground nearby with such force that his unburned body was half-embedded in the soft soil, leaving a clearly defined imprint in the grass. When the first local people arrived on the scene they found him lying sprawled on his back in the grass. To their astonishment he was still breathing, but he died minutes later. The other crew members were already dead.

The following morning, MacDonagh was allowed to go into the barn where the bodies had been taken. He wrote of Mathy:

> Yes, there he lay in death at my feet, the bugaboo of the Zeppelin raids, the first and most ruthless of these Pirates of the Air bent on our destruction. He had poured hundreds of bombs indiscriminately on the defenceless civilian population in the darkness of night – this destroyer of humble homes, this slayer of women and children! And now he had met the fate that was fitting!

The death of Mathy marked the end of a chapter in the war against airships. Although the raids continued sporadically for another year or so, the German airshipmen no longer had the same confidence in their craft and in their ability to wreak havoc on Britain. Never again would they cross the North Sea with their former sense of impunity. The days of the Zeppelin as a terror weapon were finished. By the time the raids were discontinued in 1917 – long before the war ended – 77 out of a total of 115 German airships had been destroyed, and nearly 600 of their aircrew had been killed. As Churchill wrote: 'Zeppelins were clawed down in flames from the sky over both land

and sea by aeroplanes until they did not dare to come any more.' It was a crushing blow to the enemy and an incalculable boost to British morale. The achievement was celebrated by the comedian Henry Bluff whose song 'Ten Little Zeppelins' – after so many civilian deaths, thoughtfully enjoyed by Frank – became a best-selling record in 1917.

> Eight little Zeppelins, their bravery to show,
> Were oh so very busy buzzing enemies below,
> Never saw an aeroplane climbing up to heaven,
> Until he fired his little gun – and then there were seven!

Frank Brock more than anyone else had made the triumph possible. Other factors, including more powerful aircraft engines capable of high-altitude flight, and a network of telephone-equipped observers to track aerial invaders, played their part. So did the Pomeroy and Buckingham bullets, not to mention the courage and tenacity of the pilots. But the view of men like Professor Sir William Pope and Murray Sueter was that the Brock bullet above all else signed the death warrant of the Zeppelins and made them strategically obsolete while the war was still in progress. The RNAS continued to use the bullets for the rest of the war, although the Royal Flying Corps, having initially ordered 500,000 rounds, subsequently relied on the Pomeroy, preferring its less sensitive properties.

The success of his bullet assured Frank of an important place in military history (although there would be many more successes to come) and in recognition of his achievement he was promoted to the rank of flight commander at the end of 1916. In April 1917 he was made a wing commander 'in consideration of very valuable services performed for naval and military air services.'

The deployment of the Brock bullet remained a closely guarded secret. Word of its existence reached the Russian aviation authorities in 1917, but their request for a supply of Brock and Pomeroy was turned down by the British War Cabinet, mainly on the grounds that their use abroad would increase the risk of them falling into enemy hands. In the spring of 1918, however, amid indications that Zeppelins might start operating in the Mediterranean area, the War Cabinet approved their use in Egypt on the strict understanding that pilots carrying the ammunition must never be in a position where they might be forced to land in enemy territory. The Brock bullet was also issued to seaplane stations for use in anti-Zeppelin patrols. Ten thousand bullets, for instance, were sent to RNAS Mudros on the Greek island of Lemnos.

By then Frank had long before moved on to other things. He had always been a man of many parts, and once he had achieved success in one direction he invariably turned his attention to another. In 1915, H. G. Wells, writing for *The Times*, had deplored the state of British invention. The only superior British invention thus far in the war, he had lamented, had been 'in the field of recruiting posters'.

Wells had not accounted for the likes of Frank Brock. In the autumn of 1916, Frank told G's brother, Jack Albert: 'I have finished the Zeppelins. Now I am going to do for the submarines.' And he meant it.

CHAPTER II

Father of Invention

Frank was overjoyed when G gave birth to their first child, a daughter, in 1915. It was the day of their first wedding anniversary, and in a letter of congratulation he described himself as her 're-bridegroom'. Earlier in the year the couple had bought a substantial villa in the residential suburb of Raynes Park in South-West London. They called their new home in Grand Drive 'Lilfren'. G's bump was visible by the time they moved in, and given Frank's whimsical sense of humour, Lilfren was perhaps a jocular adaptation of 'Little Friend'. It was at Lilfren that Anne Grosvenor Brock was born with the help of a doctor and midwife on 24 October. Frank's letters to G, written from a variety of war-time locations, revealed his pride and excitement. 'My own best beloved and only one (except for Anne)', began one missive.

He hoped his dark-haired little daughter would be the first of many children. The Brock clan went in for large families, and he had every intention of continuing the tradition. Shortly after the baby's arrival he was inspired to pen a hastily scribbled poem for a family friend, Molly Wilson.

> Dear Molly mine
> Just a line,
> The baby's fine
> With crystalline
> Eyes that shine
> With look benign
> And chubby chine.
> She loves to dine
> On that wife of mine
> A splendid sign.
> She's superfine
> With a gorgeous spine,
> Not serpentine
> But straight as a line,

And doesn't whine
Or peak or pine
When she's bathed at nine
In Tydman's brine.
My heart shall entwine
Like a wild woodbine
On a clinging vine.
I'm a lucky swine.
Always thine
Frankenstein

The doting husband and father decided that sea air was needed to help G to recuperate and to give Anne the best start in life. Shortly after the birth he booked them into the Alexandra Hotel in Eastbourne where he had often stayed during his pre-war visits to the town. Here, between bracing walks along the seafront, he arranged for Jasper, Weston & Son to visit the hotel in order that Anne's first formal photographs could be taken.

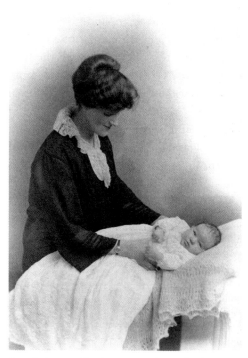

G with Anne in Eastbourne not long after her birth on 24 October 1915, exactly one year to the day after Frank and G were married and Frank left for the Friedrichshafen Raid.

It fascinated Frank to watch Anne develop. He even wrote short letters to her when she was only a few weeks old. Almost as if she were one of his inventions, he evolved theories about her and was keen to test them out. One was that children, even toddlers, have an instinctive sense of balance. To prove his point he had a miniature bicycle built for her, and propelled her down a grassy incline on it not long after she had learned to walk. To Frank's delight, and to G's relief, the theory worked and little Anne remained upright.

He and G regularly visited his parents' house in Sutton to show off the new baby at family gatherings. Having already achieved so much, Frank was held in great respect by his siblings. His sister-in-law Dorothy, who had married his brother Alan while still in

Anne on Frank's knee in 1916.

her teens, would admit years later to having been a little frightened of him, not because he was in any way unpleasant but because she was in awe of his formidable brain and all-round ability. He was one of those men whose presence transformed the atmosphere of a room.

In his war-time work he faced new challenges and wider responsibilities. Recognising that the skills he had developed with Brock's Fireworks were rare and valuable, Churchill and Murray Sueter had tasked him in January 1915 with setting up and commanding the top secret RNAS Experimental Station. Frank's brief was to think up and develop new forms of military technology, an undertaking to which he was perfectly suited. Several acres were found for him in Stratford, East London, and he was given free rein to develop the site.

Since experiments with smoke, explosives and chemicals were high on his agenda, he planned the depot's lay-out on the lines of a Brock's fireworks factory. Scores of sheds and huts were built to his specifications, all set well apart to minimise injury and damage in case of a fire or an explosion. It was a text-book formula based on his childhood memories of the premises at South Norwood, and it was greatly to his credit that no serious injury ever occurred on his watch. Almost certainly his father helped with the project. Arthur had carried out the move to the 200-acre, state-of-the-art fireworks factory in Sutton 12 years earlier, and was one of the most qualified people in the world to advise on the depot's design.

To build his team, Frank was able to pick and choose from some of the best scientific brains in the country. He put Lieutenant Thomas Slater Price, who had graduated from the University of London with first-class honours in chemistry and physics, in charge of the research laboratory and the Prussic Acid and Smoke Mixture Producing Plants. Many of the several hundred ratings he took on also had degrees in science. With a largely free hand to cook up a vast range of gadgets and devices aimed at assisting the war effort, he was able to order as much plant as he needed in the knowledge that it would be delivered to him with a minimum of fuss and delay. The depot was heavily guarded day and night to protect its vast quantity of inflammable material. Few civilians knew its true purpose. Nearly all the men employed there had one thing in common: at some point in their lives they had been to a Crystal Palace firework display and, like the pupils at Dulwich College before them, they were intrigued to be working alongside a member of the famous Brock family. Frank did not disappoint. His official service record noted that he had a 'good command of men', and with his enormous energy and big-hearted enthusiasm he had no trouble carrying them with him.

Typical of the ideas that he pioneered at Stratford were smoke floats designed to help merchant ships under attack by enemy submarines. Easy to use and cheap to manufacture, Frank's so-called 'E' floats automatically produced thick clouds of impenetrable smoke when thrown overboard, giving the ship the opportunity to escape. They required no training to use. All a seaman had to do was throw them in the water. Frank's brother, Alan, described them as 'probably one of the most ingenious purely pyrotechnical devices ever designed.' More than 200,000 of the floats were manufactured and supplied to merchant vessels. They saved countless lives.

Frank developed a system of coloured smoke signalling cartridges for British pilots to use in order to stop friendly-fire accidents in daylight. Yet another device to which he applied his inventive mind was a rocket-propelled life-saving apparatus for use at sea while another was a marine signalling system involving prisms. He also designed and brought into production one of the earliest air-to-air missiles, the Brock Immediate Rocket (immediate because there was no delay after the electrical firing button was pressed, unlike its French counterpart, the Le Prieur Rocket). Both Brock and Le Prieur rockets were intended for use against Zeppelins, observation balloons and enemy aircraft,

An 'E Smoke Float' being tested on land. The E Smoke Float was regarded by the firework historian Alan St. Hill Brock as 'probably one of the most ingenious purely pyrotechnic devices ever designed'.

Smoke float in action on the sea. (IWM HU_131 808)

and were carried and fired from tubes attached to the struts between the biplanes' wings. There were occasions in the war when these air-to-air rockets were lethal to large numbers of observation balloons. Typically four or five were carried on each side, although it was rare for them to be deployed, and there was no widespread use of air-to-air missiles until World War II. In this respect Frank was far ahead of his time. The RNAS considered his rocket far superior to the Le Prieur Rocket. An official gunnery memorandum noted:

> The Le Prieur Rockets are generally slow at getting off and do not appear to keep well and should therefore be used for practice. The Brock Rocket is half the size and weight, and leaves very quickly. These should be reserved for actual attack.

Hardly a day seemed to pass without Frank having one great idea or another. To use a firework analogy, he was the Roman candle that kept fizzing. If there were a challenge to be met, he always found it irresistible. His service record noted that he had an extensive knowledge of chemistry and physics, was 'very capable and zealous', and possessed an 'exceptional talent for devising and perfecting new devices for use during war.' On occasion he went in person to front-line trenches in France to try out his ideas. 'Frank goes to the front on Monday next but only for a few days I hope,' wrote G to their friend, Molly Wilson. 'Just for some experiments of things he's invented. I'm not going to worry because I mustn't.' Though, of course, she did.

A correspondent for *The Navy* magazine wrote of him:

> From H2O to WO2 they knew all about it, or thought they did until the wayward genius of the Commander, who never pretended to be a chemist, taught them that there were permutations and combinations to the nth degree that they had never dared to think of. Wing Commander Brock's great secret was originality. To the accepted formula he would add just a touch of the unexpected. The chemists would say it can't be done, or it wouldn't work. Sometimes it did not, but often it did, very nearly. And Brock's pioneer brain touched it a bit more— and lo! the impossible and the unexpected had arrived.

Frank's work at Stratford was observed closely by the Board of Invention and Research, which had been set up by the Admiralty in July 1915 with

Experimenting with Le Prieur rockets. (IWM Q 27503)

the aim of stimulating naval research and development. The board was chaired by the bellicose, dynamic, indiscreet, charismatic and intolerant former First Sea Lord, Jacky Fisher, who during a long and distinguished naval career had been instrumental in switching the Navy from wooden ships with muzzle-loading cannons to a 20th-century force of steel-hulled dreadnoughts, battlecruisers and aircraft carriers. Often called the greatest admiral since Nelson, he was a vociferous supporter of submarines and had foreseen that they would play an important role in any future war. He was an energetic writer of letters, which he often finished with assurances of 'Yours till hell freezes,' or 'yours till the charcoal sprouts'. The *Oxford English Dictionary* credits him with the first use of the now-ubiquitous text-speak abbreviation OMG for 'Oh My God'.

Frank was asked by Fisher to join the board's secretariat, and he regularly attended meetings at its offices in a house in Cockspur Street near Trafalgar Square. The premises were characteristically re-named Victory House by the flamboyant Fisher. Here Frank rubbed shoulders with some of the most eminent scientists of the day: Sir Joseph Thomson, the Nobel Prize-winning discoverer of the electron; New Zealand-born Ernest Rutherford, the splitter of the atom; Sir Charles Parsons, who invented the compound steam turbine; Sir George Beilby, a brilliant chemist who had patented a production method for hydrogen cyanide; and William Crookes, the octogenarian inventor of the vacuum tube.

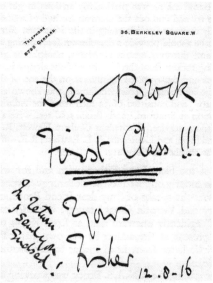

Lord 'Jacky' Fisher. One of the most influential officers ever to hold a commission in the Royal Navy. (Library of Congress)

A letter from Lord Fisher to Frank, written in his typical style and commending one of Frank's 'schemes' on which they worked together.

The ebullient Fisher referred to his team of experts variously as the Chemist's Shop and the Magi. To encourage them to think positively he placed a slogan on the wall: 'To HELL with yesterday – what's doing today?' One of his favourite sayings, borrowed from Lord Macaulay, was 'Moderation in war is imbecility.' His fervent belief in his work was summed up in a letter to Arthur Balfour, Churchill's successor as First Lord of the Admiralty: 'Man invents; monkeys imitate. This war is going to be won by inventions.'

Part of the board's work entailed evaluating the several hundred ideas it received every week from members of the public. Some of these were ingenious if fanciful, such as a suggestion to destroy the German grain crop by dropping thousands of incendiary discs on farms during dry, windy weather. Others provided moments of light relief. A proposal to train cormorants to peck away the mortar of the buildings at the Krupps armaments factory in Essen, so causing the factory to fall down and wreck the German war machine, appealed to Frank's lively sense of humour. So did a letter from a char lady who was irritated by a bad smell and thought it might be bottled up for use against the Germans.

The board took more seriously any schemes for trying to detect and destroy U-boats, however outlandish. It authorised a series of experiments in which food was placed on periscope-shaped buoys to attract seagulls, the idea being that flocks of gulls would descend hungrily on any real periscopes that appeared above the surface and give away their location. It also approved a plan for training seals to lead destroyers to submerged enemy craft by teaching them to associate the sound of submarines with food. Tests took place in swimming baths, at Bala Lake in North Wales, and in the Solent. The seagulls and the seals proved stubbornly resistant to training, but the fact that the board contemplated their use at all was an indication of the Navy's increasing desperation over its failure to combat the U-boat menace.

Fisher, now well into his seventies, became immensely fond of Frank, and treated him almost as a son. 'This Brock is A.1,' he wrote in a note to the Fourth Sea Lord, Admiral Sir Lionel Halsey. Fisher's personal slogan was 'ruthless, relentless, remorseless,' the same qualities which he had found admirable in the young Winston Churchill, and which now drew him to this brilliant young wing commander. He was enthralled by the constant stream of ideas that flowed from Frank's fertile brain (one was a top-secret proposal to attack and capture U-boats with gas) and corresponded with him regularly. One note he sent him, which probably referred to the Brock bullet, said simply: 'Dear Brock. First class!!! Yours. Fisher.'

On another occasion he wrote: 'Dear Brock. I'm greatly fascinated! May I show your paper confidentially to some of the All Highest? Yours. Fisher.' The paper which 'greatly fascinated' Fisher, and which he showed the 'All Highest' (the term he sometimes used to describe the War Cabinet), was a 13-page proposal by Frank to drive the German fleet out of the Heligoland Bight in the North Sea. Heligoland, a small archipelago a little under 30 miles off the German coast, was of immense strategic importance. Not only did it guard the main German naval base but also the Kiel canal which allowed ships of the German fleet to be transferred from the North Sea to the Baltic free from any hostile enemy threats. For most of the 19th century it had been in British hands, but was transferred to Germany in 1890 in return for swathes of territory in Africa. The Germans evacuated the civilian population and developed the main island into a major naval base, with extensive harbour and dockyard installations, underground fortifications, and coastal batteries. An important sanctuary for U-boats as well as surface vessels, Heligoland was a symbol of great national pride, not least because the lyrics to Germany's national anthem, *Deutschland über alles,* had been written on the island by August Hoffman.

Never one for half measures, Frank proposed ousting the Germans from the base by seizing the tiny German island of Sylt, some 40 miles to the south, and using it as a launching pad to attack the Heligoland Bight with asphyxiating gas prior to a bombardment by the Royal Navy. He found the use of gas as repugnant as anyone, but at least there would be no civilian involvement, and countless lives would be saved in the long run if a large number of U-boats were deprived of their base. He suggested in his paper that a full-scale rehearsal of the attack should be carried on a remote Scottish island – possibly Fair Isle – to ensure that the gas travelled over cliff faces and penetrated tunnels. At the very least, he argued, a gas attack on Heligoland would draw the German fleet into the open, and 'there is always the possibility that an undamaged airship may be found on the island.' The idea appealed to the swashbuckling Fisher, and was considered at length by the Admiralty, but like countless other war-time ideas it was eventually discarded.

Knowing Frank's capacity for hard work, Fisher pleaded with his protégé not to run himself into the ground. It was not unknown for Frank to work 36 hours at a stretch, and although he always remained in robust good health, Fisher was concerned. 'You are working too hard!' he wrote. 'I am anxious! You'll bust up! So I've written a letter to my very good friend Halsey [Admiral Sir Lionel Halsey] to do something to prevent your going to Heaven just at present by getting you some assistance.'

A paper Frank sent to Fisher in September 1916, which highlighted the replacement of General Erich von Falkenhayn as Chief of the German General Staff by Paul von Hindenburg, demonstrated his ability to think politically as well as strategically. Frank commented that Hindenburg's appointment was 'extraordinary' given the Kaiser's personal animosity towards him, and suggested there must be a 'hidden reason'. One explanation, he suggested, was that 'Hindenburg has always been an apostle of frightfulness, and the Kaiser wants to use some new military frightfulness which is too inhuman even for Von Falkenhayn.' He speculated the 'frightfulness' might be the introduction of biological warfare. Another possible explanation, he said, was that the Kaiser had secretly ordered Hindenburg to mastermind an invasion of England, with likely landings on both the north-east and south-east coasts. Though neither of these fears materialised, Fisher found Frank's ideas stimulating and thought-provoking.

The admiration Fisher had for Frank was reciprocated. The crusty old sea dog had resigned as First Sea Lord in 1915 amid fierce arguments with Winston Churchill over the Gallipoli campaign. Frank for one wanted to see him reinstated, and wrote to tell him so in early 1917. Fisher responded: 'My dear Brock. Your delightful wish for my 'prompt return' came at the same time as a long telegram from Queen Alexandra saying she was fervently praying for the same thing and for the 'Great Sea Lord to Guide'. So it's a happy omen but alas! I don't think it will come off.'

With Fisher's encouragement, Frank apparently made an important decision about his own future at around this time. According to RNAS colleagues he resolved to adopt the Navy as a permanent profession after the war. Staging fireworks shows for his father's firm was all very well, but it could not compete with the excitement, the danger and the challenges of the naval work he had undertaken since 1914, nor with the swell of the sea and the feel of a teak deck. It was not as if there was a shortage of Brock sons to take over the family business when Arthur decided to call it a day. The next brother down, Alan, was already showing a keen interest in pyrotechnics, and would make an excellent successor to his father. Frank discussed his thoughts with Fisher, who wrote to him in early 1917: 'I look forward to making a fellow called Brock an Admiral or a Duke.' In a later letter Fisher wrote: 'I arranged a plan yesterday with Tyrwhitt [Reginald Tyrwhitt, commander of the Harwich Force] to get you your deserved extra stripe and I hope it will come off.'

Always on the look-out for new ideas, Frank went to France in July 1916 to swap information with the French Ministry of Inventions. He was accompanied by Sir William Pope, the Cambridge chemistry professor who had provided advice about the Brock bullet and Jellite. Staying at the Hotel Meurice, the two men spent 12 days in and around Paris, and brought back an array of new ideas to Fisher's Board of Invention and Research. Their hosts in Paris included the brilliant French physicist Maurice de Broglie, and the Minister of Inventions, Paul Painlevé, who would become Prime Minister of France the following year. They exchanged information about Zeppelin construction, and discussed new methods of guiding aerial bombs to their targets.

The battle of the Somme was in full swing at the time, and off to the north, if the wind was right, Frank could hear the sluggish boom of artillery at Montauban, Beaumont Hamel and other shattered towns and villages on the front line. Gas was being deployed there by both sides, and the visitors were shown a new method for detecting lingering traces of chlorine or phosgene gas on the battlefield. This entailed an officer taking a slip of glass from a tube and exposing it to the air. Two moist strips of paper, one more sensitive than the other, were attached to the glass. If both became dark the air was too dangerous to breathe, and gas masks should remain in place. If only one of the two darkened, the air was fit to breathe but contained traces of gas. If neither strip darkened no gas remained in the air. It was one of many innovative ideas that Frank took back with him to England.

The two men were also given access to several top-secret installations, including the photographic units at Plessis-Belleville and Meudon air bases outside Paris. Frank was particularly impressed by a 120cm focal length camera designed for aerial reconnaissance. Made of aluminium, it was lighter than any used by British aviators, and produced impressively sharp pictures due to minimal vibration during exposure. Other inventions the visitors were shown included a system of microphones and highly sensitive diaphragms capable of detecting far distant sounds such as the rhythmic noise of an aeroplane. At a laboratory in the Sorbonne they were shown coloured screens through which objects of certain colours, such as khaki cloth and grey German uniforms, could be seen in increased contrast with their surroundings.

Thanks to the detailed report the two men wrote on their return to England, many of these ideas were subsequently adopted by the British armed forces and greatly assisted the war effort. Picking up on what he had learned at the Sorbonne, for instance, Frank obtained a range of dyes and pioneered the use in Britain of colour filters to improve sharpness of vision through goggles, binoculars and cameras under different atmospheric conditions. Before long, tens of thousands of his Brock colour filters were in production, the contract awarded to Ilford Ltd., the camera and film company.

In August 1916, Fisher put him in charge of Section 6 of the Board of Invention and Research, which specialised in bombs, bomb sights and aircraft armaments. In particular Frank worked on a method of aerial attack he had been told about in Paris. This entailed projecting bombs from an aeroplane on a distant objective along a path which formed an acute angle with the earth's surface. The method counter-acted problems with air resistance, which frequently deflected bombs off course, and ensured far greater accuracy.

Frank's activities were not confined to inventing and developing military gadgets. In June 1917 he was caught up in a minor controversy when he accepted the vice-presidency of the newly formed British American Overseas Field Hospital, a charity set up in June 1917 to establish mobile casualty clearing points close to the front line. The charity's founder was an eccentric individual named Henry Allan Ashton, known chiefly as the author of an outspoken pamphlet entitled 'Some Suggestions Regarding the Terms of Peace'. This accused the Germans of committing atrocities 'which no one a few years ago would have believed possible even among cannibals.' Under Ashton's proposed 'peace terms', Germany would be broken up into eight separate countries, her navy and air force would be destroyed or appropriated, and Allied soldiers would be allowed to dig up German gardens to find the gold secreted there by 'the cute and cunning Teutons.' Ashton said he needed £20,000 in donations to fund his charity, and promised that 'every penny, without deduction for rent, staff, office or management charges' would be spent on the proposed field hospital.

It sounded fine in theory. As well as luring Frank on board, Ashton persuaded Lady Rosemead of Datchet to become chairman, and the Duke of Atholl to be a patron. The charity had smart offices in London's Piccadilly, but all was not what it seemed. Days after the fund opened, the Charity Commission discovered that Ashton had previously been involved in fraudulent share dealings, having run public competitions for worthless shares or selling them at inflated prices. It was the end of the road for the British American Oversees Field Hospital, and Frank, along with other worthies who had accepted positions in the charity in good faith, quickly dissociated themselves from it.

Less contentiously, Frank was instrumental in initiating and equipping an RNAS station in Malta, and planned to go there himself later in the war to test out his latest ideas. The island had become known as 'The Nurse of the Mediterranean' due to the large number of wounded soldiers who were accommodated there. Of more pertinence to the RNAS, Maltese waters were infested with German submarines which preyed on merchant vessels in the Mediterranean shipping lanes, especially the busy stretch between Malta and the waters north of Crete. Under Frank's old commander Murray Sueter, the RNAS set up a major sea plane base there in 1917 and adopted many of the ideas Frank had discussed in Paris. These included a listening station which used hydrophones to pick up suspicious engine sounds, and an experimental station which specialised in developing and trialling new photographic and observational procedures, especially those involving colour filters, searching for submarines and minefields beneath the surface of the clear Mediterranean waters.

In the meantime, the question of how to counter the threat to merchant ships from German submarines nearer to home was taking up an increasing amount of Frank's time. In 1915 Untersee boats – U-boats – had accounted for 1.3 million tons of Allied and neutral shipping. This rose to 2.3 million in 1916. In December of that year Admiral von Holtzendorff, head of the German Navy General Staff, proposed upping the toll to 600,000 tons a month – or more than 7 million tons a year. He estimated that this would starve Britain into submission within five months and Admiral Reinhardt von Scheer, who had commanded the German High Seas Fleet at the inconclusive battle of Jutland, visited the Kaiser and advised him that following the battle he believed it was impossible to beat the Royal Navy. If Germany wanted to win, it had to wage unrestricted submarine warfare and starve the enemy into submission, he said. The Kaiser duly gave his approval for a more aggressive campaign, boasting that 'we will frighten the British flag off the face of the waters.' Like wolves rampaging through a flock of sheep, U-boats began savaging the plodding merchantmen as never before.

By the beginning of 1917, one ship in every four sailing in British waters was ending up at the bottom of the sea. In February and March 1917 alone more than 250 merchant ships totalling nearly 1 million tons were sunk by the underwater predators. By the end of April another 860,000 tons had slid under the surface. The losses for May and June combined ran to more than 1.3 million tons. With the support lifelines to the empire and neutral America under constant threat, food stocks began to run terrifyingly low. Supplies of wheat shrank to cover only six weeks. The Prime Minister, Lloyd George, was reluctant to court unpopularity by introducing rationing, but at his request the king urged his subjects 'to practice the greatest economy and frugality in the use of every species of grain.' Britain had seldom faced such a desperate situation. Following a council of war in London in June, Field Marshal Douglas Haig noted:

> Today, a grave and worrying matter was discussed. Admiral Jellicoe, the First Lord of the Admiralty, reported that Great Britain's shipping losses due to German U-boats would make it impossible to continue the war in 1918. This news hit like a bomb ... Jellicoe commented that there is no point in making plans for the coming year; we will not be able to carry them out.

The Royal Navy's success at countering the threat was at best patchy. During the first three months of the new campaign Germany lost just nine submarines out of a fleet of 140. U-boat production was such that any losses could be replaced almost immediately. Slow to respond effectively, and against its wishes but with the encouragement of the Prime Minister, Lloyd George, the Admiralty established a new system of trans-Atlantic convoys in the summer of 1917. This helped to reduce the losses, but it was not enough.

Part of the answer lay in denying U-boats passage through the Dover Strait. The best hunting grounds for U-boats were in the waters south and west of Britain where merchant ships converged to enter or exit the country's main seaports. To reach these prime waters, U-boat commanders opted where possible to use the shorter, southern route through the strait, and until late 1917 this remained the major highway for German submarines going to and from their various stations. Their only alternative was to enter the Atlantic via the North Sea and around Scotland, but this added weeks to their passage.

Accordingly, in 1916, the British had laid a barrage of deep mines and nets across the Dover Strait with the aim of barring passage to German ships and submarines. The brainchild of Admiral Sir Reginald Bacon, the Cross-Channel Barrage extended 18 miles from the Goodwin Sands to the Outer Ruytingen Shoals off the coast of northern France, the equivalent of laying a net between

London and Windsor. Its nets were each 100 yards long and up to 75 feet deep, and were suspended from steel hawsers held up by floats. They were policed by the Dover Patrol, a ragtag collection of destroyers, trawlers, drifters, monitors, and motor boats. If a submarine became ensnared in the net, the agitation of the floats would bring patrol boats to the spot to attack it with depth charges. If the U-boat dived, it would be destroyed by the contact mines laid at different depths beneath the nets. That, at any rate, was what was supposed to happen.

Unfortunately, Admiral Bacon's pride and joy proved next to useless. Although it hindered the progress of German submarines, it did precious little to stop them. The U-boat commanders navigated the barrage simply by floating their vessels over the top of the nets in darkness and at high water. A U-boat was a tiny target in the gloom of night, and for all their hard work and dedication, the little craft of the Dover Patrol seldom spotted the dark prowling shapes. Those U-boats which in exceptional cases took the longer route around Scotland were ordered to let themselves be seen as freely as possible so as to mislead the British into thinking that the barrage was working. It was very much in Germany's interests that it remained in place.

The upshot was that some 30 German submarines were slipping through the strait each month to infest the Atlantic and the Irish Sea. During the whole of 1916 only one U-boat was sunk in the strait. The following year only one was definitely sunk compared to 253 known to have navigated it successfully. In the words of one naval expert, they were 'passing through the Straits of Dover in an unbroken procession.'

The Admiralty's confidence in the barrage took a particularly severe knock when 14 British destroyers crossed over it by mistake without suffering a scratch. Drastic action was needed. 'Can the Army win the war before the Navy loses it?' Lord Fisher asked acidly in a private note to Frank in March 1917.

At the end of 1917 Vice Admiral Roger Keyes, aged 45, was appointed to the Dover Command in order to shake things up. He had sailed under the White Ensign since he was a boy, and was the sort of man who inspired others to give their best under all conditions. Winston Churchill believed he 'had more knowledge and feeling for war than almost any naval officer I have met.' A fresh breeze began to blow through musty corridors.

Keyes made it his top priority to strengthen the existing barrage. His longer-term aim was 'to root out the evil from its operational source.' To make the barrage more effective, he had it re-sited from Folkestone to Cape Gris Nez and equipped it with 9,500 improved mines and additional patrol craft. Next came his masterstroke. He decided to illuminate the barrage through the night with flares and searchlights, forcing U-boats to dive into the minefields instead of slipping over the top of the nets into the healing darkness. But was it possible to make flares that were powerful enough to do the job, and could they be produced in great enough numbers? Keyes knew who to ask. He had been told that if anyone could come up with what he wanted it was a brilliant young inventor based in RNAS Stratford. His name was Frank Brock.

Frank set about the task with enthusiasm and ingenuity. Calling on his knowledge of fireworks, he rapidly designed and developed what became known as Deck Flares or Dover Flares. Three feet high, with a diameter of eight inches, and weighing 90 pounds, each one burned for seven and a half minutes with the strength of 1,000,000 candle power, brilliantly illuminating an area of three miles radius. Keyes placed orders with the Brock's Fireworks factory in Sutton for 135,000 of the flares at around £9 a piece. These were distributed among 12 trawlers, which took up positions on both sides of the Dover Straits, burning several hundred flares a night between them. Any gaps were filled by searchlights operated from boats. As Winston Churchill wrote subsequently, the flares lit up the Channel at night 'as bright as Piccadilly'.

Elsewhere and to make life more difficult for the U-boats at night, Frank developed large flares which were suspended beneath kite-balloons and towed behind motor boats. In a further boost to the Dover Patrol, he designed an enhanced Very light capable of dividing into different colours to improve signalling between ships. Under his system a sequence of Very Brock Signals – VBS – was fired as a challenge to any suspicious ship. If the other vessel failed to respond with a different combination of colours, it was regarded as hostile, and offensive action was immediately taken. The arrangement was a significant advance on the slow and cumbersome hand-held signal lamps it replaced, making it harder for enemy ships to infiltrate the Strait, and reducing the risk of friendly fire.

The new arrangements paid immediate dividends. On the very first night of the beefed-up barrage's existence, *UB-56*, which had sunk four merchant ships since her launch in May 1917, was forced by the flares to dive into the minefield. She was blown to pieces with all hands lost. Over the next four weeks another four U-Boats were destroyed in the strait. One was spotted as it submerged and a series of depth charges sealed its fate. The other three, pinned in the blinding light of Frank's flares, dived into the minefield with the inevitable results. Admiral Ludwig von Schroder, commander of the Flanders *Marinekorps*, was forced to concede that the new 'light barrier', as he called it, had made the Channel passage extremely hazardous. In the face of this danger,

The trawlers of the Dover Patrol Cross-Channel Barrage carrying Frank's flares. (IWM SP_000276)

the number of German submarines infiltrating the Channel dwindled from 38 in December 1917 to one in February 1918. In all, at least 14 U-Boats were sunk while attempting to pass through the barrage, and the average life expectancy of a U-boat crew dropped to just six patrols.

One victim of the barrage was *UB-55*, commanded by Lieutenant Ralph Wenninger. The experience of her crew underlined the horror of being trapped in a doomed submarine. Wenninger had been responsible for sinking 98 ships. Only four weeks earlier he had sent the American steamer *Chattahoochee* to the bottom of the sea, along with her cargo of 120 lorries. In the early hours of 22 April 1918 he was caught up in Frank's flares some nine miles south-west of Dover. He ordered a dive, but as the boat reached 12 metres a mine exploded against her stern. Water poured in, forcing down the stern, and the crew were ordered forward to restore trim. The boat eventually settled on the bottom at a depth of some 25 metres, but water flowed into the control room and the batteries began leaking chlorine gas. As the air pressure increased, several men committed suicide by stuffing their mouths with wadding and putting their heads under water. Others tried to shoot themselves, but the damp cartridges would not fire. Finally 22 men managed to climb through the conning tower hatch and the bow torpedo hatch. The change of air pressure killed most of them, but a patrol boat picked up Wenninger and seven others after they had been in the water for an hour and a half. Wenninger would sink no more merchant ships.

Keyes deservedly took the lion's share of the credit for this important reversal in Britain's naval fortunes, but Frank's contribution was crucial. Keyes himself said of Frank:

> There was great difficulty in obtaining the materials for making the quantity of flares we required, and Brock worked with untiring energy to produce the number I wanted. A little later a strike interfered with the supply of aluminium and considerably reduced production. Brock before long devised a new system of manufacture, and from about the end of January onwards, the supply was assured. I have no hesitation in saying that Brock's ingenuity and energy gave us the means of instituting a most successful anti-submarine patrol in the Dover Straits. He worked with the most untiring energy to produce the flares for me and the results obtained through their use was wonderfully successful.

As significant as the U-boat losses themselves was the fact that enemy submarines were now increasingly forced to use the northern passage round Scotland to reach their hunting grounds in the Atlantic. The added fuel they used shortened the time they could spend haunting the shipping lanes. The results in terms of merchant ships sunk by enemy action was striking. In April 1917 the total tonnage lost was 881,000. By April 1918 the figure had dropped to 279,000. In the Channel itself the figures were even more marked, dropping from 70,000 to 8,000 weekly. Fears that the country might be starved into submission began to subside. The flares had more than done their job. Alan Brock wrote of his brother:

It can be said without fear of contradiction that no one man did more for military pyrotechny during the Great War, and possibly in no other single subject during the war was one man so invaluable. Endowed with a marked inventive ability and a phenomenal memory, and brought up as it were in an atmosphere of pyrotechny, he developed a knowledge of pyrotechnic chemistry which was extraordinary and appeared almost instinctive. The few moments he could snatch from his duties and the many he stole from sleep were devoted to the invention and elaboration of war devices.

Frank's achievements were recognised at the highest level. On 13 February 1918 he went to Buckingham Palace where King George V appointed him to the Most Excellent Order of the British Empire 'for the service you have rendered on work connected with the war.' By now his contribution to the war effort both at sea and in the air was incalculable, and the lives he had saved were countless. But Frank Brock OBE was not one to rest on his forest of laurels. In the wake of his success with the Cross-Channel Barrage, Admiral Keyes was planning one of the most dramatic and dangerous war-time missions ever attempted, and Frank was determined to be a part of it.

CHAPTER 12

Striking the Viper's Nest

Effective though it was, the new Cross-Channel Barrage was only part of the answer to the U-boat problem. For every enemy submarine that was destroyed, others managed to slip into the open sea, sometimes roughed up a little but otherwise intact. Not all started their journeys in Germany. Many were based just 65 miles from the English coast in the medieval town of Bruges in occupied Belgium – what Admiral Keyes called 'the nest of vipers'. From Bruges they threaded their way to sea along a lattice-work of beautiful canals, emerging either eleven miles away at Ostend or, more usually, eight miles away at the port of Zeebrugge (meaning Bruges on the Sea). The Zeebrugge canal was 24ft deep, enabling moderately large vessels to pass between the sea and the docks at Bruges. The shallower and narrower Ostend canal could only accommodate smaller vessels.

At any given time, up to 30 submarines were either resting or undergoing refits in their concrete pens at Bruges. For the crews, the town was a welcome respite from the dangers of war. The officers stayed in hotels and the crews were billeted in designated houses. The bar in the officers' mess was decorated with frescoes showing John Bull drinking champagne with monkeys, and carrying mottoes such as 'Life is short, and you'll be a long time dead' and 'Drink, for tomorrow you may die.' The inland haven was also a base for numerous destroyers and torpedo-craft.

Being some three hundred miles nearer to Dover than their naval ports in the Heliogoland Bight, Bruges was an invaluable outpost for the Germans. The reduction of mileage conserved fuel, lessened the risk of interception, and meant the crews remained fresher while harassing the supply ships that plodded across the Channel. There was no shortage of prey. Every few minutes, around the clock, a vessel of one sort or another left England for France carrying troops, guns, ammunition, food and fuel. A constant stream of ships poured

back the other way with casualties or men on leave. As the author 'Jackstaff'
wrote in his book *The Dover Patrol:*

> For nearly every ounce of his rations, for nearly all the uncountable millions of cigarettes
> he smokes, for much of the clothing he wears, for what he eats himself and for what he
> 'feeds' to 'Gerry' in different ways, Thomas Atkins is mainly beholden to the Dover Patrol.

The vessels carrying these essential cargoes were constantly open to attack. By
the spring of 1918 Bruges-based U-boats had accounted for some four million
tons of Allied shipping – around one third of the total – and the Royal Navy
dearly wanted to put them out of action.

The running sore of Bruges dated back to October 1914 when the city
had been over-run by reserve troops of the German Fourth Army. Since then
the British had tried several times to knock out its two satellite sea ports,
usually by shelling them with heavy artillery, but always without success. A
proposal to send in shallow-draught warships to wreck the lock gates was
abandoned, mainly because the quality of the smoke screens then available
was inadequate to cover their approach. A plan to drive the Germans out of
Flanders by land, and to capture Zeebrugge and Ostend in the process, also
failed when the third Ypres offensive became bogged down in the muddy
morass of Passchendaele in late 1917. However, the War Committee, meeting
in London on 20 November, agreed that it remained imperative to deprive
the Germans of their U-boat bases in Belgium. The minutes noted:

> There is no operation of war to which the war committee would attach greater importance
> than the successful occupation or at least the deprivation to the enemy of Ostend and
> especially Zeebrugge.

Now, at the beginning of 1918, Keyes turned his attention to a bold and
dangerous new plan. He knew that Bruges itself was too far from the sea to be
captured in a naval operation. Nor would it be feasible to take possession of
the canals that linked it to the sea. What might be possible, however, was to
block access to the canals by scuttling ships across their entrances at Zeebrugge
and Ostend. In one fell swoop this would render Bruges useless as a base and
bar the oceans to a large proportion of the U-boat fleet.

Many in the Admiralty had misgivings about the plan. They were particularly
concerned about the formidable defences at Zeebrugge. Its harbour and the
canal entrance were shielded by a curving quay wall which for sheer size had
no equal in Great Britain or the United States. Known as the Mole, a word
derived from the classical Latin term for a large pier, breakwater or causeway,
its total length was approximately one and a half miles. Completed in 1903,

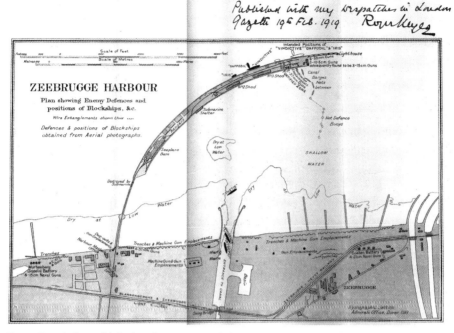

Roger Keyes' plan published in the Gazette and also sent to G by Keyes after the raid. It is possible to see the church where Frank and Hermann Künne are both believed to be buried.

and opened with great pomp by King Leopold of Belgium, it was constructed of vast concrete blocks paved with granite. Along its top ran a parapet roadway the height of a two-storey house. At its seaward end was a narrow 300ft pier ending in a lighthouse. At the other end, connecting it to the shore, was a 900ft viaduct carrying railway lines and a roadway. The viaduct's purpose was to allow the tide to flow through and prevent the harbour from silting up.

The main part of the Mole was the width of a rugby pitch and could not be effectively damaged by bombardment. According to intelligence reports, it was garrisoned by 1,000 crack German defenders, and was infested with concrete emplacements for machine guns and anti-aircraft guns. Directly in line with its tip stood the menacing Friedriechsart Battery, whose 6.5in naval guns dominated the harbour. Numerous other batteries were dotted along the Mole itself and along the shore behind it. Destroyers were normally moored against its walls, their guns ready to sweep the channel entrance in case of attack. The very idea of sneaking blockships past the Mole and sinking them in the canal entrance seemed like a suicidal fantasy, all the more so because no comparable amphibious assault in history – including two by Nelson at Tenerife in 1797 – had ever succeeded.

But Keyes knew that wars are not won by doubters, and he had numerous tricks up his sleeve. Not only did he intend to scuttle obsolescent cruisers filled with concrete in the necks of the canals – three at Zeebrugge and three at Ostend – but simultaneously he planned to deliver the Mole itself a crippling blow. In order to maintain the vital element of surprise it would have to happen on a moonless night. First, he would land 800 highly trained Marines and Bluejackets on the Mole with orders to inflict as much damage as they could. They would knock out machine-gun posts, blow up buildings, put gun batteries out of action and attempt to sink any destroyers found alongside. At the same time the viaduct linking the Mole to the shore would be destroyed to prevent the arrival of German reinforcements. This would be achieved by jamming two old submarines packed with explosives into its girders and blowing them sky high. All this mayhem had an important purpose. It would divert enemy attention from the approaching blockships. If the Germans were sufficiently distracted by an all-out assault on the Mole, it might be possible – just possible – to scuttle the ships in the canal entrance before they realised what was happening.

The action was fraught with danger, but the need to neutralise the pirates' lair at Bruges was becoming more urgent by the day. Hunger was stalking the civilian population. Many poorer families were suffering from malnutrition. Rationing of sugar, meat, flour, butter, margarine and milk had been introduced in London at the start of the year and, although the public did not know it yet, these restrictions were due to be extended nationwide. War weariness was setting in, and morale was at a dangerously low ebb. In the trenches, pea soup with a few lumps of horse meat had become the staple diet. Against this bleak background, Keyes was given the green light to let rip. With no time to waste, he pencilled in the Zeebrugge and Ostend raids for mid-March, or April at the latest.

Right from the start he took Frank into his confidence, summoning him to Dover at the beginning of the year he installed Frank in a workshop near his own office – something that was to become slightly uncomfortable later after two different accidental explosions damaged Frank's hut. Responding to one explosion, Keyes found the 'the great rocket man emerged look(ing) a bit sheepish, with singed eyebrows, collar askew, but otherwise unharmed'.

Keyes gave him a list of his requirements. The first and most important of these was a smoke screen that would mask the British flotilla as it approached Zeebrugge, and shield the blockships as they entered the harbour. Not any old smoke screen, but a fog of such impenetrable density that it would render the fleet invisible until the last possible moment. On top of this, the smoke should be devoid of any bright flames that might advertise its source and so make easy targets of the ships. This had always been a problem with previous smoke screens, which had been generated by burning phosphorus in open iron pots. The method created fierce flames, and – for obvious reasons – was especially problematic during night operations. Keyes emphasised that the success of the entire mission rested on Frank being able to produce a dense, flameless smoke. Without it the advancing ships would be blown to bits before they reached the Mole.

Keyes listed many other ways in which Frank's expertise could be used on the operation. Flamethrowers, phosphorus grenades, flares, signalling rockets, flashing marker buoys – if Frank could make them, Keyes would use them. But it was the smoke that mattered most.

Frank responded enthusiastically, but there was a price for his whole-hearted co-operation. He told Keyes he wanted to take part in the raid and to be one of the first to go on to the Mole. The admiral tried to dissuade him, telling him that his genius for inventions was too valuable to put his life at risk. He would serve his country best by remaining safely in England and working on his gadgets at Stratford. But Frank was having none of it. Firstly, he argued, he understood better than anyone how his numerous devices worked and his knowledge of them, particularly in respect of the smoke screen, would greatly assist the operation if he was there in person. Secondly, and just as importantly, he wanted to go ashore to try to locate one of the devastatingly accurate Goertz range-finders with which the German coastal batteries were equipped and which were superior to anything possessed by the British. Intelligence reports had revealed that a system of metal tubes was mounted on the Mole, and Frank believed these were probably part of the Goertz set-up. It was a hugely tempting prospect. If he could examine a German range finder, and better still bring one back with him, he should be in a position to develop a British version to match it. Frank had often told his friend Sir William Pope that he planned to snatch a range finder from under the noses of the Germans at either Heligoland or Zeebrugge. Pope had thought he was joking, but Frank was being deadly serious.

That may not have been all he hoped to find on the Mole. The war historian E. C. Coleman has speculated that he may also have been intent on investigating a much feared anti-aircraft weapon known as 'flaming onions', described in newspaper reports of the time as 'an extraordinary device of Prussian ingenuity'. British pilots described it as a 'cluster of six or eight whirling balls of fire', held together by wire, which wrapped itself round its target and set it on fire.

According to one pilot, 'the onions are shot upward from some kind of mortar … bunches of them are fired at you while you are flying over the enemy lines. The first thing you see is a big cluster of six or eight whirling balls of fire coming at you from below. They rise very rapidly, as fast as shrapnel, rotating rapidly.' A British naval officer who had seen them from his ship described them as 'rising heavenwards, hanging stationary for a few seconds, and then slowly falling in their curiously serpentine manner, for all the world like colossal snakes writhing in their death agony.' His description bore an intriguing resemblance to press reports of firework displays at the Crystal Palace: 'Rockets burst into constellations of coloured balls; some joined up and floated in chains, others whistled like a gale.'

The weapon had never been captured, but a gun for firing 'flaming onions' was known to be sited at the end of the Mole. Finding out exactly what 'flaming onions' were, how they worked, and perhaps replicating them in Stratford, would have been an irresistible attraction to a man like Frank. It was another good reason for going ashore.

The admiral was torn, but even now Frank had not finished. To clinch the matter he pointed out that Keyes himself, though crucially important to the war effort, would be taking part in the raid. If Keyes was to be allowed to risk his life, then so should Frank. At this, Keyes's opposition crumbled, and he reluctantly gave Frank the go-ahead to take part. He wrote afterwards: 'Brock's one plea, which I would have preferred to have refused – as his genius for inventions was so valuable – was that he should be allowed to get on to the Mole. I reluctantly consented.' With hindsight it was a foolhardy decision. As the war historian Deborah Lake has pointed out, it was akin to allowing the bouncing bomb inventor Barnes Wallis to fly as a bomb-aimer on the Dambuster raids in World War II.

It is probable that Frank had another unspoken reason for wanting to go to Zeebrugge. Given that he had lost so many friends during the war, and bearing in mind his undoubted courage, it would not have been surprising if he craved the chance to take on the Germans in person. Here was an opportunity to settle a few scores.

Whatever the reasons, Keyes was not the only one to have concerns about his participation. When Frank broke the news to G, she found it impossible to hide her fears. Her own deep love for him apart, she was – as she revealed to him – expecting their second child in the autumn. She hoped Frank might change his mind, but she knew it was a forlorn wish. Besides, as he kept assuring her, he had been born lucky. He was not going to come to any harm. G was not superstitious, but it did not help matters when Frank accidentally

Frank and a fellow officer on the quay at Dover before the raid. Frank's face has aged markedly over just four years. The inhalation of toxic gases didn't help but like many British officers he carried heavy responsibility and frequently worked for periods exceeding 24 hours without sleep.

broke a looking-glass. Didn't that mean that bad luck was coming his way?

Having been promised his place at the forefront of the raid, Frank turned his mind to producing a smoke screen that met Keyes's requirements. He established a base in Dover on 24 January and, in the words of the admiral, 'he set to work with feverish energy.' He transferred three officers and 87 men from Stratford to secret workshops and laboratories at the naval dockyard in East Cliff. Most were billeted in private houses, sleeping ten to a room in hammocks.

In the shadow of the famous white cliffs they began working round the clock to produce not only the required smoke screen but an array of other devices that were wanted for the mission. The smoke was given top priority, and Frank quickly came up trumps. Using chloro-sulphonic acid – a colourless liquid obtained from the reaction of hydrogen chloride gas with sulphur trioxide – he developed a compound that, when injected under pressure into the hot exhausts of motor launches and coastal motor boats, and into the funnels of destroyers, created a dense smoke screen which hung low over the water and was far superior to anything that had been produced before. Just as importantly, it was devoid of a tell-tale flame. The toxic compound had to be handled with great care. It did not tolerate carelessness. An officer on board one of the ships destined to take part in the raid required medical treatment after he gassed himself while tinkering with one of Frank's smoke cylinders. But in every other way the chloro-sulphonic acid did the job to perfection. Looking as delighted as if he had been offered the crown jewels, Keyes described the results as 'wonderful'.

A tactician as well as an inventor, Frank also suggested a previously untried way of deploying the smoke. The earlier plan to attack Zeebrugge's lock gates

Frank's experiments with smoke on land at RNAS Wormwood Scubs before the raid.

had entailed laying down a smoke screen some five miles from the target in a wind speed of five or six mph. It was dismissed at the time as being too long and laborious. Frank told Keyes he believed there was a better way. He proposed that coastal motor boats should go in close to the Mole – to within a few yards if possible – and lay smoke screens at full speed as they dashed to and fro across the flotilla's line of approach. He set up a series of sea trials and proved to Keyes's satisfaction that such a method could be highly effective. Sold on the idea, Keyes gave Frank a free hand to fit out a posse of 30 coastal motor boats accordingly.

Then, at the end of February, came a blow. It emerged that the manufacturers of the chloro-sulphonic acid needed to make Frank's smoke could not supply sufficient quantities in time for a mid-March attack. Only 19 of the required 82 tons had been delivered. Even an April assault now looked unlikely. At the rate the acid was arriving, it might not be possible to mount the raid until August, by which time the war could well be over. Keyes took the news badly, describing it later as 'an unpleasant shock'. He summoned Frank to his office and discovered he was already aware of the problem and was working on an alternative system of producing smoke from another liquid, stannic-chloride, carried in cylinders. Over the next two nights Frank trialled the new system in front of a sullen Keyes, but the admiral was unimpressed. While the stannic-chloride proved efficient at breaking up searchlight beams, the weight of the cylinders was too heavy to be carried in sufficient numbers on the motor boats. At best the system would be good for an hour and a half. For an operation which might extend from midnight to dawn and beyond, it was a non-starter.

The firebrand admiral did not hide his irritation. In what may have been the only time in his military career that Frank was the subject of official criticism, Keyes wrote to Admiral Beatty, Commander-in-Chief of the Grand Fleet, telling him that even if the rest of the preparations for the raid were completed (which he conceded was unlikely) the lack of effective smoke ruled out a mid-March operation. He added:

> Brock means well, I believe, and has been invaluable in providing the latest trench warfare devices and special rockets and flares – but I am afraid he is unreliable and he has certainly let me down in the matter of smoke.

Keyes's verdict on the fiercely loyal and energetic inventor of the Brock bullet and the Dover Flare was borne out of frustration, and possibly because he wanted to divert attention from other problems that were holding up the mission. He was an impulsive man who was quick to criticise, and he probably regretted the comment as soon as he had made it. The truth, as he well knew, was that obtaining special materials was an extremely difficult task when the output of every large firm in the country was already earmarked for other purposes. It was made that much harder because the need for secrecy meant the demands from Dover could not be supported by explanations as to their purpose. While Frank continued his experiments with stannic-chloride, Keyes adopted a new, more constructive tack. He contacted the Admiralty and urged it to use every means possible to deliver the required 63 tons of chloro-sulphonic acid to Dover by the beginning of April.

The root of the problem quickly emerged. Chloro-sulphonic acid was a key ingredient of several synthetic products. One of these was the sugar substitute, saccharin. The main producer of saccharin was the pharmaceutical firm of Burroughs, Wellcome & Co, which marketed it under the trade name Saxin and sold it in large quantities to diabetics. As it happened, questions about the possible health risks of saccharin had been raised in the House of Lords the previous year. Despite a reassuring answer from the Board of Agriculture, there remained lingering doubts about its safety. This provided a perfect excuse for the government to have it withdrawn from the market. The Admiralty appealed to the War Cabinet, and days later the manufacture of Saxin was temporarily shut down. All supplies of chlorosulphonic acid were diverted to Frank's workshops, and for several weeks diabetics and dieters drank their tea unsweetened, grumbling about yet another war-time shortage and quite unaware that they had helped to put the Zeebrugge operation back on track.

As smoke screen production returned to full swing, any misgivings that Keyes had briefly harboured about Frank were quickly forgotten. One of Frank's trials in the Dover Strait was so successful that the fog he generated refused to dissipate itself for three days, resulting in complaints from mercantile captains about the inaccuracy of the Admiralty's weather forecasts. Balancing the ledger, Keyes would write of Frank afterwards:

> During the weeks of preparation I saw him constantly, and his services were simply invaluable to me …. The value of Brock's contribution to the undertaking was simply incalculable … he was always full of the most optimistic enthusiasm and this sometimes led him into undertaking more than was humanly possible to carry out under war conditions of production. Nevertheless he was incapable of contemplating failure and set to work with extraordinary energy to develop every possible source of supply.

Numerous other devices wanted for Operation *Z-O* – as Keyes, with a surprising lack of subtlety, had code-named the mission – were by now taking shape in Frank's workshops. One requirement was special buoys. A night attack in enemy waters would make it difficult for the armada to reach Zeebrugge with the accurate positioning and timing needed. Ordinary buoys might be spotted by the Germans if laid too far in advance of the operation, and would take too long to be lowered on the actual night. What was needed were buoys that would burst into light when placed in the sea by a single boat and which would guide the ships of the attacking force to their destination. Frank designed and delivered the prototype in the shape of a floating calcium flare within 24 hours.

Smoke screens for the larger ships in the armada, created by feeding solid cakes of phosphide and calcium into containers of water, were also developed and successfully tested. So were flares to be dropped by aircraft and flare rockets to be fired by surface vessels. Frank suggested QF (Quick-Firing) guns would be needed for use on the main assault ship, and managed to obtain some through his close contacts in the Trench Warfare Department. In a well-guarded storeroom his men stockpiled portable flamethrowers and phosphorus grenades for use on the Mole. Also in production were two powerful oil-fed flamethrowers designed to blast the German gun batteries on arrival at the Mole and hopefully to put them out of action before the assault parties went ashore. A seaman who saw Frank and his men testing one of these fearsome weapons on the deck of a ship recalled:

They sent a spray of liquid fire over the quarter-deck and I should not care for an embrace of that kind. There was something horribly fascinating about the long flames curling and twisting in the air like luminous serpents.

Frank was in a unique position to speed up the acquisition of vital components needed for the raid. As well as ordering material and equipment from the Air Board and from Stratford, he had no hesitation in asking his father for assistance whenever it was quicker and easier to do so. 'I will be glad if you will make me the following,' he wrote to Brock's in March. 'Twelve volley firers with two-minute delay and four chances, with four 16ft tails of instantaneous fuse … further, 300 Incendiary Grenades according to the pattern designed by me, to be fitted with four-second delays.' A day later he wrote: 'Gentlemen, I shall be glad if you will prepare for me 300 light rockets,' and proceeded in his letter to provide precise specifications. These and other orders were fulfilled within days and arrived in secret consignments from Sutton. Arthur was as keen as Frank to land a stinging blow on Kaiser Bill, that old and pompous acquaintance of his from the Crystal Palace days.

Captain Alfred Carpenter, who had been selected to command the main attack ship, and who was in regular contact with Frank in the run-up to the raid,

'Flame projectors, far exceeding anything hitherto known, were mooted. Brock produced them also.' – Captain Carpenter VC. RN. (IWM HU_131 799)

'[Frank] also designed immense flame throwers for the Vindictive...'. (*Naval Memoirs*, Sir Roger Keyes). One of the two large static flamethrowers provided by Frank for the *Vindictive* shown at an IWM Zeebrugge exhibition in 1961. (IWM MH_006896)

was dazzled by his ability to meet almost any requirement quickly and efficiently. Always buoyant, always positive, Frank frequently attended conferences in the captain's cabin to discuss all aspects of the operation. Together he and Carpenter calculated exactly where the smoke screens needed to be laid. Keyes recalled:

> The greatest credit is due to Brock and Carpenter for the way in which these details were worked out, and the clarity of the instructions. If the wind would only remain fairly constant between the limits given, I felt confident that the smoke-making arrangements would enable us to close our objective without annihilation. I would not have undertaken the enterprise had I thought otherwise.

Carpenter, who believed Frank was a 'natural for special operations' described him as a 'whizz-bang man and warrior-poet dedicated to the art of warfare as much as to the pursuit of intellectual study and reflection.' He wrote afterwards: 'No matter what our requirements were, Brock was undefeated. With a highly scientific brain he possessed extraordinary knowledge of almost any subject.' He also applauded Frank's self-confidence and optimism, these being key to maintaining morale among the hard-working RNAS workforce from Stratford. 'His geniality and humour were hard to beat,' noted Carpenter. 'But of all his qualities, optimism perhaps held first place. At times we, who were far from being pessimistic, thought his optimism excessive, but it was justified absolutely with regard to the success of the enterprise.' In the words of one of Carpenter's officers,

Lieutenant Commander Robert Rosoman, Frank was simply 'the clever devil who invented the smoke screen upon which the success of the venture hinged…'

One nervous new recruit was said to have remarked on his first day in Dover, 'I've never done a job with live explosives before' to which Frank replied, 'I've never done one without.' Frank was seen as 'superbly well organized and controlled – a creature of habit' who worked his way through carefully constructed lists of tasks he laid out each day. He required as much from himself as from others. Christopher Sandford, writing in his *Zeebrugge* book, described how on one occasion, 'wanting to assess the waterproof qualities of a particular explosive compound (Frank) had stripped off and swam two miles out into the straits of Dover with a waxed polythene bag filled with volatile chemicals tied to his waist. One of the team waiting anxiously for his return remembered the sight of "the skipper, semi-naked, body thickly oiled in workshop grease, and only the whites of his eyes visible through a mask of slime" calmly emerging to announce, "Well boys, I'm alive!".'

Frank's optimistic nature typically demonstrated itself when he telephoned Captain Henry Halahan, who had been selected to command the naval storming party, to speak to him about some aspect of the raid. He mentioned in passing the looking-glass he had broken, prompting Halahan to remark jocularly: 'That means seven years of bad luck.' Frank replied instantly: 'Never mind, it shows that I'm going to live for another seven years anyway.'

Not that he failed to consider the possibility of death. During the final build-up to the raid, most of the men sought quiet corners at the end of the day to write home. One of Frank's letters to G contained important practical advice. A year previously he had been involved in an angry exchange of letters with the Ministry of Munitions, which was trying to claim ownership of the Brock bullet. He had told the Ministry that their action was 'absolutely out of order'. He successfully fought off their claim, forcing the ministry to concede that the bullet was his and his alone. He was, however, still concerned about the amount of royalties he would receive from his invention.

If he was killed, he told G, she should press his claim for a generous award. In 1916 the Munitions Inventions Department had decided that a total of £70,000 should be awarded to those involved in ending the Zeppelin scourge. At a fraction over 31 per cent, Frank's share of this sum had been calculated as less than that of Pomeroy's at 35 per cent. The lower level of Frank's award was due to the fact that some of his work on the Brock bullet was considered a facet of his 'day job' as a naval officer, whereas Pomeroy had worked in a purely private capacity. Frank was not happy with this computation. It was his contention the bullet fell outside the scope of his official RNAS duties because it had been developed at his own expense and in his spare time. Not only that. Both he and the pilots were in no doubt that Brock bullets had been primarily responsible for the early successes against airships. In his letter to G, he urged her to push for an award at least as great as Pomeroy's if he was no longer around to do so himself.

By the end of March, Keyes' plans were in place. The ships were ready, the men selected, and the equipment all in good working order. Dover teemed with four-stripe captains. Detailed drawings of the ports at Zeebrugge and Ostend had been obtained from engineers who had worked on their construction and who were now refugees in France and England. British aviators, using the type of camera pioneered by Frank himself, had photographed every portion of the Mole from almost every conceivable angle, and artists had made a plasticine model of it for the assault parties to study.

Finding men for the mission – and they were all volunteers – had been easy. Even though Britain was tired and its manpower reservoir was running low, officers and enlisted men signed up for the mission in droves. None were told the identity of the target. They only knew that it was to be an operation of immense importance and great danger. They were given training in night fighting, bombing, bayonet attacks and trench raiding. Winston Churchill, now Minister of Munitions, told the Royal Marines taking part: 'You are going on a daring and arduous stunt from which none of you may return, but every endeavour will be made to bring back as many of you as possible. Should any of you, for any reason whatsoever, desire not to go you may on dismissal of this parade go to your company office, hand in your name and not a word will be said.' Not one man dropped out. As Captain Carpenter recalled: 'It was generally conceded that the Hun, wherever he was to come to close quarters with such antagonists, would have an uncomfortable evening.'

Among those selected for the mission was a detachment of 34 RNAS men from Stratford, chosen by Frank from a large group of volunteers and christened the 'Pyrotechnic Party'. They would assist with the smoke-making equipment and operate the fixed flame throwers that would blast the Mole's gun batteries. Some would go ashore with hand-held Hay Flame Guns and phosphorus grenades to deliver further nasty surprises. This select team, none of whom had seen action before, was despatched to Wembley for battleground training during February and March. Although all had been warned by Frank of the dangers, they were as determined as their commander to be at the centre of the action. One, Air Mechanic Sidney Hesse, recalled:

> I must have been mad! They told us beforehand that a lot of us wouldn't come back. They said that if you hadn't given your parents a photo, then you should get one because we

probably not get another chance. At the last moment they gave us a chance to pull out. I volunteered, so I'll go. I'm not sorry.

All told, 78 craft had been designated to take part in the raid on Zeebrugge, and a further 59 in the simultaneous assault on Ostend. An elderly three-funnelled cruiser, the 5,600-ton *Vindictive,* on which Frank would sail, had come out of retirement to lead the attack on the Mole. It had been equipped with a false top deck and 18 wooden ramps to get the landing parties on top of the 29ft high sea wall as quickly and as efficiently as possible. The ship bristled with newly installed weaponry. An 11in howitzer had been mounted on the quarter-deck, a 7.5in howitzer on the forecastle and another on the false deck. Prominent on its upper deck were two mattress-protected steel shelters, fore and aft, in which Frank's men had installed his two deadly flamethrowers. Given the fire hazard inherent with so much wood built into the new structures on *Vindictive's* decks and the warmth of the reception she would likely face, men were later comforted by the way all exposed timber would be doused with a mysterious 'anti-fire mixture' supplied by Frank.

Vindictive was a strange-looking craft, and Captain Carpenter recalled that one man remarked as he boarded it: 'Well, it's darned good to be aboard a blessed something, but I'm blowed if I know what she is.' Able Seaman Wilfred Wainwright, who had been selected to join one of the landing parties, recalled: 'There is no denying it she was ugly, as she lay there, a veritable floating fortress, a deathtrap fitted with all the ingenious contrivances of war that the human brain could think of, but we took unholy pride and a fiendish delight in her.' Anyone walking round the ship during the build-up to the attack was liable to hear blood-curdling yells and see a party of men charge round a corner with fixed bayonets and brandishing loaded ash sticks called knob-kerries as they hurled themselves at an imaginary foe. In a letter home, Engineer Commander William Bury gave an unintended significance to his words when he wrote: 'We quite expected to put up a good Brock's Benefit if hit.'

In all, some 1,700 men had been selected to take part in the Zeebrugge raid in various capacities. Of these, 600 Royal Marines and 200 navy Bluejackets were to go ashore at the Mole. Those for whom there was not room on *Vindictive* would sail behind her on two tough old Merseyside ferryboats, *Iris* and *Daffodil.* The advantage of these unlikely combat vessels was that they drew less than nine feet of water, so enabling them – with luck – to cross minefields. Three obsolete light cruisers, *Thetis, Iphigenia* and *Intrepid,* had been chosen to end their careers blocking the entrance to the Zeebrugge canal, each carrying an adroitly placed cargo of concrete to make them hard to move once they had been scuttled. Once the blockships were in place, their crews would be picked up and taken to safety in small boats under the cover of Frank's smoke, although Keyes had warned them it was more likely they would end up as prisoners of war. That was assuming they were lucky enough to survive in the first place. As one of *Vindictive*'s gunnery officers, Lieutenant Commander Edward Hilton Young, recalled:

> I think that everybody was fairly sure that *Vindictive* would go down with a great many casualties, and that a certain number would get picked up by the small craft or struggle ashore and be made prisoner. At any rate there was some sort of chance that one might come through, and since there was a chance it was unnecessary to confront too definitely an unwelcome possibility.

Two old C-class submarines formed the other important element of the operation. Packed with five tons of amatol, they would proceed to the arches under the Mole viaduct and be blown up. Again, if all went to plan, their crews would be whisked to safety. Other vessels making up the armada included a protective covey of destroyers and, crucially, a flotilla of 33 motor launches which, among other tasks, would lay Frank's smoke screen during the approach. A further 18 coastal motor boats would inject whatever mayhem they could. Over-seeing the operation from one of the destroyers, HMS *Warwick*, would be Keyes himself.

Now it was a question of waiting for the right conditions of moon, tide, wind and weather. A high tide was crucial for positioning the landing ramps on top of the Mole. A light northerly breeze to waft Frank's fog towards the Belgian coast was also essential. Code-breakers in the Admiralty's top secret Room 40 had found a way of intercepting and deciphering encrypted radio reports of the weather conditions at Bruges issued by the Germans to their submarines and patrols. These would be used to give the boats laying Frank's smoke screen the exact direction of the wind.

On 7 April, with the approach of favourable weather conditions, Keyes told the assault parties where they were headed. Until then they had assumed they were going to France, probably to defend Calais in the face of rapid German advances towards the Channel. When they learned the real objective of the expedition they broke out in cheers. RNVR officer Commander Patrick Edwards wrote later:

> I thought it was quite hopeless, but, oh my goodness, it was quite gloriously hopeless. It was desperate; but I realised our position and the frightful losses the U-boats were inflicting on our shipping were also desperate … how lucky I was to be in it.

Able Seaman Wainwright recalled:

> The magnitude of the scheme overwhelmed us, the sheer audacity of tackling a place like Zeebrugge.

There was similar delight when the commander of the marines, Lieutenant Colonel Bertram Eliot, outlined the details to his men on board one of the support ships, HMS *Hindustan*. Frank stood near him to answer questions about the smoke screen. Colour Sergeant E. F. Tracey remembered:

> The Colonel was roundly cheered, which broadened the smile on his face. And standing not far away was the inventor of the smoke screen (which was to save lives) Wing Commander Brock RNAS of Brock's Fireworks.

Waiting was agony. The men champed at the bit. Every day they could feel a bat-like stirring in the air, the distant thunder of the guns in France and Flanders, the sound of British soldiers fighting for their lives against a renewed German onslaught. Freed from fighting on the Eastern Front following the Russian exit from the war after the Bolshevik Revolution of 1917, Germany was concentrating all her forces on the Western Front in one last offensive. Her aim was to defeat the British and French armies before the fresh but untried troops of the United States could turn the tide. The initial success of the new German offensive brought Britain nearer to defeat than at any other time in the war. By 21 March, the enemy had advanced an astonishing 28 miles. The Allies had their backs to the wall. Up and down the country newspapers were scanned apprehensively every morning as people wondered how it would all end.

In Dover everyone from Keyes downwards was desperate to get going and do their bit to hit back at the enemy. At last the moment came. Or so they thought. On the evening of 11 April, Keyes told the ships to 'raise steam', and the motley fleet set off towards the Belgian coast. Everything depended, Keyes knew, on the wind being in the right direction to blow Frank's smoke shorewards. He wrote later:

> My thoughts constantly turned to the assault on Santa Cruz in the island of Tenerife in July 1797, when Nelson's impatient ardour impelled him to undertake a hazard, which was foredoomed by the state of the weather.

For several hours, everything seemed to be going to plan. Demolition charges for use on the Mole were brought on to *Vindictive*'s upper deck. Ammunition was made ready, and small arms inspected. Emergency lighting and gas masks were tested. Frank checked and re-checked his two large flamethrowers. Keyes ordered the first of a series of coded one-word signals declaring that Operation Z-O was on. Hopes were high.

Then, when they were fewer than 90 minutes from their destination, the wind changed from north to south. Keyes was 'horribly tempted' to continue all the same, even though he knew that Frank's blanketing shroud would be blown back in their faces. He recalled: 'I went through a pretty difficult time

HMS *Vindictive* fully rigged and on her way to Zeebrugge. (Paul Kendall Collection)

during the next few moments. I knew that every man in the expedition felt as I did, keyed up for the ordeal. How they would hate to be called off and then asked to undertake it all over again.' As Captain Carpenter reflected later: 'He who risks nothing attains nothing. Discretion is the better part of valour. What was it to be?' Finally Keyes made his decision. The fleet turned back.

He explained to the disappointed men the next day that without an effective smoke screen they 'would not have a dog's chance' of completing the mission. He wanted, he told them, to have 'a great success, not a heroic disaster.' He wrote later:

> I swore before Heaven that I would take them alongside the enemy, but they must trust me and wait until I considered that we could undertake the business with a fair prospect of success. Their shout of approval and ringing cheers lifted the awful cloud of depression, and I think we all felt happier. At any rate I know I did.

Two nights later the armada set off again. On this occasion Frank, held up by administrative work on shore, nearly missed the sailing. He had to be taken out to *Vindictive* on a destroyer, along with a letter from Keyes declaring: 'We must push in tonight.' But it was not to be. This time near gale-force winds forced the flotilla to return to port after only two hours.

Another nine long days went by. The men on the ships, unable to go ashore in case information about the raid leaked out, forbidden even to send or receive letters, grew increasingly frustrated. It was like living in a vacuum. Keyes described it as 'the most trying week of my life.' Then, on Monday 22 April, the conditions looked promising again. Keyes resolved that this time there would be no turning back. He knew that the Admiralty, already concerned that security had been stretched to the limit, would not allow another cancellation. It had to be third time lucky.

CHAPTER 13

Brock of the Mole

Even now the weather was far from ideal. The northerly wind, essential for the success of Frank's smoke screen, was erratic. The moon was full and visibility off the Belgian coast was good. There was a risk that the collection of destroyers, launches, old submarines and Mersey ferry-boats would be spotted by the Germans while still miles from Zeebrugge. Nevertheless, Keyes, straining at the leash, knew it was now or never.

Over the weekend Frank had managed to slip home to South London to see the pregnant G and two-year-old Anne. He also found time to play a round of golf at his local course, Raynes Park (later Malden Golf Club), with a fellow member, K. B. Bayliss. No one could have guessed from his cool, confident demeanour on the tees and fairways that he was about to play a key role in one of the most daring raids in history.

Dressed in khaki, as required of all members of the raiding parties, he arrived back in Dover early on the morning of 22 April, his trademark pipe clamped firmly between his teeth, his cap slanted jauntily to the left. Although he was still fighting fit, the war had aged him, and he looked older than his 33 years. In his arms he carried a mysterious wooden case marked: 'Explosives – Handle with great care.' People stared at it as he climbed *Vindictive*'s gangway. What was Brocky up to now? Did the case contain some fiendish new invention to be deployed on the Mole? One thing was certain. Here was a man not to be messed with. During a recent trip home he had succeeded in bringing down a snipe on the wing while practising with a revolver. Frank Brock clearly meant business.

To add to his mystique, he was now in the extremely rare position of having held commissions in all three branches of the armed services – possibly the only man in World War I to have done so. He had begun the war in the Army as a temporary lieutenant in the Royal Artillery, before transferring to the Navy three months later as a lieutenant in the Royal Naval Air Service. At the beginning of April 1918 the RNAS had merged with the Army's Royal Flying Corps to become the Royal Air Force. Although in practice Frank was unaffected by the change, and still sported the gold stripes of a naval commander on his khaki, he was now officially listed as an acting lieutenant colonel in the RAF. It was yet another striking aspect of his remarkable career.

At 5.00 pm, after Frank had posed for a group photograph with Captain Carpenter and other senior officers on the deck of *Vindictive*, the fleet set sail. Earlier in the day, Roger Keyes's wife, Eva, had walked down to the pier to say goodbye to her husband on the flagship, HMS *Warwick*. She told him that the next day was St George's Day – he had not realised this – and that England's patron saint was sure to bring the mission good fortune. Her parting words were to beg him to use 'St George for England' as the fleet's battle cry. A little before nightfall, the armada mustered near the Goodwin Sands. As the sun set, a strange quietness fell over the ships as the men reflected on what lay ahead. Frank was not alone in wondering if he would see the sun rise again in the morning.

Recalling his wife's plea, Keyes sent a semaphore signal from *Warwick* to Captain Carpenter on *Vindictive*: 'St George for England'. After a brief pause, Carpenter's reply flickered back: 'May we give the dragon's tail a damned good twist.' Operation *Z-O* was on. Earlier, Frank's curious wooden case had been hoisted gingerly on to the *Vindictive*'s upper deck. With an enigmatic smile he carried it to Captain Carpenter's fore cabin. Fellow officers crowded round inquisitively and clapped him on the back when they saw what was inside. Like a conjuror producing rabbits from a hat, Frank lifted out several bottles of vintage port.

During a convivial dinner in the fore cabin, Frank shared out some of the port with four other officers – Captain Henry Halahan, the commander of the naval storming parties and, incidentally, a fellow old boy of Dulwich College; Lieutenant Colonel Bertram Eliot, commander of the Marines contingent; Eliot's second-in-command, Major Alexander Cordner; and Commander Seymour Osborne, the gunnery officer. There were toasts to a successful mission, and a vow to polish off another bottle or two during the homeward voyage. '*Detur Soli Deo Gloria*' ('Glory be Given to God Alone') intoned Frank and Captain Halahan, remembering their old school motto as they clinked glasses. There may even have been time for cigars. Ever practical, Frank kept in his pocket a tiny silver cigar-cutter shaped like a clown.

Beneath the joviality, there was inevitably an undercurrent of foreboding. Nobody was in much doubt as to how the odds lay. They knew that going ashore would be something akin to playing Russian roulette, but with five of the six chambers loaded. As it turned out, only one of the five men sitting round the table in Captain Carpenter's cabin that night would still be alive six hours later.

Having so recently returned from seeing his family, even the normally ebullient Frank was in a reflective mood. Earlier in the day he had taken aside Lieutenant Commander Arthur Langley, one of his colleagues from the Experimental Station at Stratford, and told him about his daughter Anne, adding: 'If I come back from this stunt and she asks me what I did in the war I shall be able to tell her.'

The Belgian coast was drawing closer. Frank's calcium flares, laid a few hours earlier, were leading the attacking force to its destination with total accuracy. There was hardly any motion of *Vindictive* in the calm sea. Only the squeaks and rattles down below, and the wind singing in her rigging, were a reminder of the ship's remorseless advance towards Zeebrugge. Though Frank did not know it, somewhere beneath him on the sea floor lay the wreckage of Lieutenant Wenninger's *UB-55*, destroyed that morning after she was pinned in his Dover Flares and forced into the mines of the Cross-Channel Barrage. Already that day, he had helped to deliver another deadly blow against the Germans.

Moonlight silvered the North Sea. Off to the east the summer lightning of the restless artillery in Flanders rose and fell on the horizon. From the bridge of *Warwick*, Roger Keyes could see every vessel of his rag tag flotilla sharp and clearly defined in the baleful glare of the full moon. With her hinged landing ramps sticking out, the *Vindictive* looked rather like a giant beetle with eighteen legs on her port side. The shapes of destroyers and the white curl of their bow-waves were visible to starboard. Off to the rear came the blockships, accompanied by a posse of small boats. Visibility was a worrying eight miles or more. Keyes mentioned this to the ship's captain, Wilfred Tomkinson, who responded drily: 'Well, even if the enemy expects us, they will never think we are such damned fools as to try and do it in bright moonlight.'

At 10.30 pm the flotilla split into two, with the Ostend force altering course for its separate destination. Zeebrugge was now just 15 miles away and the Germans still had no idea they were coming. *Vindictive* sailed on in silence with her faithful ferry-boats, *Iris* and *Daffodil*, at her heels. Her mascots, two black cats, Mr Thomas and Mrs Tabitha, roamed unconcernedly about the lower part of the ship. Perhaps they, or perhaps St George himself, were responsible for the good luck that now came the fleet's way, for suddenly the rain began to fall in fat, hard drops. Clouds obscured the moon and a welcome mist descended over the water. Visibility was reduced to less than a mile. Although the weather was now in the fleet's favour, the rain and cloud prevented any aircraft cover (so much for Frank's aircraft flares) but that was a small price to pay for the inky darkness that now enveloped them.

Frank donned his greatcoat and went out into the salt-damp night. The tension and expectation made him want to flex his muscles. He carried with him, as he always did, a pocket edition of the New Testament, his favourite possession. His knowledge of its contents was comprehensive, and he touched the book for good luck as he strode along the upper deck. It was 11.00 pm. One hour to go. The thought uppermost in his mind was the weather. Would the wind remain favourable for his fog? Beneath a lucky horseshoe attached to one of the funnels – given to *Vindictive* by Eva Keyes – he carried out a final check of his deadly flamethrowers and buoyed up their operators with words of encouragement.

Satisfied that all was in order, Frank began arming himself to the teeth. Mills Bombs, manufactured at his father's Sutton factory and his own design of phosphorus incendiary grenades (intended to fire and destroy anything that took his fancy on the Mole) joined the two holstered pistols at his side. Mindful that it might be necessary to repel boarders at Zeebrugge and that the plan of attack envisaged close-quarter action on the Mole, several of the officers going ashore armed themselves with the 1900 pattern cutlass. With its distinctive broad blade, black grip and knuckle-guard it was the Navy's favourite edged weapon but Frank was seen to arm himself with his private short sword, curved like a scimitar and possibly acquired on one of his many foreign travels. Even now he had another weapon to fall back on. He patted his pocket and felt his Intelligence-issue knuckle-duster inside it. If all else failed, he was fully prepared to slip it on and use his fists. Burglars embarking on a night's thieving must feel like this. The final additions to his equipment were a set of spanners and the obligatory gas mask. There was no knowing what the Germans might throw at them, and he was ready now for whatever the night had in store.

He exuded confidence. His remarkable imperturbability was an inspiration to those around him, particularly the men from the experimental station at Stratford, who were bracing themselves for their first experience of battle. With his cutlass and pistols, and with a tot of vintage port inside him, he had the determination and athletic confidence of the Pirate King in Gilbert & Sullivan. This was a man you would want by your side in the jungle.

At 11.15 pm the order for 'action stations' was given. The men of the bayonet-and-bomb brigade who were to go on to the Mole had spent the voyage sleeping, reading and playing cards down below. Men like Private Jim Clist, who now scooped up the pennies he had won and placed them in his breast pocket as protection against the bullets and shrapnel he expected to encounter. His friend, Private Fred 'Curly' Freeman, convinced he was going to be killed, cut off a lock of his hair and gave it to Clist as a memento. (Freeman would be dead within the hour, but Clist survived.)

Tots of rum were ladled out to those who wanted it. Then they all wished each other good luck, said goodbye in case they did not make it, and clattered up the iron stairways. From the steel shelter containing the aft flamethrower, Frank watched them assemble on the main deck, shoulder to shoulder in five ranks, waiting to be let loose. At 11.30 pm the Blankenberge light buoy bobbed past. This told Frank that they were five miles from Zeebrugge. Rifles were loaded. Soft clicks confirmed that bayonets were fixed. The surgeons discreetly prepared their operating instruments. The chaplain, Charles Peshall, said a prayer. Everyone spoke in whispers. Almost the only noise was the propellers breaking the water. Frank was perhaps thinking of Kipling's 'Hymn Before Action':

> Ere yet we loose the legions –
> Ere yet we draw the blade,
> Jehovah of the Thunders,
> Lord God of Battles, aid!

Not far from Frank, Lieutenant Edward Hilton Young, commander of one of *Vindictive*'s guns, turned a Nelsonic blind eye to the cigarette ends that were glowing in the dark in breach of the regulations. The waiting men, he decided, should be allowed a little leeway. He wrote later:

> Up till the very last moment that night it was impossible to realise with any vivid conviction that the great adventure was actually about to happen. The ship was stealing along in such profound silence, the sea all round was so completely tranquil, the darkness was so limitless and so empty, that it seemed as if we might go on thus for ever. So the minutes passed until now it was a quarter to twelve, and suddenly there came a shock of conviction – we must be within a mile or two of the Mole, and we are holding our course; in ten minutes we shall be into it.

Like wolves in the dark, the coastal motor boats had slipped ahead of the flotilla. Now, as they ran up close to the great concrete finger of the Mole, they began belching out Frank's artificial fog. Clouds of dense smoke billowed across the water, rendering the main body of the fleet invisible. The Germans were confused. They could see no further than a few yards. What did this wizardry portend? What was Tommy up to? Did the skittering motor boats

Motor launches laying smoke. (IWM HU_130 292)

herald a full-scale attack, or were they just up to a bit of mischief? Was there something out there in the fog or wasn't there? Their searchlights poked at the smoke like nervous, probing fingers. Star shells soared, hung, disappeared. The commanding officer of the Mole battery, Kapitanleutnant Robert Schutte, an experienced professional who was known to his gun crews as 'The Pope of the Mole', ordered his guns to fire blind. Small-arms fire spattered the water. All to no avail. The German projectiles passed harmlessly over the invisible flotilla. The searchlights and pirouetting star shells were unable to pierce the acrid smoke. All the enemy could see was a wall of fog. Thick, impenetrable fog.

On *Vindictive*, visibility was down to barely a yard. The forecastle could not be seen from the bridge. The other ships in the armada were hidden from her in the fog. Cocooned in her own world, the old cruiser pushed on through the loppy water at 16 knots. The men on board counted the seconds. They were nearly there. Foul-smelling and metallic-tasting it might be, but the Brockish vapour was working a treat. Nipping backwards and forwards in front of the Mole, the motor boats kept belching out dense white clouds of Frank's concoction. When the first German star shell went up, *Vindictive's* helmsman, Petty Officer Edwin Youlton, turned to the ship's First Lieutenant, Commander Robert Rosoman, who was standing next to him, and remarked 'We shall get it in the neck, now sir.' Rosoman recalled:

I said 'Yes, I expect so,' but we didn't. I wondered why. Soon I realised that the smoke screen was so good that we could not see the star itself until it had climbed over the artificial fog bank, and so realised the Hun could not see us.

On the bridge of *Vindictive*, Captain Arthur Chater of the Royal Marines peered into the fog in gratitude. 'Star shells started coming over us and we realised how well we were being concealed by the smoke,' he said afterwards. The same thought was going through the mind of Edward Hilton Young:

> As each star fell into the smoke screen that now covered the sea, unless it was within a few hundred yards of us, it was eclipsed as a star and became a large, vague nebula. Although then there was plenty of light about, a few hundred yards from the ship everything was blotted out in wreaths, eddies and whirls of glowing vapour. The German gunners, I imagine, were peering into the vapour, unable to perceive any definite object in the shifting, dazzling glow, and wondering what in the name of goodness was going to come out of it.

In the same vein, Leading Seaman William Childs recalled: 'The artificial smoke screen had been started, and one could scarcely see two yards ahead. The smoke screen was splendid, due to the efforts of Wing Commander Brock, of firework fame.' Ordinary Seaman William O'Hara summed it up in one short sentence: 'We were invisible to the enemy.'

Captain Carpenter was equally impressed, subsequently describing Frank's smoke screen as 'the thickest pea-soup fog' he had ever encountered. He could see nothing through it except the diffused glow of German searchlights and gun flashes. These, fortuitously, were now acting as an aid to navigation and guiding them towards the Mole. 'The screens were so efficient that they undoubtedly prevented the enemy from discovering our presence until we were close to our objective,' he wrote later. On board *Warwick*, Roger Keyes said a silent prayer of thanks to Frank. He would write later: 'The smoke screens were entirely responsible for enabling the whole force to close unseen … a good many people had good reason that night to be thankful for Brock's smoke.' Colour Sergeant E. F. Tracey summed it up with the words: 'Thanks to Wing Commander Brock we were safe … it was good to see the smoke screen drifting towards the Mole and further in like a sea fog.'

As the armada closed in, a marine on *Vindictive* accidentally discharged a shot while loading his revolver. This caused a rattled companion to do the same. Yet thanks to the density of the smoke screen the Germans still had no idea of what was descending on them.

And then, at this critical moment, St George perversely switched sides. At four minutes before midnight, when the *Vindictive* was only a quarter of a mile from the Mole, the wind changed from the northeast and came from the south instead, blowing away Frank's protective blanket of fog. As Captain Carpenter reflected afterwards: 'There is nothing so fickle in the life of a sailor as the wind.' To the German soldiers watching from the Mole, the *Vindictive* looked like a 'phantom ship' as she emerged from the smoke. For a moment they did not react. Possibly they were stunned into disbelief. Then, as the British cruiser became clearly visible, lit from end to end by star shells and the merciless glare of searchlights, they launched all the high explosive they could muster at her.

Instantly the sea around *Vindictive* and the ships nearest her churned with German shell bursts. The six guns on the Mole Extension – four 105mm and two 88mm – could not miss. They blazed away at *Vindictive*'s side and her upper works at almost point-blank range, ripping away pieces of her superstructure. Machine-guns raked the decks with streams of red tracer bullets. Her funnels were shot through like colanders. A German destroyer moored in the harbour joined in the firing. Strips of luminous green beads – the infamous 'flaming onions' – shot into the sky and lost themselves in the clouds. 'I can't see anybody getting out of this lot,' one of Frank's RNAS volunteers, Sidney Hesse, thought to himself.

The packed marines and seamen fell in horrifying numbers. One shell alone killed some 30 men. Lieutenant Colonel Eliot and his second-in-command, Major Cordner, who had dined with Frank hours earlier and drunk his port, died simultaneously when a shell hit the fore-bridge. Another of Frank's fellow diners, Captain Halahan, the man who had warned him the previous month that he faced seven years of bad luck, was fatally felled by machine-gun fire. Marine Ernie Clist recalled:

> We were packed like sardines. When the Germans got on target, they gave us hell, the row was deafening … there must have been thirty or forty of our chaps laid out on the deck, killed or wounded.

At this point Frank himself appears to have had a lucky escape. It seems likely that a bullet penetrated his greatcoat and smashed into a 1901 halfpenny in one of his pockets. That would explain the bent and battered coin that was found in his greatcoat later, Queen Victoria's famous profile almost unrecognizable from the bulging impact of the bullet but for the moment he remained unscathed. His luck was holding, as it had done all his life. Gripping a speaking tube, he barked orders to the operators of the flamethrowers and told them to prepare for action.

It took four hellish minutes for *Vindictive* to close the gap to the Mole. Captain Carpenter called for full speed, steering the shortest course to the

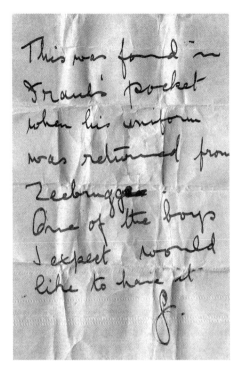

This was found in Frank's pocket when his uniform was returned from Zeebrugge. One of the boys I expect would like to have it. G.

The bullet-damaged halfpenny recovered from the pocket of Frank's greatcoat, which he left behind on the *Vindictive* when he went ashore to fight on the Mole. G gave it to her daughter Anne for one of Anne's sons.

stone mass looming up before him. The ship trembled as her turbines drove her forward. Parts of her deck and superstructure were ablaze, and flames shot from the gaping holes in her lacerated funnels. The ventilators, bridges and chart house were riddled with bullets and shrapnel. Her guns roared back defiance but could not silence the German batteries. The noise of the battle could be heard in at least four countries – in Belgium, Holland, France and across the Channel on the Kent coast. Seaman Wilfred Wainwright recalled:

> Every gun in the *Vindictive* that could bear had now given tongue and the night was made hideous by the nerve-racking chatter of the pompoms, the deep bell-like boom of the howitzers and trench mortars, and the all pervading rattle of musketry and machine-gun fire; it was hell with a vengeance.

Even now, the small boats kept pouring out Frank's smoke in a bid to protect the armada. Edward Hilton Young recalled:

> Quick as thought, one of the motor craft grasped the situation and dashed forward, leaping – almost flying – across the waves with furious haste, pouring out smoke as she came. She

swung across our bows, right between us and the batteries and under the very muzzles of their guns, and vanished into her own smoke unharmed. It was a gallant act, and glorious to see.

Finally, at one minute past midnight, Carpenter swung *Vindictive* hard against the Mole. She was precisely 60 seconds behind schedule. Her screws thrashed violently. Bobbing up and down like a cork in the frothing water, she was unable to close the gap between her hull and the wall, making it impossible to position the gangways. Salvation arrived in the shape of the ferry *Daffodil*, which shoved *Vindictive* against the Mole and held her there. As the gap reduced, the surviving members of the storming parties clambered over the mass of dead and wounded on the decks and prepared to scramble ashore. Unfortunately the wash caused by the ship's speedy arrival had ground her against the wall, smashing landing ramps not already wrecked by enemy gunfire. Only two of the 18 ramps built to get the stormers ashore were still intact. To make matters worse, the swell had caused *Vindictive* to overshoot her intended position by some 300 yards, and the stormers were faced with a section of the Mole they found unfamiliar.

High up on the port side of *Vindictive*'s foretop, unprotected by the sea wall which now shielded most of the rest of the ship from the enemy's guns, Frank's two flamethrower cabins endured a blitz of machine-gun bullets and shrapnel. Every German gun within two miles was trained on the bucking and rearing cruiser, which rang like a gong from the constant pounding. The pyrotechnics were noisier and more brilliant than anything Frank had laid on at the Crystal Palace, the White City or anywhere else. Lance Corporal George Calverley, on board *Iris*, described the maelstrom of shells as being like Dante's Inferno. Such was the carnage on *Vindictive*'s upper deck that the chaplain felt compelled to risk his life time and again to assist the over-worked stretcher teams.

Frank had originally hoped to deploy the flamethrowers against the enemy's gun emplacements, but these were frustratingly out of range because the cruiser had not arrived at the designated spot. Instead he decided to use them against any Germans who might be sheltering near the ship. This moment represents an early example of how many conflicting accounts emerged of the raid. The established British position suggested that having seen his artificial fog utilised to such good effect, he had high hopes for the flamethrowers, but was to be disappointed. Lighting the ignition apparatus of the aft flamethrower, he gave the order to switch on. The oil ran its course, but at the last moment a piece of shrapnel destroyed the ignition system, narrowly missing Frank himself. Instead of emitting a flame, the nozzle spurted out jets of thick and extremely

'The Storming of the Mole', a famous painting by Charles De Lacy. It shows *Vindictive* being held against the Mole by the ferry *Daffodil*. Marines and Blue jackets storm ashore while the night sky is lit by gunfire and Frank's illuminating rockets designed to show the block ships where the Mole ended. (Author's copy, framed in wood taken from *Vindictive*'s decks after the war)

inflammable oil over the decks. Things were no better at the forward cabin. The flamethrower's nozzle was shot away just as Lieutenant Arthur Eastlake gave the order to switch on, rendering it useless. Almost simultaneously another shell cut its oil supply pipes, sending gallons of oil pouring into the first-aid post beneath the conning tower.

However, one German soldier sheltering in a building closer to the northern end of the Mole subsequently reported the 'monstrous scene' that he had witnessed when a jet of liquid fire from the *Vindictive*'s upper deck ignited a flash grenade held in a friend's ammunition belt. 'The accursed individual (had) become a screaming human beacon', he said.

Whatever the truth, the flamethrowers were done for and standing there listening to cries of 'I'm hit, I'm hit!' Frank was said to have remarked 'It's awful to feel so ineffectual'. Never one to dwell on setbacks and realising there was no more he could usefully do on the ship, Frank decided the time had come to reap the dividends of all those months of hard work and

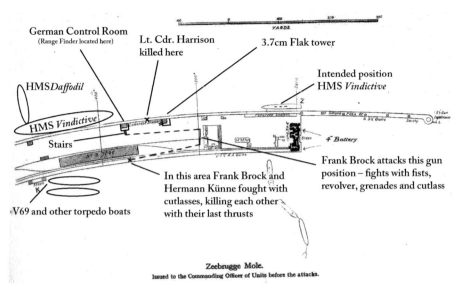

German Control Room
(Range Finder located here)

Lt. Cdr. Harrison killed here

3.7cm Flak tower

HMS *Daffodil*

Intended position HMS *Vindictive*

HMS *Vindictive*

Stairs

4" Battery

Frank Brock attacks this gun position – fights with fists, revolver, grenades and cutlass

In this area Frank Brock and Hermann Künne fought with cutlasses, killing each other with their last thrusts

V69 and other torpedo boats

Zeebrugge Mole.
Issued to the Commanding Officer of Units before the attacks.

Frank's likely journey on the Mole. It is not known whether he managed to get onto the lighthouse extension. Reports were contradictory in the immediate aftermath of the Raid but M. Ryheul's recent detailed study is confident of his last movements.

inventiveness and go ashore. His blood was up and he wanted to give the Germans a kicking. His latest phosphorus grenades needed to be tested in action and there was also the matter of his booty in the shape of the Goertz sound-ranging apparatus that he was sure was on the Mole. Perhaps, too, he hoped to find those lethal 'flaming onions' so feared by British pilots, and tonight very much in evidence. One way or another, there was no stopping him from leaving the ship. Handing over command of the pyrotechnics to his chief assistant, Lieutenant Graham Hewett, he flung off his greatcoat and ran through the witches' brew of smoke and flames to the forward gangway. Several of his RNAS ratings from Stratford followed him. One, a man named Oxenbury, was felled by bullets as he left the flamethrower hut, but Air Mechanic Roland Entwisle, who had been trying to help ignite the aft flamethrower, managed to stay with him.

By now the two surviving ramps had been secured to the Mole under almost impossibly dangerous conditions. They rose and fell violently above a black 30ft chasm as *Vindictive* bucked and reared in the turbulent waters created by her wash. Somehow keeping their balance, a naval raiding party led by Lieutenant-Commander Bryan Adams and a Royal Marine party under Captain Chater swarmed up them on to the Mole parapet. The air above their heads crackled with machine-gun bullets. Frank was close behind. Reaching the forward ramp, he found himself having to climb over several dead bodies at the edge of the deck. One of the men lying there, Lieutenant Harold Walker, the son of a general, was still alive, his left hand and lower arm smashed by gunfire. Waving his remaining arm, he shouted: 'Good luck to you, good luck', as Frank and Entwisle stormed up the see-sawing ramp and arrived on the Mole parapet.

Dropping down to the floor of the Mole, Frank sprinted forward and caught up with Adams's depleted raiding party. Without waiting for the area to be secured, he made his way to the front ranks. An unidentified member of the group later told the *Northern Daily Mail*:

> We were one of the earliest crowds to go over and Commander Brock went ahead. It was a fearful job getting over the brow, but the Commander dropped down on to the Mole, a distance of at least ten feet. 'Come on you boys,' he shouted, and one by one we followed him.

The small band of men faced a situation not unlike that of the Light Brigade at Balaclava. Their aim was to attack and, if possible, silence the German guns on the Mole's lighthouse extension which, if not put out of action, might prevent the blockships from reaching the canal entrance. This meant advancing 250 yards through a storm of fire. As Seaman Wainwright described it:

> Once on top of the Mole one was assailed by the overwhelming feeling of nakedness and maddening desire to go forward at all costs and stop the hail of death that swept the Upper Mole. Sense and reason were replaced by insane fury and the events that followed cannot be remembered coherently; it was a horrible nightmare of sweating and cursing men thirsty for blood, the sickening 'sog' of bayonets and of shots at close quarters.

With the rest of Adams's raiding party Frank sprinted towards the Mole extension in the face of intense fire from one or more machine guns. Speed was the thing, he knew. Speed and ruthlessness, and to hell with what might be coming at you. Press forward with your attack and think of nothing else. To a rugby forward like Frank it all came naturally.

After forty yards or so he spotted a stairway, at the bottom of which several Germans were sheltering. He threw a Mills bomb down the steps and fired at the men with his pistol. As the enemy soldiers made a dash for the safety of a moored destroyer, Able Seaman Albert McKenzie took aim and accounted for several of them with his Lewis gun. McKenzie told his brother in a subsequent letter:

> There was a spiral staircase which led down into the Mole, and Commander Brock fired his revolver down and dropped a Mills. You ought to have seen them nip out and try to get across to the destroyer.

The German control tower on the Mole. At the front and looking out to sea is the observation post where Frank inspected the range-finder. (Johan Ryheul Collection)

The flak tower against which Commander Harrison charged with his cutlass drawn, cut down by bullets and killed as he did so. (Johan Ryheul Collection)

The party arrived at a squat concrete look-out post. Above it was some equipment which Frank believed was part of a Goertz range-finder. He told Adams he intended to go inside to investigate, and a seaman lobbed a Mills bomb into the building in case it contained any Germans. There are different accounts as to what happened next. Some reports say that Frank produced spanners and wrenches from his pocket and entered the deserted observation post before climbing up to examine the range-finding apparatus above it. Adams never saw him again after this point. He subsequently concluded that it was around now that Frank met his death, probably from machine-gun fire.

But Frank was far from dead. Numerous reliable accounts, including Keyes's official report to the Admiralty, indicate that he did not spend long at the look-out post and was quickly on the move again with the intention of catching up with the others. Why did he spend such a short time there? It is possible that a brief examination of the equipment told him all he needed to know. Equally, the apparatus may have been incomplete. The all-important microphones, stopwatches and recorders may have been situated further along the Mole. A simpler explanation is that he did not want to miss out on a good scrap. He had seen dozens of men killed on *Vindictive*, and many more on the Mole itself. Honour would have dictated to a man like Frank that he should be at the centre of the action, avenging the deaths of his comrades rather than crouching in a concrete hut.

According to Air Mechanic Entwisle, who had accompanied him off the ship, a machine-gun opened up as Frank sprinted forward again. He recalled:

> I dropped down behind some gear; just at that moment it was very dark and very smoky, and I saw Commander Brock either fall forward or commence to run. I could not say which. When the firing had stopped, I crawled round to see where I had last seen Commander Brock, but there was no sign of him.

As it turned out, Frank was not done for, as Entwisle had feared. His Alamo was yet to come. After Entwisle lost sight of him, he was seen charging towards the lighthouse extension on the Mole, his cutlass in one hand, a pistol in the other, and taking on the crews of two German guns virtually single-handedly. At one point, according to awed witnesses, he used his fists to send them flying after he had emptied his revolver.

Being at the receiving end of a Brock uppercut, albeit one delivered in strict accordance with the Marquess of Queensbury's rules, would not have been a pleasant experience. As a heavyweight boxer, Frank packed a mighty punch. As one of his friends later wrote to *The Times*:

> He was the sort of man who would never dream of going back. I can imagine him being on the Mole at Zeebrugge, and if he lost his revolver, fighting on with his fists.

A sergeant of the Royal Light Marine Infantry told the *Coventry Evening Telegraph* on his return to England:

> Brock rushed among the gun crew, fighting out with his naked fists and knocking over the enemy who tried to bar his path. Behind the brave officer came our men in increasingly large numbers. The Germans put up a hard fight, but they were driven back step by step, and all through one of the finest sights I have ever seen there was Commander Brock letting Jerry have it with his fists. Every time he got his fist a Fritz went home, or at least went down. Very soon they gave him a wide berth, contenting themselves with firing at him. I can't say what happened to him. He disappeared from sight soon after that.

A German marine officer, quoted a fortnight later in *Thomsons Weekly News*, told a similar tale. He spoke of a British officer who seemed to be entirely devoid of fear:

> He did not seem to mind anything. He rushed straight at the first gun, and with his fists he struck out at the gunners, knocking down four of them and putting the rest to flight. The men at the other gun positions tried their hardest to get into action before this attack reached them, but it was all to no purpose. The brave British officer and his men were on top of us, and had overpowered our gunners before they could do anything. I saw clearly that it was this daring officer who was our greatest danger, and I ordered my men to fire on him. It was true there was some danger of hitting our own men, but it was important to knock out the brave British officer, and if that end was achieved I did not care about anything else.

This tallies with another account of the fighting given to the *Northern Daily Mail* by a British warrant officer:

> There were Huns near us in a nest surrounded by barbed wire, but we stormed that and reached one of the guns on the Mole. Commander Brock, single-handed, attacked the gun's crew and we captured the gun and put it out of action. Then we went further along the Mole, and in the light of the star shells, I saw the officer fighting the crew of another gun. The last time I saw him he was removing one of the locks of the gun. He shouted to us to go on, and said he was coming too, but I never saw him again. Another man says that just before we went back to the ship he saw Commander Brock wounded, and being held up against the side of the Mole by two marines, who refused to leave him.

It seems probable that the officer being held up against the side of the Mole was Captain Tuckey of the Royal Marines who had been helping men back towards the *Vindictive*. Even now, though possibly injured, Frank evidently refused to call it a day. German accounts of the fighting suggest that he and a handful of other survivors went on to attack a moored motor torpedo boat, the *V69*, which they believed was a threat to *Vindictive*.

According to more than one report, Frank was on the point of planting demolition charges to blow up the vessel when the group was attacked by a German unit led by Oberleutnant Adolf Rodewald. There followed a savage hand-to-hand fight in which every available weapon was used – rifles, knives, cutlasses, coshes, boots and fists.

It is likely that one of the men in the deadly encounter was Hermann Künne, a 20-year-old crewman from torpedoboat *S53* in which he had served in the battle of Jutland two years earlier and which was now moored beside the V69. The Englishman he took on was almost certainly Frank. German reports speak of Künne attacking an officer armed with a revolver and cutlass and slashing him across the neck with a cutlass. The British officer, though desperately wounded, stabbed the German as he fell.

A German gunnery officer who witnessed the fight, Richard Pollicke, gave a slightly different version of events. He said the British officer, who was on the point of laying demolition charges, stabbed Künne first, and was then stabbed in the neck by the German. Both bodies were found a few feet apart and though nothing can be stated for certain, all the evidence suggests that the British officer was Frank and that this was how he met his death.

This is certainly the firm view of Flemish military historian Johan Ryheul, who has studied the fighting on the Mole in minute detail over several decades. Ryheul believes that all other British officers wearing khaki were reliably accounted for as having been killed elsewhere: Captain Tuckey who died and was being held up against the parapet and Lieutenant-Commander Harrison who died on the parapet walkway attacking the flak tower in the bravest of diversionary charges. No other British officer could have fitted the German description of the Briton who fought and died with Hermann Künne because no others made it to this part of the Mole. He believes that Frank was alone and unaccompanied when he met Künne. No other British bodies were found in that location and had others been with him and escaped they would have reported what they had seen.

As Captain Carpenter commented afterwards, the conditions on the Mole made it impossible to give a connected account of the fighting. It remains possible that Frank died during his earlier headstrong dash towards the German guns. It was a very intense and confusing battle. The only thing we can be completely sure of is that Frank never returned to *Vindictive* and that, like a true rugby player, he played the game to the end.

CHAPTER 14

The Finest Feat

Frank Brock was such a larger than life character that many of those who took part in the raid refused at first to accept that he had been mortally wounded. Commander Seymour Osborne, the sole survivor of the dinner party held on *Vindictive* on the evening of the raid, told a journalist on his return to Dover: 'I don't think he is dead. He is like a cat with nine lives. I should not be surprised to hear he is a prisoner.' The same unwillingness to believe that Frank had been killed was widespread for days afterwards, even though the First Lord of the Admiralty, Sir Eric Geddes, in a statement about the raid to the House of Commons on 24 April, said it had been reported to him that Frank was dead. Five days later a correspondent for the London *Evening News* wrote: 'I am delighted to learn from a very well-informed source that Commander Brock was undoubtedly alive, although wounded, when the British withdrew from Zeebrugge.' At the beginning of May, *Flight* magazine wrote:

> There appears to be some chance that Commander Brock may still survive as a prisoner of war … it is to be hoped therefore that he may some day be able to receive the greeting in this country which should await his return.

Others were less given to wishful thinking. One day after the raid, Frank's second-in-command at Stratford, Lieutenant Commander Arthur Langley, wrote to G:

> I cannot tell you how sorry everybody here is at the news of Commander Brock. All the officers ask me to express very real sympathy with you. Stratford seems impossible without him – for he and it seemed to be one and the same thing, and we find it impossible to believe that he is gone.

Whether they thought he might still be alive, or had given him up for dead, everyone who returned from Zeebrugge was agreed on one point. Frank's smoke had prevented a full-scale massacre, and it was down to him that they had lived to tell the tale. Survivors in a military hospital in Deal read about their exploits in the *Daily Express* beneath the headline 'Enemy surprised by fog screen.' The day after the raid one of the wounded there was given a tot of brandy by an orderly. The man in the next bed said: 'Give me a drop of that, sir … I want it to celebrate Brock's Benefit.'

The verdict of Admiral Keyes was that Frank's contribution had been 'incalculable'. And so it had been. His smoke had been deployed during every part of the operation on that remarkable night. Twenty minutes after the midnight arrival of *Vindictive*, the three blockships, *Thetis*, *Iphigenia* and *Intrepid*, had emerged near the seaward end of the Mole from a world that had been reduced by his swirling fog to five square feet. They were right on time and fully intact, having delayed their approach to gain maximum advantage from the diversionary attacks on shore. They had just enough coal in their bunkers to complete the one-way journey. All items of copper and brass had been removed from them, since the Germans were known to be short of both.

Thetis led the way, guided by great illuminating rockets fired from *Vindictive*'s stern by one of Frank's pyrotechnical experts, a man who had never been to sea before or seen action. Weighed down with cement and concrete, she slipped past the lighthouse into the harbour. The entrance to the Bruges canal was just one nautical mile away. Eight minutes sailing time. So far so good.

Only now did the enemy, distracted by the assault on the Mole, realize the true purpose of the raid. They were quick to respond, and as *Thetis* emerged from the fog she ran into withering fire from the guns on the Mole extension. Water poured into her badly holed hull, and with both her engines out of action she slammed into a sandbank 300 yards short of the canal entrance. For the time-being she was out of the game, but even now her guns kept blazing, drawing most of the enemy fire on herself and away from her two consorts, *Intrepid* and *Iphigenia*.

Engines pounding, the two other blockships ploughed on towards the canal. With Frank's blinding smoke pouring from her stacks like a volcano, *Intrepid* edged past *Thetis* and reached the coastline almost unscathed. Her captain, Lieutenant Stewart Bonham-Carter, nosed his ship into the canal entrance and swung her across the width of the channel. Satisfied that she was placed correctly, he ordered his men into the accompanying motor launches. Then he turned the firing keys and blew the bottom out of the concrete-laden ship. With four satisfying thumps she settled into the water.

Iphigenia followed suit a few minutes later. With skill and patience, her captain, Lieutenant Edward Billyard-Leake, aged just 22, forced her bow into the silt between the bank and *Intrepid*, herded his men into the rescue boats and blew the charges in the ship's bowels, bedding her down on the canal bottom. Even now the blocking operation was not finished, for *Thetis* had managed to get her starboard engine working. Pushing herself off the sandbank, she edged closer to the canal entrance and scuttled herself crosswise, creating yet another headache for the U-boats and torpedo boats in Bruges. As the crews of all three blockships were rushed away in the escape boats to waiting destroyers, they were again cloaked by Frank's smoke. Thanks to his pyrotechnics, nearly all would make it home to Dover.

While this was going on another surprise was being sprung. Away to the right, one of the obsolete British submarines, *C3*, ploughed doggedly through the darkness towards the viaduct linking the Mole to the shore. A motor skiff was slung across her back, rather like a pannier on a donkey. The Germans held their fire as she emerged from Frank's fog, perhaps hoping that the vessel would become trapped and could be captured intact. With some amusement they watched *C3* smack into one of the viaduct's arches at nine and a half knots – a case, so they thought, of woeful seamanship. Unable to keep the smirks off their faces, they watched and waited.

C3's commander, Lieutenant Richard Sandford, set the fuses for 12 minutes and scrambled into the skiff with his small crew. Discovering the craft's propeller was broken, the men took to the oars and began paddling for their lives. Still having no idea what was about to happen, the Germans at last opened up with rifle and machine-gun fire. 'They couldn't hit a pussy cat,' remarked Sandford drily. Seconds later a bullet smacked into his thigh. Two of his crew were also hit. The skiff had managed to struggle about 200 yards when, with a brilliant flash and a colossal roar, *C3*'s five tons of amatol shattered the night, sending a tangle of girders, railway sleepers, guns and lumps of concrete flying into the air. Everyone in the vicinity felt the explosion. Petty Officer Harry Adams on *Daffodil* recalled: 'It shook heaven and earth – the ships quivered and trembled – the nearest approach to an earthquake one could imagine.'

As well as destroying power and telephone cables, and knocking out searchlights, the explosion blew a 90ft hole in the viaduct itself. This left the Mole no longer connected to the shore, so putting paid to any German hopes of summoning reinforcements. *C3* had done her job, and all her crew survived. Her back-up, *C1*, being no longer needed, turned round and headed back across the Channel.

Throughout this activity, the destroyers *Warwick*, *Phoebe*, *Myng*, *Mansfield* and *North Star* provided smoke screens as and when necessary, mainly in the vicinity of the Mole. A damaged tank on *Myng* enveloped her in smoke and gas, but there was no panic, and the prevailing view was that the unintended fog saved the ship from being blown out of the water.

With the blockships in place, and the viaduct smashed, the mission was complete. It was 12.50 am – around the time of Frank's deadly encounter with Hermann Künne. Watching events from *Vindictive*, Captain Carpenter knew it was time to head for home. Incredibly his ship was still afloat, but she was jammed with dead and wounded, and the swashbucklers on the Mole were still taking casualties. A series of short blasts from *Vindictive* was supposed to signal the withdrawal, but her siren had been shot away. *Daffodil* used hers instead, but it was badly damaged and the best it could manage was a tinny squeak. Over the next 20 minutes the survivors from the assault parties fell back, fighting a series of rear-guard actions as they did. They carried with them their wounded and some of their dead. Frank was nowhere to be seen. As the last stragglers came on board, Carpenter looked out across the Mole. He could see many bodies, but none that moved. When he was satisfied that no one else was going to appear out of the gloom, he gave the order to cast off.

The German batteries were still blazing away as *Vindictive* and her tough little companions, *Iris* and *Daffodil*, pushed away from the Mole at 1.10 am. Their box of tricks was depleted but not empty. Out belched more of Frank's smoke from stacks and canisters, even denser than it had been on the approach, sheltering them all the way out. All the enemy could see of *Vindictive* was the glare of the flames from her funnels illuminating the upper part of the fog. Only *Iris* nearly came to grief. A shell hit her bridge, killing the captain and knocking out her navigating officer and quartermaster. As she drifted off course, she was struck by more shells. Then a motor launch cut between her and the shore batteries and spewed out more Brockish fog. A providential shift in the wind carried the smoke to shore, screening *Iris* from the guns and allowing her to limp off into the welcome darkness. Not a single man on either *Vindictive* or *Daffodil* was lost during the withdrawal despite the almost point-blank presence of the enemy's guns. Throughout it all, *Vindictive*'s lucky horseshoe remained attached to her middle funnel.

Over the course of the last century the success or otherwise of the raid on Zeebrugge has been widely debated, but no one has ever questioned the importance of Frank's contribution. Sir Eric Geddes, in praising the mission in the Commons, described his smoke screens as 'one of the essentials of success'. Captain Carpenter concluded: 'Without the smoke the operation would have failed.' Petty Officer Albert Pointer of the *Daffodil* recalled: 'The smoke screens were what helped us. They hid us going in and they hid us coming out … I escaped without a scratch.' In *The Zeebrugge Raid 1918,* published in 2008, the military historian Paul Kendall wrote:

> If it was not for Brock's smoke screen the author does not think anyone would have returned home from the raid. The German batteries along the Belgian coast would have sunk the entire flotilla and the raiders would either have been killed or taken prisoner. He had certainly prevented a massive disaster for the Royal Navy and Royal Marines.

The enemy, too, recognised the value of Frank's smoke. An account of the raid written after the war by Captain Charles Schultz revealed that 200 German officers and men placed on the Mole to protect aircraft sheds were unable to take part in the fighting because 'the difficult conditions of visibility made it inadvisable for them to leave the vicinity of the Airplane shed.' Schultz added that some of the shore batteries had been unable to fire at *Vindictive* during the landing 'because of the dense fog which continued throughout the attack, enveloping everything.'

Recalling the dash for home, the *Vindictive*'s Lieutenant Edward Hilton Young, wrote:

> Thick black fumes were eddying about the decks from our smoke apparatus…each moment we expected the crash and the flame; but the moment passed, and still the silence of the ship's progress was unbroken…astonishment came into my mind. How much longer than I expected it was taking before the bad time began…and then I realized with a flash that while I had been waiting and wondering a good ten minutes had passed…so by the biggest wonder of that night of wonders, we re-passed the batteries, not only unsunk but also unhit. Confused by our smoke screen and flurried, no doubt, by what was happening on the Mole, the Germans dropped behind us every shot they fired, in a furious and harmless bombardment in our wake.

Captain Chater of the marines recalled: 'As the ship withdrew, we expected to be heavily shelled. Clouds of smoke were released aft, which, although asphyxiating to those of us who were on deck, hid us from the enemy, and to our surprise we were not hit.' Colour Sergeant E. F. Tracey's verdict was: 'We would have undoubtedly been sunk but for the immediate action of a motor launch rushing in to shield us with smoke.'

It must have been about now, as the survivors of the raid thanked their lucky stars for Frank's fog, that they began to wonder about the whereabouts of its inventor. Tales began to circulate about his heroic dash towards the German positions and his dispersal of enemy gunners with his bare fists. Some said they had seen him remove the breeches from captured German guns and fling them into the sea. There was talk that he had been wounded. Someone thought he might have been hit by a shot fired from a moored destroyer. Others stated they had seen him being tended by two marines. Possibly he had been taken prisoner. Perhaps he was dead. No one was quite sure.

But for now there was little time to reflect on his fate. The sick bays on *Vindictive*, *Iris* and *Daffodil* were crammed with casualties, row upon row of jaded faces the colour of dry parchment. The surgeons were overwhelmed. Engineer Lieutenant Commander Bury recalled: 'We had no room to separate out the dead from amongst the living, so thickly were they packed.' One man, Private 'Chitty' Chittenden, who had lost both legs, brushed away anyone who came to help him with the words: 'Don't worry about me, look after the others.' From *Iris* came the signal: 'For God's sake send some doctors. I have a shipload of dead and dying.' On *Daffodil* Lieutenant Harold Campbell, with blood streaming down his face from an eye wound, smoked a cigarette and sang 'The End of a Perfect Day'.

Beneath grey, matronly clouds, the ships arrived back in Dover one by one. Each received a noisy and ebullient welcome from the crews of berthed craft. The euphoria peaked when *Vindictive* hove into view at 8.00 am. She brought with her a quarter of a ton of masonry and concrete debris from the Mole as a souvenir of her visit. During the return journey the gallant old cruiser had had yet another narrow escape when she nearly hit a floating mine. Among her survivors were her two mascots, Mr Thomas and Mrs Tabitha. So tight had been security that when Captain Carpenter's wife received a telegram from a thoughtful young officer in Dover assuring her of her husband's safety – 'Operation successful – Husband quite all right' – she assumed he had been struck down by appendicitis.

Daffodil was towed in five hours later by the destroyer *Trident*. *Iris* chugged home in mid-afternoon, down by her stubby head but still moving under her own steam. That afternoon Admiral Keyes's wife went round Dover buying every red rose she could find and gave one to each of the wounded to wear for St George's Day.

The sea-going vessels had suffered remarkably light casualties. Two motor launches were destroyed, and the destroyer *North Star* was sunk. HMS *Phoebe*, spewing Frank's smoke as fast as she could, managed to scoop up many of *North Star*'s crew.

If the ships came off lightly, the men did not. Of the 1,700 who took part in the raid, 206 died, 412 were wounded or missing, and 19 were taken prisoner. Among the dead were three of Frank's RNAS men from Stratford, Air Mechanic First Class Ernest Poole, Air Mechanic First Class Cedric Wilkinson and Mechanic Second Class John Rouse.

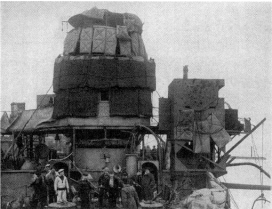

HMS *Vindictive* after the raid. One of the two steel shelters containing Frank's flamethrowers is visible on the right.

Frank himself was listed as missing, but Keyes for one held out little hope that he had survived. On 25 April he wrote to G from Dover:

> I am so very distressed that your gallant husband is missing and I deeply sympathise with you in your sorrow and anxiety. As I told the Admiralty, without the wonderful smoke which he invented, and developed here in Dover, it would have been impossible to undertake the operation and his services were invaluable to me throughout the weeks of preparation. His loss to the Service is simply irreparable, but I still fervently hope that he may have fallen into the enemy's hands alive. Knowing his gallant spirit, however, I cannot but feel that the chance is remote unless he was found unconscious and spared. If your husband is dead, he gave his life in a very heroic enterprise in which he was intensely interested and towards the success of which he contributed greatly.

Sadness overwhelmed those who had worked closely with him. On 25 April, Frank's London secretary Barbara Rowe wrote to Arthur Brock's assistant in Sutton: 'I do not want to intrude but just to express my heartfelt regret that they, his many friends, and the nation should have lost such a splendid officer. You understood Cdr. Brock so well and will know how sadly I miss him. There were days when things were difficult but he was very soon sunny and bright again. I just loved him and feel proud that I was privileged to work for him for nearly three years.'

Two days later there was similar gloom among officers and men about Frank's chances. On 27 April the RNAS ratings in Stratford stood in silence on the parade ground as a mark of respect, and sent a message to G: 'We desire to tender you and your family our heartfelt sympathy in this time of anxiety; and to express our admiration and pride at the gallant conduct of our Commanding Officer, Wing Commander Brock, and those of our ratings associated with him in the hazardous and brilliant exercise of 22 April.' Officers from Stratford gathered in memory of their dead chief in a London restaurant, The Holborn, where Commander Langley told them how Frank had mentioned to him that if he returned from Zeebrugge he would be able to tell his daughter what he did in the war. Langley added: 'He did not come back, but that little girl will be able to find out what her father did, recorded in the history books.'

The respect accorded to Frank by his men was demonstrated in a poem 'Not at Half-Mast!' written the day after the raid by W. Roberts from the RNAS Experimental Station 'in memory of the boys from Stratford who fought and fell.' Dedicated to their commanding officer by way of his picture at the top of the page and sent to G, it summed up Frank with the words 'This was a man!'

> Not at half-mast our flag, but waving proudly
> Full in the breeze, floating victorious.
> E'en though as yet we cannot mention loudly
> Zeebrugge glorious.
>
> Not at half-mast! Straight to the Mole they steered them –
> This was indeed the Drake-cum-Nelson touch!
> Shades of the mighty dead looked down and cheered them.
> Mourn not too much.
>
> Not at half-mast! Our boys faced hell like heroes –
> Faced hell and gave it, fighting to the last,
> Firing the sheds and stores like very Neros
> Ere the hour passed.
>
> Not at half-mast! For Brock himself did lead them –
> His master mind conceived th' heroic plan.
> He knew the risks they ran, counted and shared them.
> This was a man!
>
> Not at half-mast! Messmates we loved return not,
> Yet in our hearts their memory aye shall last.
> Bowed though our heads, yet floats on high our Ensign –
> Not at half-mast!

Frank's family was quick to accept the inevitable. In Sutton the grieving Arthur closed the Brock's factory for a day in his son's memory. Although Frank's parents and siblings took solace from the knowledge that he had contributed so much to the war effort, G's desolation was not eased by pride in his achievements. Headlines like that in the *Daily Sketch* – 'Brock's Great Fight – Commander Beats German Gun Crew with Bare Fists' – were of no comfort to her. Nor was the headline 'Brock's Benefit' which was used by numerous newspapers, such as the *Middlesbrough Daily Gazette*, to capture the spirit of the raid. She wrote to her best friend:

> Dearest Mollie. What can I say to you? You know what I am suffering. My heart is so full of agony there is no room in it for the pride I ought to feel. To his family this pride in what he did is a great comfort to them. Pray God it may come to me some day. I am grateful for your dear letter which I dare not read again and therefore cannot answer.

In May, the Fourth Sea Lord, Admiral Sir Hugh Tothill, wrote to G consoling her on her 'irreparable loss.' He told her: 'In time to come I trust it may be some solace to you to know how gallantly and nobly your husband was fighting when he laid down his life for his country.' In August G received a letter from Buckingham Palace recording the king and queen's 'deep regret' that Frank was now officially confirmed as dead. Nonetheless, she clung to the faint hope that the information was wrong. At the end of October she sold back his 500 shares in Brock's Fireworks to the firm 'on the proviso that if he turns up they shall be sold back to him at the same price.' When the war ended two weeks later, and there was still no sign of him, that final vestige of hope vanished.

Accolades poured in. Henry Major Tomlinson, one of the army's official correspondents, described Frank's death as 'a loss of the gravest description to both the Navy and the empire'. In his official report on the raid to the Admiralty, Keyes recorded his indebtedness to Frank 'for the indispensable share he had in the operation.' He tried to discover what had happened to Frank and wrote to update G on several occasions, including one where he enclosed his map of the Mole. The *Daily Mirror* declared: 'His presumed death closes gloriously a career of conspicuous usefulness.' An obituary in *Flying* magazine, which coincidentally appeared next to an item bout the death of the great German flying ace, Manfred von Richthofen – the Red Baron – called Frank 'a man of men'. *The Crystal Palace Advertiser* commented: 'His was one of the most valiant deaths at Zeebrugge.'

There were many who thought that Frank should have been awarded a Victoria Cross, which in 1918 was the only gallantry medal that could be won posthumously. Admiral of the Fleet Sir Reginald Tyrwhitt was one of the most famous naval figures of WWI. As Commodore Tyrwhitt, he served as commander of the powerful Harwich Force of cruisers and destroyers and was known to the entire Navy, the press and virtually every household in the land as 'Com.T'. He worked closely with Frank and wrote to G's brother Jack Albert shortly before the Armistice '[Frank was] chiefly connected to the Harwich Force for the development of a system of signalling by means of prisms .... His death was a great blow to me as I liked him so much, besides which I had the greatest admiration for his wonderful brains and endurance." They became good friends, devising schemes together. For example, the proposal to attack Zeebrugge with smoke and gas screens submitted by 'Com.T' to the Admiralty on 7 May 1917 was credited by the commodore to Frank. In December 1918, he wrote to G from his ship *Curacoa*:

> The few lines I wrote to your brother only very inadequately express what I really felt for your husband, who I had not only a great admiration for but also real affection. He was one of the greatest gentlemen I have ever met and I can't say more than that. I only hope the Admiralty will do what they ought to do. It is most unfortunate that they cannot award the only honour that is applicable ie the VC. I have a ramrod which belongs to a rifle he used to keep on board my ship and I will send it to you if you tell me where.

If the eye-witness accounts of his final moments are accurate, his bravery more than merited a VC, but in the wake of a night when there was no shortage of gallantry, and when the reports of what happened on the Mole were confusing and often contradictory, his name did not go forward. Some, like his friend, Lord Fisher, thought this an outrage.

Captain Carpenter, who was one of those who did receive a VC, wrote that 'it would be difficult for anyone to speak too highly' of Frank. He went on:

> He was a rare personality. An inventive genius, than whom the country had no better, it was his brain that differentiated this blocking enterprise from all previous attempts in history in one most important particular. The difficulty of reaching the destination in the face of a strenuous opposition had hitherto brought failure, but he provided an antidote in the form of a satisfactory artificial fog designed to protect the blockships from the enemy's guns during the critical period of approach.

Among other tributes was a eulogistic verse in 'Well Done Vindictive', a poem by a Church of England clergyman and writer, Hardwicke Rawnsley, which was published in *United Service Magazine*:

> Of him who with magician skill
> Wrought clouds to blind the foe
> To save us from the fiery hell
> Thro' which we steered – the shot and shell
> Too soon to lay him low

Amid the widespread praise for Frank, and for the raid in general, there was a nagging concern. Had the mission actually succeeded? Some in the Navy thought not, and over the ensuing months and years the view took hold that it had been a heroic failure. The Germans were quick off the mark in playing down the effects of the assault. A communiqué from Berlin on 23 April, while noting the use of Frank's 'thick veil of artificial fog', made light of the raid as a whole, claiming it had made little difference to their ability to get their boats to sea. Two days later they rammed home the point by boasting that one of their smaller submarines, *UB-16*, had worked her way past the scuttled ships at Zeebrugge. So much for the blocking operation. The truth was, said the Germans, that the reckless English had been sent packing with a bloody nose. German casualties during the assault had been tiny compared to those of the attackers, with figures of ten killed and 16 wounded often cited. Not only that, but the simultaneous raid on Ostend had been an out-and-out failure. Even the British could hardly deny that. As at Zeebrugge, Frank's smoke had been deployed there in large quantities, but the blockships designated to seal the canal met a blizzard of enemy fire and became grounded around a mile and a half east of the channel entrance. Nineteen men were killed and 30 wounded during an utterly fruitless operation. (A second attempt to close off the Ostend canal the following month, using *Vindictive* as a blockship, also failed.)

Rivalry and jealousy among British naval chiefs reinforced the view that the raid on Zeebrugge had not succeeded. Vice Admiral Sir Reginald Bacon, still smarting that Keyes had replaced him as head of the Dover Patrol the previous year, questioned the value of the mission. Keyes himself fell out with Captain Carpenter, whom he thought was trying to take too much credit for the operation, and complained in a letter that the assault on the Mole had been a failure because *Vindictive* had overshot her assigned position. He did not mean that the operation as a whole had been a failure, only that the assault had not sufficiently distracted the enemy from the blockships as they moved into position. This was strictly accurate but in due course the word 'failure' was wrongly assumed by others to refer to the entire mission.

Keyes's own Intelligence Officer, Captain Herbert Grant, added fuel to the flames, describing the raid as 'the most consummate folly'. Complaining that 'Keyes believed his own heroics,' he stated that 'nothing is more distasteful to me than thinking or writing of the Zeebrugge attack and often I wish that I had nothing to do with the affair.' Perhaps some of his ire was born of his admiration for Frank, of whom he wrote to G two days after the Raid 'I only knew your husband since February when we were connected in preparation for the Zeebrugge operations. I am proud to say I saw in a very short time his sterling qualities, wonderful scientific knowledge combined with the most practical commonsense. With all this he was so wonderfully modest of his abilities, did not in fact appreciate them to the extent we outsiders did.' Another of Frank's devoted friends and a strong critic of the Raid was Lord Fisher. He had long disliked Keyes and was furious about Frank's death.

'My dear friend Brock, of imperishable memory and Victoria Cross bravery, wickedly massacred at Zeebrugge.'

On top of these criticisms there was a growing feeling that Zeebrugge had not been a nut worth cracking in the first place, and that its importance had been exaggerated by the Royal Navy. The improved Cross-Channel Barrage had already been making life increasingly difficult for German vessels in the Flanders flotilla, and by the early spring of 1918 some two thirds of the attacks on British merchant shipping were being launched from enemy ports to the north. Any suggestion that the U-boat menace had been crushed in a single act of bravado and derring-do at Zeebrugge was not credible.

But those who dismissed Operation *O-Z* as having been ultimately futile were a long way wide of the mark. In operational terms alone it achieved significant if not dazzling results. The attempt to neutralise the less navigable Ostend canal may have failed, but there is ample evidence that access to the canal at Zeebrugge was restricted for a considerable period after the raid, whatever the Germans may have said about the matter. The author E. C. Coleman has convincingly argued that *UB-16*'s supposed passage through the canal two days later was a sleight of hand, pointing out that it was not backed up by any photographic evidence. In fact, the first enemy wireless message intercepted by Naval Intelligence after the raid had warned: 'Until further notice, the canal entrance at Zeebrugge is blocked at low water and obstructed at high water. U-boats will use alternative ports.' A fortnight later two captured German airmen were overheard telling a fellow prisoner that high command regarded the raid as 'completely successful' and 'a serious mishap'. Sergeant Harry Wright, who had been taken prisoner on the Mole, was told by one of his captors, a German petty officer, that 'the German navy thought highly of our raid and compared it with a German operation of attacking Dover Harbour with units of their fleet.'

Four weeks after the raid, aerial reconnaissance indicated that 12 German destroyers, 11 torpedo boats and at least seven U-boats were 'bottled up' at Bruges like 'salmon in a pool', with up to 12 more trapped U-boats probably lying unseen in submarine pens. A month later the same number of vessels still appeared to be trapped. At the end of July, the RAF reported that the canal remained 'completely shut off by our sunken ships.' Even allowing for British exaggeration, it is clear that the raid on Zeebrugge caused considerable disruption to the Bruges-based flotilla. Not until January 1921 did post-war salvage crews completely clear the channel, and in a German report on the raid published in 1929, Captain Karl Schulze conceded that the canal entrance at

Zeebrugge 'was impassible except at high tide' for three weeks. By pretty well any measure, many tens of thousands of tons of allied shipping were saved.

That said, the real significance of Zeebrugge lay not in what it achieved operationally but in the galvanizing effect it had on British morale. Napoleon stated that in war the morale is to the physical as three is to one, and the unusual and spectacular nature of the attack caught the public imagination as seldom before. People were hungry for good news, and the Admiralty milked Zeebrugge's propaganda value for all it was worth. Its triumphant announcement of the raid on 24 April made no mention of the heavy British casualties. Nor was there any talk of *Vindictive* arriving at the wrong location or of the problems she encountered with her ramps. Instead 'nothing hindered the orderly and speedy landing by every gangway' and 'the Huns had fled in terror when faced with British bayonets.' By the same token the failure at Ostend was attributed to nothing more than a freak change in the wind.

The mission's place in history was cemented by the award of eight Victoria Crosses for Zeebrugge (more than in any single action except Rorke's Drift) and three for Ostend. Admiral Keyes was knighted and received a St George's Day telegram from King George V:

> Most heartily congratulate you and the forces under your command who carried out last night's operation with such success. The splendid gallantry displayed by all under exceptionally hazardous circumstances fills me with pride and admiration.

The public was thrilled. Everyone was cheered by this gallant flash of the old sea-dog spirit, and from the king downwards the excitement was unalloyed, dispelling the national gloom like one of Frank's Dover Flares. Here was undeniable proof that Britannia still ruled the waves. The operation re-established faith in the Royal Navy (badly dented at Jutland two years earlier) and in the armed forces in general. No longer could the Navy be taunted with the words of a popular poem:

> What is the British Navy doing?
> We have the right to ask,
> In this mighty war that's being waged,
> Do they fulfil their task?

For Winston Churchill, Zeebrugge gave the Navy back 'the panache that was lost at Jutland.' He wrote subsequently that the raid 'may rank as the finest feat of arms in the Great War, and certainly as an episode unsurpassed in the history of the Royal Navy.' The Archbishop of Canterbury spoke of the raid as being 'the sort which makes a man hold his breath in admiration of the magnificent courage and skill involved in such an enterprise.' The Prime Minister, Lloyd George, described it as 'one of the most gallant and spectacular achievements of the war'. Admiral Sir Walter Cowan said: 'It's done more for the honour of the Navy than anything in this war.' The Secretary of State for War, Lord Milner, declared: 'Never has the banner of St George floated over more magnificent fighting men.'

All over the country, survivors of the raid returned home to a hero's welcome from their communities. Thousands lined the roads when Petty Officer George Pemberton from *Daffodil* and Air Mechanic John Lomax arrived back in Blackburn. Thousands more welcomed the Royal Marines on their return to Plymouth and showered them with chocolate. In the House of Commons there were cheers when Sir Eric Geddes revealed the details of the attack to MPs. An equivalent outpouring of enthusiasm had not been seen the relief of Mafeking at the turn of the century.

At a time when the enemy had been making dramatic advances across the Western Front, Zeebrugge restored Britain's confidence in its ability to win the war. The country had shown it could inflict a humiliating defeat on an enemy who had seemed invincible, reviving the certainty of ultimate victory. For the British troops in France and Flanders, driven back by the German spring onslaught, it came as a badly needed stimulant to morale to learn that the Royal Navy had delivered a stunning blow behind enemy lines. Among those who sent congratulations from the Western Front was Field Marshal Sir Douglas Haig, who told Keyes: 'St George's Day was indeed a fitting date for such a daring feat of arms.'

An uncritical press reflected the nation's jubilant mood. A *Punch* cartoon showed the ghost of Drake congratulating Keyes. 'Bravo, sir. Tradition holds my men singed a King of Spain's beard, and yours have singed a Kaiser's moustache.' *The Army and Navy Gazette* declared: 'Honour to all who took part in the raid. In the words which Shakespeare puts in the mouth of Henry V before Agincourt: "He that outlives this day, and comes home safe, will stand a tip-toe when this day is named."' The *Saturday Review* commented: 'No incident in the long war by sea and land has more deeply touched the popular imagination … it reads like a chapter from one of Henty's novels or a passage from Southey's *Life of Nelson*.' Under the headline 'An Epic Story', the *Daily News* declared: 'In all the heroic records of this war, on sea and on land, this episode, by its scale and its circumstances, stands out in bold relief.' The tub-thumping author 'Jackstaff' wrote in his book, *The Dover Patrol*, published soon after the raid: 'The glorious adventure of Zeebrugge showed the whole world that the British seaman of today is made of the same stout stuff as his forefathers.'

There was more lavish praise in Keble Howard's book, *The Glory of Zeebrugge,* published within weeks of the raid. The book hugely over-stated the military success of the operation and was so full of inaccuracies that it was subsequently disowned by some of the naval officers who were interviewed for it. Nonetheless it was lapped up by an excited public. Howard, whose usual genre was science fiction, concluded portentously:

> Zeebrugge, therefore (and Ostend no less) means this to Empire. It means that the Empire's Navy, as well as the Empire's Army, is ready, eager, and able to resist with all its courage, all its science, and all its force the domination of the world by Prussia. Zeebrugge means just that and all that. Though to the unimaginative but a swift and sudden blow in the night, it ranks in glory and importance with Waterloo, Trafalgar, and the Battle of the Marne.

Abroad, too, the raid was hailed as an outstanding success. The French newspaper *Le Matin* called it 'the finest feat in the naval history of all times and of all countries.' French officers and men who had taken part in the Ostend raid sent a telegram to Keyes with the message:

> Proud to serve under the same Commander as the British ships, whose dash and courage they have witnessed at Ostend, and deeply honoured at his high praise. The French units will be happy to again fight in their ranks, and to strive to equal them in their bravery.

The New York Sun declared that the Royal Navy 'has set a standard of excellence unsurpassed in the history of the world,' and proudly but erroneously told its readers that Americans had taken part in the raid. In Australia, press coverage benefitted from the presence of Australian servicemen on *Vindictive*. 'A brilliant exploit – the nation thrilled' went one headline. 'A naval epic with tales of inspiring gallantry' ran another. 'A Whiff of Nelson's Days' declared Queensland's *Rockhampton Morning Bulletin*, adding that the Germans had 'bolted en masse in every direction.' According to one Australian report, the attackers had boarded a number of German destroyers where they had found the enemy in their 'nightgowns' and 'tapped their heads with stout sticks.' In Belgium, the jubilation was, if anything, greater than in England, and the raid came to be seen as the spark which lit the flame of freedom. A Belgian nun wrote: 'Bless the English. Everything was so successful that it may well be considered a miracle, and a major defeat for the Germans.'

By the same token the raid was a damaging blow to German morale out of all proportion to its military weight. In the space of little over an hour the Royal Navy had disproved the notion that Britain was on her knees and incapable of fighting back, so robbing the German soldier of his belief that the war was as good as over. The reported words of a German official based in Bruges – that 'the hopes of the Fatherland were buried at Zeebrugge' – was an absurd exaggeration, but fears that the Allies were in the process of landing an immense force on the coast of Flanders in the wake of the operation sparked immediate preparations to evacuate the town. At the same time the raid put paid to any German hopes of releasing men and resources from Belgian coastal defences and throwing them into the main battle on the Western Front. On the contrary, fearing further amphibious assaults, they were forced to send reinforcements from the Heligoland Bight to defend Zeebrugge.

There was even praise for the raid in the German press. *The Hamburger Nachrichten* said that 'the attack was carried out by the British with great skill and extraordinary pluck.' The Berlin-based *Lokal Anzeiger* commented:

> In German naval circles it is recognised unhesitatingly that the British attempt on Zeebrugge was undertaken with extraordinary skill, while the greatest gallantry and dash were shown in its execution.

Abroad too, international financiers who had witnessed the astonishing advances made by the Germans in their spring offensive noted Zeebrugge and saw that the British could still fight. In a purely military sense Zeebrugge was not especially significant, but in terms of morale it was one of the high points of the war, comparable only to that other great operation in which Frank had played a central role – the shooting down of the first Zeppelins. No country can successfully prosecute a war for long if the majority of its citizens are disillusioned, disheartened and disenchanted. Operation *Z-O* replaced despondency with optimism, and in this respect the raid was not only a triumph but arguably a turning point in the conflict.

The man who made the mission possible – 'Brock, the gallant optimist, whose inventions had been so invaluable to us,' as Keyes wrote of him – need not have put himself in harm's way, but it was not in his nature to shy away from danger. The call of duty, and the moral imperative of doing the right thing, were too deeply ingrained. 'Nothing in his life was more characteristic of him than the manner of his leaving it,' noted the Dulwich College Roll of Honour. The war historian Barrie Pitt observed in 1958 in his book *Zeebrugge – Eleven VCs Before Breakfast*:

> The more one reads his notes, his letters, and the opinions of those who knew him best, the greater certainty arises on one point: had he known of his fate beforehand, he would still have gone gaily forward to meet it.

Believed to be the funeral of those who died in the raid. The church and graveyard remains today and is visible on Admiral Keyes' plan (see page 163). (Johan Ryheul Collection)

Frank's numerous attributes included a phenomenal memory, ferociously inquiring mind, a powerful intellect, an inventive genius, physical courage, the ability to inspire others and a very great ability to get things done. Along with his patriotism, his love of literature and his sense of humour, they combined to make a truly extraordinary man. Had he lived he would undoubtedly have gone on to achieve great things after the war, and would almost certainly have played a crucial role in the second great conflict with Germany a quarter of a century later.

As the military historian Paul Kendall in his major work *The Zeebrugge Raid 1918* published in 2008, concluded: 'Brock was a brilliant, charismatic man whose loss was not only a tragedy for his family and those who knew him, but a national loss.'

In an effort to seek closure, the family, torn by the pain of a son who had disappeared, dispatched Frank's immediate younger brother and later acclaimed author Alan St. Hill Brock, to Zeebrugge to see if he could find out what had happened to Frank. Without the knowledge gained in recent years from the German archives by the Belgian military historian M. Johan Ryheul and therefore unaware of Herr Pollicke's description of the fatal fight in which Künne stabbed the British officer through the neck, Alan sought help from the chief of local police who invited the local gravedigger to attend. A few lines taken from Alan's detailed notes would seem to confirm M. Ryheul's careful research, although at the time, with no concept of a swordfight in his mind, Alan believed the wound referred to must have been a bullet:

> The Chief of the Local Police Station fetched the gravedigger who said he helped to make the grave and put the bodies in the coffins, which had been made at Ostend and sent to Zeebrugge. He said all were in khaki (Frank was indeed wearing khaki). The gravedigger was unsure of the number of rings on their sleeves but said there were three officers and described them as 'captain', 'lieutenant' and 'under-officer'; the two latter were smaller men, one having red hair. The 'Captain' was in the grave on the extreme left; he said he remembers he was a tall, well built man with dark hair; he had only one wound piercing the neck from side to side…

Included in the file of Alan Brock's notes is a handwritten sheet which appears to be the funeral speech of a German officer burying a number of marines:

> You see before you the bodies of four English Marines who died fighting against us. They are our enemies but they are dead. They can never again take up arms against the fatherland. They are soldiers. We are soldiers and we are giving them an honorable (sic) military funeral and we hope they will do the same for our dead. They are now in a land where there are no enemies or countries or frontiers, but only one God for all men and all men for one God.
>
> They are Englishmen. England is the most cruel the most tenacious and the strongest of our enemies. It is she who caused the war. What they have done is heroic but it is done in vain. Their plan has failed. Our submarines will still go out to strike a death blow at the heart of England and we will fight on until we have gained the peace for which we are striving.

The German officer need not have worried about unequal treatment. At exactly the time *Vindictive's* task force was setting out for Zeebrugge, Manfred von Richthofen, the German fighter ace known as 'The Red Baron', was being buried by the Allies with full military honours.

CHAPTER 15

Brock's Benefit

Frank Brock's bullets helped to end German hopes of supremacy in the air. His flares played a key role in preventing U-boats from starving Britain into submission. His smoke was essential to the success of a naval venture regarded by some as a watershed moment in the war. Add to that his other contributions – the Friedrichshafen raid, the signalling systems, his work with colour filters, the E-floats that saved the lives of countless seamen, his heroism on the Mole – and it is clear that he was one of the most significant figures of World War I. It did not end there. Many of his ideas remained in use long after his death. Immediately after the Zeebrugge raid, Admiral Keyes gave orders for all destroyers and coastal motor boats in the Dover Patrol to be fitted with Frank's smoke-screen devices. The same method of creating smoke with chlorosulphonic acid was introduced into the exhaust pipes of tanks for use on the battlefield and was still being employed 30 years later.

A WWI tank laying Frank's smoke. (IWM HU_136827)

King George V had met Arthur several times and had met Frank at least once at his investiture for the OBE in early 1918. This picture shows the king visiting the Mole after the war ended. He was accompanied by Admiral Keyes and the area where Frank and Künne fought is to the right in the picture. (Johan Ryheul Collection)

During World War II RAF pathfinders illuminated targets with the flares he invented. The air-to-air missile technology he pioneered grew into a key component of air warfare.

He has no known grave, although he was probably one of two unidentified British officers whose bodies were retrieved from the Mole by the Germans after the raid and who were buried alongside each other in a small cemetery at St Donaas church in Zeebrugge. Their identical white headstones, maintained by the Commonwealth War Graves Commission, are inscribed with the words 'A British Officer of the Great War'. The other unidentified officer buried there was probably Lieutenant Commander Arthur Harrison, who also died storming the Mole. To this day local people leave photographs of both men beside the two graves.

Others who died that night, both British and German, lie in the same churchyard. Among them is Hermann Künne, the 20-year-old German rating who, if the eyewitness accounts are correct, died at the same time as Frank during their savage swordfight. In 1937 the Kriegsmarine named a destroyer after him – the 2,400-ton *Hermann Künne* – a rare distinction for an ordinary seaman. The German Navy clearly thought he had done something exceptional that night, stopping a dangerous, perhaps overwhelming British momentum. Although nothing is stated in their archives, it must be assumed that they knew he was responsible for Frank's death.

Frank is widely remembered in his beloved England. Shortly after the end of hostilities, Sir Roger Keyes unveiled a memorial cross at St Saviour's Church, Raynes Park, dedicated to the 95 men of the parish, Frank included, who fell during the war. In a short address he said of Frank: 'His name will always stand for ingenuity, resource, courage, determination to win, and indomitable pluck.' A stained-glass window is dedicated to him in the same church.

Frank is also commemorated on Cheam War memorial in Surrey (near his father's Sutton home), on the Richmond Rugby Club memorial, on the Dulwich College war memorial, and on a memorial in Brookwood Cemetery, Surrey. The latter was erected by G in honour of Frank and of her two deceased brothers-in-law) both of whom had served in the Royal Navy. An epitaph at the base of the Brookwood memorial is taken from Tennyson's *Ode on the Death of the Duke of Wellington*:

> Not once or twice in our rough island story
> The path of duty was the way to glory

Frank is also remembered every year at Malden Golf Club, where his friends clubbed together after the war to pay for the Brock Cup. This was inaugurated in 1919 and is still played for every Armistice Sunday. The cup carries an engraving of *Vindictive* alongside the Mole and stands on a plinth believed to be made from wood from *Vindictive*. Another memento of the raid in which Frank died is the Zeebrugge Bell, which once hung on the end of the Mole and was rung by the Germans to warn of a British sea or air attack. After World War I the king of the Belgians presented it to Dover, and today it is housed on the front of the former town hall, where it is rung every year at midday on St George's Day in honour of the men who took part in the assault. Arthur Brock, that great pyrotechnist, outlived his son by two decades. While thankful that his other sons had survived the war, he never fully recovered from Frank's death. In November 1918, just as the war was ending, the shock and pain of losing his first-born son were eased when G gave birth to another girl. She was named Francesca in Frank's honour, and Sir Roger Keyes became one of her godfathers.

In the years immediately following the war Sir Roger did his best to find where Frank was buried, keeping G aware of his attempts. This letter is dated 13 January 1920 and written from HMS *Lion* in Devonport:

Alan St Hill Brock, 1886–1956, wearing the Savage Club tie. Born two years after Frank, Alan was an architect, pyrotechnist, historian and novelist. His two published histories on fireworks remain widely acknowledged as the preeminent works in this field.

When I was in command of the squadron looking after the German fleet at Scapa Flow I was able to do one or two good turns for Admiral von Reuter. He promised to find out quite definitely who were buried in that grave and in fact sent me a copy of the letter he wrote to the German Admiralty. Then I left Scapa and 2 months later, before I succeeded in getting a reply, he sank his ships and became a prisoner of war. It became impossible to communicate with him …. I will not rest until I find the information…

In the late 1920s, Arthur and his eldest surviving son Alan St. Hill Brock, the architect and talented future historian of the story of fireworks, largely rebuilt the Philharmonic Hall in Langham Street into a handsome brick and stone office building next to the BBC. Naming it Brock House and for several years with a Brock's Fireworks showroom on the ground floor and a top-rated explosives' magazine on the roof to hold its stock, the building was a major home to the BBC for over 80 years, the corporation only vacating it in 2018.

After the war, G looked after her daughters and went back to running her hat business in the West End of London from Maddox Street and Sloan Street, visiting Paris several times a year to select the latest models. In 1927 she married Frank's younger brother, Christopher. With the help of her brother, Jack Albert, she pursued Frank's claim for proper financial recognition of the Brock bullet, successfully arguing that 'he placed his scientific knowledge at the disposal of the State and therefore the claim to an award in respect of his invention should not be prejudiced on account of his being temporarily in the Service.' Honour was satisfied when the Royal Commission on Awards to Inventors praised Frank's work and made an award of £12,000. The Admiralty Ordnance Council awarded a further £7,000. The total was the equivalent in today's money of around 2 million pounds, and reflected the enormous value the powers-that-be placed on the Brock bullet. G died in Sussex in 1964.

A poignant photograph of G as a war widow with her two young daughters, Anne and Francesca, published in the *Ladies' Field Magazine,* March 1921.

Anne Brock, who had been just two and a half when her father died, claimed for the rest of her long life that she had a single memory of him bouncing her up and down on his knee. Whether or not this was a genuine recollection or just wishful thinking, she never stopped adoring him and like him, she was blessed with a phenomenal memory. For a brief period in the 1930s she worked for the family firm, helping with display teams and also as Arthur's secretary. Dying in 2014, not long before her hundredth birthday, Anne married three times and for many years was a president of the Kipling Society, no doubt inspired by her parents' love of his poetry which she knew, in its entirety, by heart. Her first husband, a naval officer

Anne Brock as an adult.

Francesca Brock as an adult.

named Frank Fletcher, perished during World War II. In 1944 she married a commando, David Smee and later, Gordon Shelford. Frank and G's youngest daughter, Francesca, married a surgeon Anthony Partridge and today, Frank's descendants are a growing band.

After World War II, Arthur Brock continued to run the family firm with flair and gusto. In July 1919 Brock's played a prominent role in the official peace celebrations, during which thousands of Frank's surplus Dover Flares were deployed at parties and bonfires up and down the country. The climax of the celebrations was a huge display organised by Arthur and Alan beside the Serpentine in London's Hyde Park, the fireworks being taken to the site in part by a requisitioned German army Mercedes Benz lorry. The display included portraits of the king, queen and Britain's military leaders, and boasted the greatest concentration of aerial fireworks ever fired. It was the first national firework spectacle to be staged in central London since the end of the Crimean War more than 60 years earlier. A reporter from the *Warrington Guardian* confessed: 'Never in my life have I seen such fiery wonders, and never since the world began had such fireworks as these been seen before.'

Arthur's eye for publicity remained as keen as ever. In 1921 he assisted with an experiment on Hampstead Heath in London in which several tons of fireworks were sent skywards to see if they could produce rain. 'Within a few moments,' reported journalists, 'there were thirty or more clouds in the sky ... but no rain.'

The previous year Brock's firework displays had been revived at the Crystal Palace. The debut show was a reproduction of the battle of Jutland. This was so realistic that one newspaper reporter was moved to point out: 'One realises that here at least the Cinematograph is hopelessly outdone.' The Crystal Palace shows remained a popular attraction for many years, and climaxed with a dazzling display to celebrate King George V's Silver Jubilee in 1935. The following year they came to an abrupt end when a disastrous fire – in no way attributable to its most famous element – robbed Londoners of their favourite resort. As the *Daily Mirror* reported: 'Spectacular to the last, the Crystal Palace, famous for its magnificent firework displays, went out in the greatest and most awe-inspiring show in its history.' Ironically, one of the exhibits on the world trade display inside had been a new, ultra-modern fire engine, lauded for its capacity to produce a more forceful stream of water than ever before.

Brock's Fireworks remained based in Sutton until 1932. That year Arthur moved the firm to a 207-acre site at Woodhall Farm, Hemel Hempstead, in order to expand production. With sales of fireworks still buoyant, and with public displays as popular as ever, the company employed upwards of 500 people. In keeping with Arthur's lifelong commitment to his workforce, he built houses for his employees, and provided them with a social club and sports facilities. He named the streets where he housed them after the 18th-century London pleasure gardens where the original pyrotechnist Brocks had made their money – Vauxhall Road and Ranelagh Gardens. As a mark of his elevated status, he acquired a Rolls Royce and chauffeur.

Arthur died in 1938 aged 80 at his home Chesham Bois, ten miles from Hemel Hempstead. Even in photographs taken of him in old age he kept his face pointed to the right so that the disfiguring results of the accident he had suffered in his youth were not visible. Under the leadership of his sons, Frank's brothers Alan, Bernard, Christopher and Roy the firm continued to sell millions of fireworks a year and to play a prominent role at great national occasions. During World War II the factory once again performed a vital role in providing countless pyrotechnics to the forces. In July 1941, the Royal Navy carried out Exercise Brock, perhaps named in recognition of the family's contribution. The exercise explored the use of illuminating flares in the Western Approaches and it was said that Lord Lovat of the commandos was a not infrequent visitor to the factory throughout WWII.

For the victory celebrations in London to mark the end of World War II, Brock's directed a spectacular fire and water display from the side of the Thames in front of the king and queen, along with Princess Elizabeth and Princess Margaret. More than eight tons of fireworks were used in the show, and it earned glowing reviews. In an article for the *News of the World*, A. P. Herbert wrote:

> Burn the Thames does – and bravely. Her muddy waters turn red, turn silver and gold and green...while Handel's Water Music is heard on the water once again...one by one 200 rockets soar with a roar from her ancient breast, sprinkling the sky with scattered stars.

After the war a new manager, Tim Bennett, was brought in but at least two of Frank's other brothers continued to play an active role in the firm. In 1947 Roy Brock supervised many displays and the fireworks for Princess Elizabeth's 21st birthday celebrations during the royal tour of South Africa, while Christopher Brock directed a centenary display for the city of Dunedin, New Zealand in 1948. Brock's also played an important role in the Festival of Britain in 1951 and was responsible for the official display for the coronation celebrations of Queen Elizabeth II in 1953.

In the 1950s the company expanded its production sites into Swaffham, Norfolk. Brock's and its head chemist, Ron Hall, developed and patented an entirely new type of pyrotechnic product based on extruded resins. These produced some novel and pleasing effects, and were in world-wide demand, particularly in the United States. Frank's nephews, Bernard's sons John and Benjamin Brock, entered the firm and later still, Frank's grandson, Anne's son Harry Smee, was to do the same.

Just as the company had assisted the building of empire in the 19th century, so, in the 1950s, 1960s and 1970s it helped to mark its dismantling, providing most of the official displays as the United Kingdom stepped down from its imperial role and independence celebrations were held around the world.

By the late 1960s Brock's was feeling the strain, its site under pressure from the fast-expanding Hemel Hempstead which the government had designated a 'New Town' in the early 1950s. In the 1970s the company relocated its production to Sanquhar in Dumfriesshire but during the second half of the 20th century Britain's fireworks industry began to lose its sparkle. The new health-and-safety culture, while successfully cutting the grim annual toll of firework injuries, extinguished some of the allure the season once held.

After China began to open up in the late 1970s it became increasingly difficult to compete with cheap imports. British manufacturers went out of business or were taken over by the Chinese. There is still demand in the UK for (almost exclusively) imported fireworks but matters were not helped by the seemingly unstoppable American juggernaut that started promoting Hallowe'en at the expense of Guy Fawkes Night.

Brock's remained in Sanquhar until 1987 when Standard Fireworks bought the company and transferred production to Huddersfield, severing all connections with the Brock family in the process. In 1998, Standard Fireworks was in turn taken over by Black Cat Fireworks, and all manufacturing was moved to China, with Huddersfield becoming the sales, marketing and distribution centre for the combined operation.

The term 'Brock's Benefit' long ago dropped out of general use. One of its last airings was by the distinguished *Daily Telegraph* leader writer T. E. 'Peter' Utley, writing about the Conservative politician Michael Heseltine in the 1970s. Utley accurately predicted that Heseltine would have to do more than his famous Brock's Benefit display in his annual speech to the Conservative Party Conference if he were ever to gain his party's leadership.

Firework displays remain a popular if less frequent form of public entertainment than before, but a century after Frank's death they have changed in character. Today's displays, partly because of the size of the audience, are mainly aerial in nature and can be repetitive if of a high standard. Laughter, once an expected crowd reaction in almost all displays, is rarely heard. Many pyrotechnical experiences have been lost, probably for ever, either because the expertise has died, or because they would be too expensive to build, or because the risks associated with the old ways have increased to unacceptable levels. Firework portraiture, 'living fireworks', 'transformation set-pieces', huge wheels and other intricate devices are spectacles of the past. No longer do spectators thrill to elaborate reconstructions of great naval battles and natural disasters, or watch aerial huntsmen pursue aerial stags across the night sky. Long gone are the days when they were mesmerised by the sight of pyrotechnical tightrope walkers, boxers and bicyclists, or gasped at the whistling 'pigeons' which whizzed from nowhere and raced hither and thither along unseen wires.

Had Frank lived, he would have undoubtedly urged his father to add the raid on Zeebrugge to his pyrotechnical repertoire. Not that Arthur needed any persuading. In June 1929 he despatched his son Alan with a team of technicians to Douglas Harbour in the Isle of Man. The harbour's 19th-century breakwater bore a passing resemblance to the Mole, albeit on a smaller scale, and here the Brock's team re-created the St George's Day raid to Arthur's pride and satisfaction.

The display featured real ships under the command of Edwin Youlton who, as a young petty officer, had been at the helm of *Vindictive* on that extraordinary night 11 years earlier. And, of course, there were clouds of wreathing, eddying smoke. A local journalist described the scene:

> First we saw a dense cloud of smoke creep across the mouth of the harbour. This part of the pageant was so true to the real thing that some of the blockading ships had difficulty in finding their way through. While this was going on, shadowy small craft crept into the harbour itself and started to create confusion by discharging torpedoes at enemy destroyers alongside the Mole. The whole inferno was reproduced as faithfully as possible by Brock's, with shrapnel crackling over the Mole, 8in shells exploding, machine-guns rat-tatting, bombs bursting, ships blowing up and going down majestically in a great dull red glow. We saw the *Vindictive* creeping into the harbour to act as a decoy, the historic storming of the Mole, and figures hurrying to and fro from the Mole itself surrounded by every form of explosive. All the episodes of this wonderful but terrible night were reproduced on a small but accurate scale.

One of the spectators at the display was an elderly woman who was seen to be weeping amid the clash and din. She had lost a son on the Mole. For Alan it was an emotional moment too, but he did not let his feelings affect his usual high standards. It was a typical piece of Brock professionalism, and Frank, that greatest of enthusiasts, would have been delighted with the results.

Appendix I: Brock Family Tree

The names of the pyrotechnists are given in heavy type.

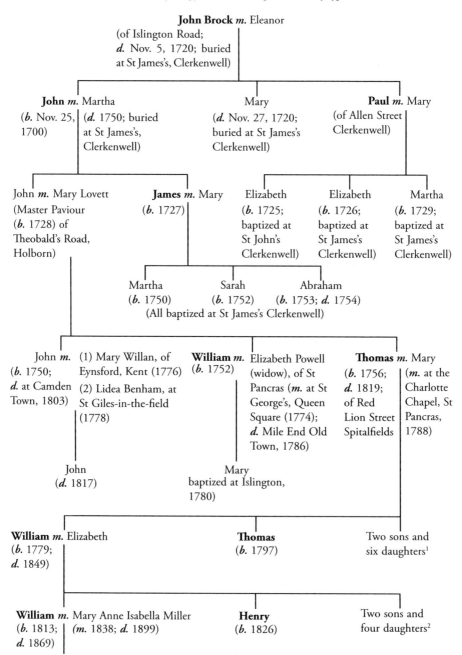

John Brock *m.* Eleanor
(of Islington Road;
d. Nov. 5, 1720; buried
at St James's, Clerkenwell)

John *m.* Martha
(*b.* Nov. 25,   (*d.* 1750; buried
1700)   at St James's,
                Clerkenwell)

Mary
(*d.* Nov. 27, 1720;
buried at St James's
Clerkenwell)

Paul *m.* Mary
(of Allen Street
Clerkenwell)

John *m.* Mary Lovett
(Master Paviour
(*b.* 1728) of
Theobald's Road,
Holborn)

James *m.* Mary
(*b.* 1727)

Elizabeth
(*b.* 1725;
baptized at
St John's
Clerkenwell)

Elizabeth
(*b.* 1726;
baptized at
St James's
Clerkenwell)

Martha
(*b.* 1729;
baptized at
St James's
Clerkenwell)

Martha
(*b.* 1750)

Sarah
(*b.* 1752)

Abraham
(*b.* 1753; *d.* 1754)

(All baptized at St James's Clerkenwell)

John *m.*   (1) Mary Willan, of
(*b.* 1750;   Eynsford, Kent (1776)
d. at Camden   (2) Lidea Benham, at
Town, 1803)   St Giles-in-the-field
                (1778)

William *m.* Elizabeth Powell
(*b.* 1752)   (widow), of St
               Pancras (*m.* at St
               George's, Queen
               Square (1774);
               d. Mile End Old
               Town, 1786)

Thomas *m.* Mary
(*b.* 1756;   (*m.* at the
d. 1819;   Charlotte
of Red   Chapel, St
Lion Street   Pancras,
Spitalfields   1788)

John
(*d.* 1817)

Mary
baptized at Islington,
1780)

William *m.* Elizabeth
(*b.* 1779;
d. 1849)

Thomas
(*b.* 1797)

Two sons and
six daughters[1]

William *m.* Mary Anne Isabella Miller
(*b.* 1813;   (*m.* 1838; *d.* 1899)
d. 1869)

Henry
(*b.* 1826)

Two sons and
four daughters[2]

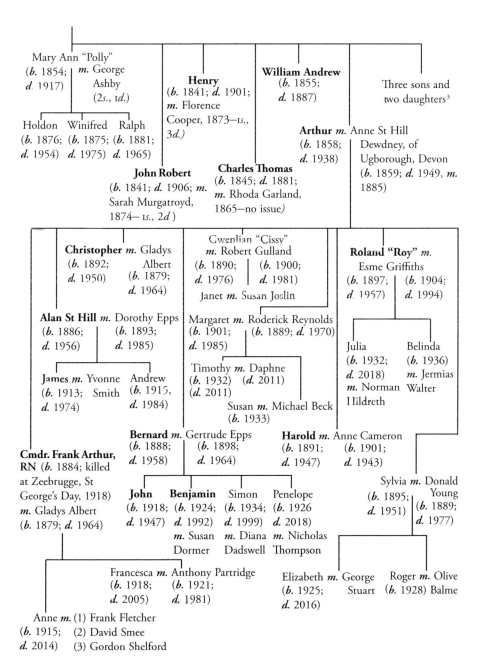

Mary Ann "Polly" (*b.* 1854; *d.* 1917) *m.* George Ashby (2*s.*, 1*d.*)

Holdon (*b.* 1876; *d.* 1954) Winifred (*b.* 1875; *d.* 1975) Ralph (*b.* 1881; *d.* 1965)

Henry (*b.* 1841; *d.* 1901; *m.* Florence Cooper, 1873—1*s.*, 3*d.*)

William Andrew (*b.* 1855; *d.* 1887)

Three sons and two daughters[3]

Arthur *m.* Anne St Hill Dewdney, of Ugborough, Devon (*b.* 1859; *d.* 1949, *m.* 1885)

John Robert (*b.* 1841; *d.* 1906; *m.* Sarah Murgatroyd, 1874— 1*s.*, 2*d.*)

Charles Thomas (*b.* 1845; *d.* 1881; *m.* Rhoda Garland, 1865—no issue)

Christopher *m.* Gladys Albert (*b.* 1892; *d.* 1950) (*b.* 1879; *d.* 1964)

Gwenlian "Cissy" *m.* Robert Gulland (*b.* 1890; *d.* 1976) (*b.* 1900; *d.* 1981)

Roland "Roy" *m.* Esme Griffiths (*b.* 1897; *d.* 1957) (*b.* 1904; *d.* 1994)

Janet *m.* Susan Joslin

Alan St Hill *m.* Dorothy Epps (*b.* 1886; *d.* 1956) (*b.* 1893; *d.* 1985)

Margaret *m.* Roderick Reynolds (*b.* 1901; *d.* 1985) (*b.* 1889; *d.* 1970)

Julia (*b.* 1932; *d.* 2018) *m.* Norman Hildreth

Belinda (*b.* 1936) *m.* Jermias Walter

James *m.* Yvonne Smith (*b.* 1913; *d.* 1974) Andrew (*b.* 1915; *d.* 1984)

Timothy *m.* Daphne (*b.* 1932) (*d.* 2011) (*d.* 2011)

Susan *m.* Michael Beck (*b.* 1933)

Bernard *m.* Gertrude Epps (*b.* 1888; *d.* 1958) (*b.* 1898; *d.* 1964)

Harold *m.* Anne Cameron (*b.* 1891; *d.* 1947) (*b.* 1901; *d.* 1943)

Cmdr. Frank Arthur, RN (*b.* 1884; killed at Zeebrugge, St George's Day, 1918) *m.* Gladys Albert (*b.* 1879; *d.* 1964)

John (*b.* 1918; *d.* 1947)

Benjamin (*b.* 1924; *d.* 1992) *m.* Susan Dormer

Simon (*b.* 1934; *d.* 1999) *m.* Diana Dadswell

Penelope (*b.* 1926 *d.* 2018) *m.* Nicholas Thompson

Sylvia *m.* Donald Young (*b.* 1895; *d.* 1951) (*b.* 1889; *d.* 1977)

Francesca *m.* Anthony Partridge (*b.* 1918; *d.* 2005) (*b.* 1921; *d.* 1981)

Elizabeth *m.* George Stuart (*b.* 1925; *d.* 2016)

Roger *m.* Olive Balme (*b.* 1928)

Anne *m.* (1) Frank Fletcher (*b.* 1915; (2) David Smee *d.* 2014) (3) Gordon Shelford

[1] Benjamin (*b.* 1781 and John (*b.* 1783), Harriott (*b.* 1784), Mary (*b.* 1786), Sophia (*b.*1788), Elizabeth (*b.* 1790), Elizabeth (*b.* 1792) and Sarah (*b.* 1795).

[2] Thomas (*b.* 1815) and John (no dates in family bible) and Elizabeth, Ann, Elizabeth (no dates in family bible), and Emma (*b.*1828; *d.*1865).

[3] William (*b.* 1839; *d.* in infancy), Alfred (artist; *b.* 1845; *d.*1874; m. Anne Morley, 1861 (1*s.*, 1*d.*)), and Samuel (dentist; *m,* Louisa Tabot, 1874 (4*s.*, 1*d*)), and Isabella (*b.* 1849; *d.* 1917; *m.* Daniel Thurston, M.D., 1885 (1*s.*, 1*d.*)), Alice (*b.* 1853; *d.* 1854).

Appendix II: Firework Set-Pieces and Portraiture

Charles and his younger brother Arthur Brock invented a new artform. They developed outstanding depictions of people and events, representations that were to become world famous.

Using the recently discovered fireproof material asbestos (almost a century before the dangers to health were discovered) they patented 'living fireworks' which were then used to show a comic scene and to bring laughter to all displays.

Drawing with coloured fire on huge screens 60 or 80 feet high, the Brocks perfected the art of capturing the instantly recognisable faces of rulers, potentates and the famous. These could be used to stir up patriotic singing or political emotions as when Charles showed Disraeli's face emerging from his favourite flower, the primrose (a 'transformation piece') or when Arthur used the faces of Dreyfus at the height of that scandal or when he placed a face of Kitchener next to that of Gordon following the battle of Omdurman with the single word 'Avenged'.

As an important part of British diplomacy, the Brocks helped to project what is now sometimes described as 'soft power' by generating joy and positive feelings in the hearts of shahs, sultans, emperors, kings, viceroys and their peoples. Looking down across the heads of tens of thousands from the royal box at the Crystal Palace, the honoured guest would press a button (a fascinating concept itself in electricity's infancy) and fire their own portraits, using the latest invention, the electric current.

Around the world, the company's creative skills were employed to fire massive displays, helping to project harmony and pleasure across the Empire, particularly when coronations were being celebrated. Often sending several teams to a large country, Brock's would be ahead of the visiting British royalty, ready to open the heavens and amaze millions of expectant subjects when the prince or the king arrived.

The Brocks were By Appointment to several monarchs and gave displays for many more. On one occasion the Sultan of Turkey was so impressed by what he saw in London that he hired the company to spread some happiness across the Bosphorous, hoping to gain some credit from his grateful subjects.

Beyond portraiture and at a time long before coloured electric lights, the cinema, TV, or even widespread colour printing, the Brocks pioneered massive set-pieces, hundreds of feet long and up to 100 feet high to relay the latest 'big news' events from around the world. Combining entertainment with current affairs, they used countless small fireworks or 'lances' with miles of instantaneous gunpowder fuse known as 'quick match', skilfully drawing an animated picture.

The set-piece, 'The Destruction of Pompeii' at the Crystal Palace in the summer of 1886 (see page 31) was just one of many developments the company introduced to the world of pyrotechny in the second half of the 19th century. This contemporary description from a journalist captures perfectly the intense, overwhelming excitement and anticipation experienced at the Crystal Palace or anywhere else in the world by an audience facing a Brock's display – an audience that overwhelmingly lived lives with little access to 'art' compared to modern times and none of the artificial and technological stimuli now thought essential for existence:

> By this time the Royal guests had come out onto the balcony leading from the Queen's Corridor. The Princess touched an electric cord communicating with a set device, which instantly burst ablaze, depicting in the brightest hues and tints of fire the national emblems of the rose, shamrock and thistle, presently changing into fire portraits of the Prince and Princess of Wales. Then followed the most superb and brilliant pyrotechnic display ever beheld. Messrs. Brock and Co. have long been famous for their unequalled skill in this branch of the art, but they even surpassed all their former efforts on Saturday night. Anything more splendid and magnificent than the fireworks on that occasion, has never been witnessed. The device representing the eruption of Mount Vesuvius and the destruction of Pompeii, is simply a masterpiece. The huge crater towering high above the noble buildings and public edifices in the valley beneath and belching forth a perfect avalanche of fire was simply stupendous. The thousands who gazed awe-struck on the mighty combustion, hissing and crackling like a hundred huge furnaces, must have wondered how art could contrive such a vivid *vraisemblance* to the most remarkable natural phenomenon of the world. This magnificent and marvellous spectacle was followed by a host of other beautiful effects, all of which went to make up a most brilliant display, but which it is impossible to describe in detail. The Royal *fête* at the Crystal Palace on Saturday June 26th 1886 will long be remembered by those who were fortunate enough to be present. It will be a red letter day for all time to come in the annals of the Crystal Palace. (*The Primrose Record*, 3 July 1886)

'The Battle of Manila Bay', 1898.

It took the resources of the world's largest and most famous firework company to develop and produce 'The Destruction of Pompeii'. Another, even larger, production twelve years later in 1898 was the very successful set-piece, 'The Battle of Manila Bay'.

Although the cameras and photographic techniques of the day were unable even to begin capturing the visual and emotional impacts of the shows, there is a contemporary photograph taken of the set-piece in action. Details from the official Brock's press release and an article from a newspaper at the time, reproduced here exactly as they were, give a clear indication of what was involved in an artform that is long forgotten.

Brock's press release – Thursday 19 May 1898

Notes re FIRST DISPLAY of the Thirty-fifth Season of C. T. Brock and Co.'s uninterrupted connection with the Crystal Palace.

It had been the unremitting endeavour of the Crystal Palace Pyrotechnists to keep 'CRYSTAL PALACE' FIREWORKS *facile princeps* by the constant introduction of novelties in mechanical and other devices, and by inventing new colours, aerial effects, etc., and, above all, by making the principal set piece, if possible, topical, artistic and true in every detail.

The Set Piece this season is a representation of the Battle of Manila Bay (No. 24 in the programme), which, besides being the most stupendous ever produced, is also the most complete in its approach to realism. An endeavour has been made to show how the up-to-date armaments of the United States ships, the brilliant gunnery and seamanship of their crews, reduced the ships of Spain to battered, sinking wrecks, while, at the same time, a tribute has been paid to the memory of the gallant Spanish seamen, who, to their lasting fame, so gloriously died fighting for their country.

THE BATTLE OF MANILA BAY

This stupendous set-piece is by far the largest ever produced, being nearly 700ft. in length.

On the right, as we face the picture, the American Fleet is seen steaming along in line, the Olympia (flag ship), leading, and, the others being in the following order: Baltimore, Raleigh, Petrel, Concord, Boston.

On the left, in the distance, is the Cavite fort, and standing round Manila Bay further to the left are Spanish vessels, Reina Christiana, Isla de Cuba, Isla de Luzon, Don Antonio de Ulloa, Don Juan de Austria, Castilla, Valasco, Mindanao, El Cano, General Lezo, and Marques de Duero.

THE ENGAGEMENT

Is commenced by a sullen roar as the Olympia opens fire with her 8in. forward guns. The Cavite forts are blown up; the Don Antonia de Ulloa sinks slowly, while her crew, under colours nailed to the mast, fiercely fight into the arms of death. Masts and spars are falling, huge rents and breaches appear in hull and sails, tangled rigging and smoking chaos testifying to the deadly work of the American projectiles. The Castilla now catches fire, and fearful explosions rend her frame as the awful carnage continues. Amid the crash of broadsides and the scream of shot and shell hurtling through the air, the Spanish ships slowly sink or become battered wrecks.

Response in the magazine *Tit Bits*, 21 May 1898, 'Sinking a Fleet in Two and a Half Minutes'

The thousands of people who visit the Crystal Palace on the first night of the firework season will be fortunate in viewing a descriptive picture of the recent Battle of Manila.

Mr. Brock, who is world-renowned for the unique character and novelty of his firework displays, is ever on the search for something up-to-date and when it was known that war had been declared, he immediately decided that a grand firework display should be given at the Crystal Palace, illustrating the first big battle of which news should come to hand. As soon as it was heard that an important engagement had taken place off Manila, preparations were immediately made to obtain the fullest and most minute particulars of the scene of the battle and the ships that took part in it.

The inquiries were successful and two artists on the staff of the company immediately set to work and sketched an outline drawing of the battle. This, of course, was drawn to scale, and after completion, the work in connection with the display was at once commenced. Sections of the picture were drawn in chalk, on the floor of a shed specially built for the purpose, and after the artists had finished, a number of boys were set to work to construct in cane and laths the designs desired. Frames made of laths, divided into equal squares, were then prepared, and on these the designs were fixed.

The set piece will be 690ft. (over an eighth of a mile) in length, and 70ft. in height. A tremendous amount of woodwork is required, and the whole of the frames will extend to nearly 50,000 square feet. For the last five weeks twenty carpenters have been at work on these, and another twenty men have been engaged in filling up and fixing on the fireworks. Over ten miles of quick-match will be used, and nearly a million coloured lights will be consumed. The fireworks burnt will weigh nearly 2000lb., and over thirty different shades of colours will be shown.

The scene as depicted on the frame will be an exact reproduction of the scene that took place in the Bay. To the right will be seen the nine American ships, headed by the Olympia; and to the left, the fort and the line of Spanish ships, backed by the Bay.

The Spanish Fleet will, of course, be totally destroyed, and every moving incident in the now historical battle will be faithfully depicted; a life-like picture being given of a sinking of the *Don Antonio de Ulloa*, with colours flying, and the burning of the *Castella*.

Although this unique display will only last for two or three minutes, during that time no fewer than 500 shells will be thrown from the two fleets, and it will require the services of no fewer than 100 men to quicken the huge framework into a beautiful picture of fire-belching batteries and ships. The total cost of this short encounter amounts to £500.

Firework portraits

For a set-piece, transformation piece or portrait one of the artists was commissioned to draw a likeness of the subject (or the news event to be shown) crucially in the case of a portrait, using a profile or semi-profile view. The picture would then be transferred onto graph paper, with a certain number of squares representing the wooden frames onto which the image would be attached. The wooden frames would be laid out on the assembly room floor and split cane or laths would be used to follow the lines of the artist's drawing.

Into the cane would be inserted double headed nails at short intervals and onto the pointed end of each would be impaled a lance. These lances (clearly visible in some of the images below) would be connected with a 'quick match' fuse. Large wheels and lattice work devices were complicated in design and beautifully intricate in display with a great many colours and subtle hues used to excite the senses.

One of the small sketches below shows the men lifting an enormous device into position using a system of ropes and pullies to gear up or leverage the strength they had to offer.

In some of these photographs, the cameras of the day have captured the individual burning lances as pinpoints of light whereas the flowing or eruption of sparks from each lance usually led to the eye perceiving lines of fire. As the *Sketch* newspaper put it in 1900: 'It is impossible to represent adequately by photography the marvellous effects Mr. Brock secures but the night views give some notion of the perfection attained in the art at Sydenham.'

The following images show different aspects of Brock's firework portraits and set-pieces.

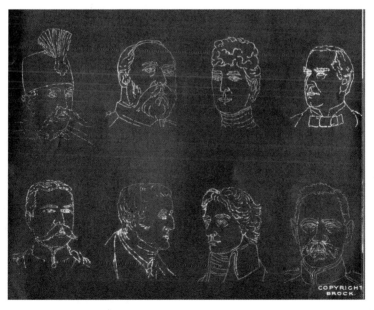

Each firework portrait was 60 feet high. Top row from left: The Shah of Persia Kind Edward VII, Queen Alexandra, unknown – possibly Lord Milner. Bottom row from left: Field Marshal Lord Kitchener, the Duke of Wellington, Admiral Lord Nelson, Field Marshal Lord Roberts.

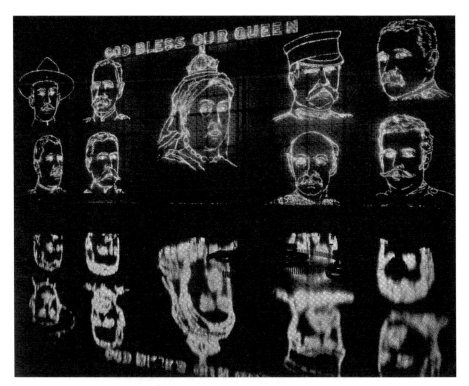

Queen Victoria and her leading generals from the Boer war.

Queen Victoria with two of her sons, Edward Prince of Wales and Arthur Duke of Connaught, with their wives Princess Alexandra and the Duchess of Connaught.

The Viceroy Lord Curzon and the Duchess of Connaught during the Delhi Durbar 1903

The electric button being pressed in the royal box by the second shah of Persia to attend Crystal Palace displays. (*The Graphic*, 30 August 1902)

A display at Mysore, India, during the king and queen's state visit in 1906.

A vice regal display at Agra, India, to welcome the amir of Afgahnistan in 1907. In the 1980s the author discussed the Amir's visits to India with a woman who was by then approaching her hundredth birthday. She told the author that when she met this Amir at a tea party on one of his subsequent pre-WWI visits to India, he had explained to her that the only way to keep order in his country was to blow miscreants from the ends of heavy guns. The Amir's fellow guest on that occasion, Vere Marsden, was to become, like Frank Brock, a great grandparent to the author's children.

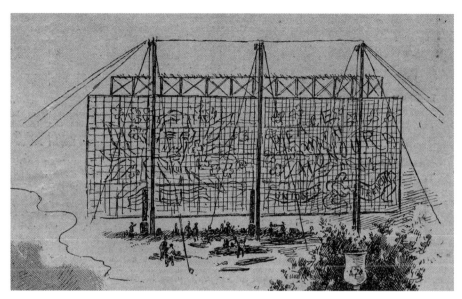

An illustration showing a transformation piece – flowers to portrait – being erected. (*Sporting and Dramatic News*, April 1888)

Preparing the giant set-pieces. Note the lances connected by the quick match fuse.

A policeman rehearses the 'living fireworks'. Notice the lances are joined by quick match. These performances were guaranteed to produce much laughter at every display.

Perhaps the greatest curiosity of recent years in the way of firework displays has been centred round the living fireworks. The 'fighting cocks' greatly amused the Shah when he was over here, and the 'boxing men' caused unbounded delight to the emperor of Germany. (*The Strand Magazine*)

An illustration showing a large device being erected using pullies. Also see the Mysore display on page 234 for similar devices in action. (*Sporting and Dramatic News*, April 1888)

Appendix III: The Trials of the Brock Anti-Zeppelin Bullet

Notes on one of several trials carried out on the Brock anti-Zeppelin bullet, submitted 17 February 1916

The Bullet which has just been devised and perfected by Flight Lieutenant F.A. Brock shows distinct promise in sinking Zeppelins. It appears almost certain that a Zeppelin coming within range of a Lewis gun with these bullets will be either set on fire or forced to descend. The bullets will function at extreme ranges with velocity of about 100 ft. a second, and appear to be reasonably safe with rifle or machine gun, for, if a premature occurs, no damage is done to weapon or user.

The result of the final unofficial trials by Air Department, which took place on Monday, 14th February, was that the Lewis gun with a Zeppelinette target with about 20 inches of exhaust gases between the hydrogen ballonet and the air, fired the target at the 7th shot.

Firing at a range of 800 yds. On fabric targets in a high wind very good practice was made, and all the bullets except one exploded in passing the 3rd target, the majority in the 2nd or 3rd, or between these two screens

It is proposed to make official trials on Tuesday next. 22nd February at 11 a.m.at Kingsnorth, weather permitting. A double balloon, having inert gas between balloons, will be fired at in the air and Zeppelinettes will be fired at on the ground.

These bullets have been proved of considerable use against heavier than air machines; also one bullet will cause enough damage to the main spar or interplane strut to bring about the destruction of the machine.

If these trials are successful it is thought that arrangements might be made to arm troops in the United Kingdom with it. Even if they did not hit a Zeppelin at great heights, at least they would have a good chance of seriously damaging it if it flew at low altitudes, as occurred during the last raid in the Midlands.

It is also proposed, weather permitting, to carry out a trial at the same time of slipping an aeroplane from an S.S. Airship. The S.S. envelope to be used is not a new one and will probably be lost. The cost when new is £600.

It is proposed that Members of the Board and others wishing to view the trials should leave Victoria by the 9.16 a.m. train for Chatham, where arrangements will be made for cars to meet the train and take the party on to Kingsnorth.

Director of Air Services
17th February 1916
A/c 325

A memorandum written by Frank Brock explaining his involvement with the bullet's development, dated 21 November 1917

Civil Assistant to D.A.S (Director of Air Services)
With reference to the letter dated July 24th 1917, from the Ministry of Munitions inventions Department and to the letter of the 15th January 1917 from the Secretary of the Admiralty to the Controller of Munitions Inventions Department, I submit the following with reference to the invention and development of the "Brock" Bullet.

At the beginning of 1915, following an unsuccessful attack on a Zeppelin by Flight Commander Bigsworth with incendiary bullets, a belief arose that the exhaust gases from the Motors were led in between the outer and inner fabrics thereby producing a layer of inert gas which formed a sufficient protection against any incendiary projectile.

At that time I was in charge of the Intelligence Section of the Air Department and commenced to work to produce a bullet which would explode between the first and second fabrics in such a way that the hydrogen could connect with the outside air.

The first official trials took place at Shoeburyness with a Winchester Rifle against fabric targets (See N.O. Paper 27488) and were so successful that I was instructed to proceed with the experiments.

Further official trials took place on October 26th, 1915, when a balloon surrounded by CO_2 was ignited with a Lewis Gun. The range at that time, however, was very short but the sensitive nose was improved until the bullet functioned at 800 yards.

Considerable opposition was then aroused as the bullets were held to be explosive and therefore against the Hague Convention.

However, in the middle of 1916 the issue of quantities was commenced.

Up to that time the whole of the cost of experimenting and of the supply of some thousands or rounds had been borne by myself and during all the experiments carried out between 26th October 1915 and July 1916, the "Brock" Bullet never once failed to ignite a balloon whether surrounded by exhaust gases or not, and I believe I am correct in stating that no other Bullet up to that time had succeeded in firing a balloon at a range over 200 yards unless "Brock" Bullets were in the mixture. Brock Bullets have been present in every mixture used successfully against Zeppelins, and, in view of the results obtained during experiments, it is contended that the Brock Bullets have been the chief factor in destroying this menace on land and at sea.

I am informed unofficially that, following the letter of January 20th 1917, at the Conference mentioned therein, an award was granted to me.

It is therefore submitted that the Board of Admiralty may approve the payment to me of such an Award as the Controller of Munitions Inventions may grant and, further, that such award should certainly not be less than that received by Mr. Pomeroy.

(Sgd.) F. A. Brock
Wing Commander RN

Appendix IV: Frank's Thoughts on Hindenburg's Appointment by the Kaiser, Sent to Admiral 'Jacky' Fisher, 7 September 1916

The dismissal of von Falkenhayn as Chief of Staff in favour of Hindenburg is so extraordinary, in view of the fact that Hindenburg, because of an old quarrel, is personally unpopular with the Kaiser, and the Kaiser is not a big enough man to forgive, that there must be some hidden reason. There would appear to be two probable explanations:

1. That as Hindenburg has always been an apostle of frightfulness in War, and has always advocated the use of every possible means by which an enemy can be made to sue for peace, it is possible that the Kaiser is desirous of using some new military frightfulness which is too inhuman, even for von Falkenhayn, if so, it is difficult to imagine on what lines such frightfulness might work.

   The only lines on which the enemy have not yet moved is upon the dissemination of disease.

2. Another explanation may be that the Kaiser or his Councillors have devised a scheme which von Falkenhayn considers unsound, and is acceptable to Hindenburg. If this is so, in view of the temperament of the man, such a scheme would perhaps be a desperate thrust, carried out through a Neutral Country, and this is improbable, for if the Germans forced Switzerland and beat Italy, they would be no nearer winning the war, and there is no other Neutral Country, the forcing of which would by purely military operations greatly affect the War.

The only possible salvation for Germany would appear to be the invasion of England on as large a scale as possible, and this, carried out by a leader, careless of the sacrifice of men so long as the thrust got home, should be quite feasible.

Such a plan might well consist of a feint on a large scale on the North East Coast, even if involving the total loss of say 30,000 men, together with an attempted landing on a still larger scale from Belgium on the South East Coast.

The advantage of an attempt from Belgium, apart from the short sea voyage, would be that such a force could be concentrated without due remark.

The smaller concentration in the North could be carried out under the pretext of the fear that Denmark was about to enter the War, and it is noticeable that this fear is already being expressed in certain German papers.

Appendix V: Poetry after Zeebrugge

The morale-boosting raid at a very difficult moment in the war and the outpouring of patriotic fervour encouraged the creativity of poets at the time. Here is one of several that were published.

LEST WE FORGET

THE STORMING OF THE ZEEBRUGGE MOLE
Saint George's Day, 23 April 1918
Dedicated to and accepted by Vice-Admiral Sir Roger Keyes, KCB in 1918

The night was dark with fitful showers,
On Zeebrugge's sandy coast;
No lights came from the hidden forts,
Where lurked the Teuton host.
The Mole stretched out a giant arm,
As if to bridge the main,
And only sounds of breaking foam
Came midst the falling rain.

But. Lo! – from out the murky gloom
A phantom form appeared,
With lengthy hull and funnels tall,
Upon the Mole she steered,
And with her two of lesser size
Stole forth in grim array,
While other shapes crept slowly towards
The dark, forbidding bay.

Bold Keyes contrived with martial skill
No blow of his should fail.
He vowed that on St George's Day
He'd 'twist the dragon's tail!'
So on the *Warwick's* narrow deck
He waited for the hour,
To harry Shroeder's pirate nest
With Britain's naval power.

The fickle wind rolled slowly back
The curtain screen of smoke,
And then the Germans knew their fate,
And every cannon spoke.
Lights flashed on high on every side,
And streamed across the sea,
While thunders rolled in anger deep,
Upon the shore and lea.

Far distant guns joined in the song
That shook the sea and sky,
And 'midst their song there rang aloft
Old England's battle cry!
The fire-balls gleamed like emerald stars,
The bullets fell like snow,
The brave Marines had one reply –
'Now over, boys, you go!'

The Mole was gained – the stormers passed
Across that bridge of Hell,
And well the old *Vindictive's* decks
The tale of carnage tell.

Brave Elliot fell and Halahan –
And Brock and many more,
But nothing checked the heroes left,
Who swept the pier and shore.
And while they held the foe at bay,
In bomb and bayonet fray,
The blocking cruisers reached their goal,
And barred the channel way.

Then, with a parting salvo sent
By every British crew,
Vindictive smoking – belching fire
Put out to sea anew.
And in the shadows of the night,
Was lost as but a speck,
But Carpenter had left his mark
Of slaughter, fire and wreck!

Oh, England, mourn thy gallant sons,
Marines and sailors too,
Who died like paladins of old,
To King and Country true.
But dry thy tears for every age,
Their glory shall extol,
So when ye hail Saint George's Day
Remember Zeebrugge Mole!

By Baron De Santa Maria, K. S. J.

Select Bibliography

Aspinall-Oglander, C. *Roger Keyes*, London Hogarth Press, 1951

Bennett, J. (Jackstaff) *The Dover Patrol*, Grant Richards, 1919

Bennett, L. *Churchill's War against the Zeppelin 1914–18*, Helion, 2015

Bilbe, T. *Kingsnorth Airship Station*, History Press, 2013

Brock, A. *Pyrotechnics – The History & Art of Firework Making*, Daniel O'Connor, 1922

Brock, A. *A History of Fireworks*, George G. Harrap & Co., 1949

Carpenter, Captain A. F. B. *The Blocking of Zeebrugge*, Herbert Jenkins, 1922

Castle, I. *London 1914–17 The Zeppelin Menace*, Osprey, 2008

Castle, I. *The Zeppelin Base Raids*, Osprey, 2011

Charman, T. *The First World War on the Home Front*, André Deutsch, 2014

Charman, T. *The First World War on the Home Front,* Carlton, 2014

Coleman, E. *No Pyrrhic Victories: The 1918 Raids on Zeebrugge and Ostend*, Spellmount, 2014

Colligan, M. *Canvas Documentaries*, Melbourne University Publishing, 2002

Corbet Anderson, J. *The Great North Wood: With a Geological, Topographical and Historical Description of Upper, West and South Norwood,* Blades, East & Blades, 1898

De Syon, G. *Germany and the Airship 1900–1939*, John Hopkins University Press, 2002

Dorling, T. (Taffrail) *Swept Channels*, Hodder & Stoughton, 1935

Dudley, E. *Monsters of the Purple Twilight*, Harrap, 1960

Fegan, T. *The Baby Killers: German air raids on Britain in the First World War*, Pen & Sword, 2007

Fullerton, A. *Sixty Minutes for St George*, Michael Joseph, 1977

Gardiner, I. *The Flatpack Bombers*, Pen & Sword, 2009

Gems, J. *The Story of Malden Golf Club*, MGC, 1990

Gollin, A. *No Longer an Island*, Stanford University Press, 1984

Grey, C. *Bombers*, Faber & Faber, 1941

Hawes, J. *Englanders and Huns*, Simon & Schuster, 2014

Hedin, R., *The Zeppelin Reader: Stories, Poems, and Songs from the Age of the Airship*, University of Iowa Press, 1998

Hilton Young, E., *By Sea and Land: Some Naval Doings*, T. C. & E. C. Jack, 1924

Hiney, T. *Raymond Chandler, A Biography*, Chatto & Windus, 1997

Hoare, P. *Wilde's Last Stand – Decadence, Conspiracy & The First World War*, Duckworth, 1997

Hodges, H. *God's Gift, a Living History of Dulwich College*, Heinemann, 1981

Holland, C. and Phillips, R. *The Great War Letters of Roland Mountfort*, Matador, 2009

Howard, K. *The Zeebrugge Affair*, George H. Doran, 1918

Hoyt, E. *The Zeppelins*, Lothrop, Lee & Shepard, 1969

Kelly, J. *Gunpowder: Alchemy, Bombards and Pyrotechnics*, Basic Books, 2004

Kendall, P. *The Zeebrugge Raid 1918*, Spellmount, 2008

Keyes, R. *The Naval Memoirs of Sir Roger Keyes*, Thornton Butterworth, 1935

Lake, D. *The Zeebrugge and Ostend Raids 1918*, Pen & Sword, 2002

Lancaster, R. *Fireworks – Principles and Practice*, Chemical Publishing, 1972

Marder, A. J. *From the Dreadnought to Scapa Flow, Vol V: The Royal Navy in the Fisher Era*, Oxford University Press, 1970

McGreal, S. *Zeebrugge & Ostend Raids*, Pen and Sword, 2007

Paddock, T. *A Call to Arms: Propaganda, Public Opinion, and Newspapers in the Great War*, Greenwood, 2004

Partington, J. *A History of Greek Fire and Gunpowder*, Heffer, 1960

Piggott, J. *Palace of the People – The Crystal Palace at Sydenham 1854–1936*, Hurst, 2004

Pitt, B. *Zeebrugge – Eleven VCs Before Breakfast*, Cassell, 1958

Russell, M. *The Chemistry of Fireworks*, Royal Society of Chemistry, 2009

Sandford, C. *Zeebrugge*, Casemate Publishers, 2018

Stoney, B. *Twentieth Century Maverick – The Life of Noel Pemberton Billington*, Bank House Books, 2004

Storey, N. *Zeppelin Blitz: The German Air Raids on Britain during the First World War*, History Press, 2015

Terraine, J. *Business in Great Waters: The U-Boat War 1916-1945*, Mandarin, 1990

Thomson, J. *Recollections and Reflections*, G. Bell, 1936

Warner, P. *The Zeebrugge Raid*, William Kimber, 1978

Werrett, S., *Fireworks: Pyrotechnic Arts and Sciences in European History*, University of Chicago Press, 2010

White, J. *Zeppelin Nights – London in the First World War*, Bodley Head, 2014

Williams, T. *Airship Pilot No. 28*, William Kimber, 1974

Williams, T. *A Mysterious Something in the Life, Raymond Chandler, a Life*, Aurum, 2012

Willis, F. *A Book of London Yesterdays*, Phoenix House, 1965

Wroth, W. *The London Pleasure Gardens of the Eighteenth Century*, Macmillan, 1896

Index